Blackwell Great Minds

Edited by Steven Nadler

The *Blackwell Great Minds* series gives readers a strong sense of the fundamental views of the great Western thinkers and captures the relevance of these figures to the way we think and live today.

blackwell great minds

newton

Andrew Janiak

WILEY Blackwell

This edition first published 2015
© 2015 Andrew Janiak

Registered Office
John Wiley & Sons, Ltd, The Atrium, Southern Gate, Chichester, West Sussex,
PO19 8SQ, UK

Editorial Offices
350 Main Street, Malden, MA 02148-5020, USA
9600 Garsington Road, Oxford, OX4 2DQ, UK
The Atrium, Southern Gate, Chichester, West Sussex, PO19 8SQ, UK

For details of our global editorial offices, for customer services, and for information
about how to apply for permission to reuse the copyright material in this book please
see our website at www.wiley.com/wiley-blackwell.

The right of Andrew Janiak to be identified as the author of this work has been asserted
in accordance with the UK Copyright, Designs and Patents Act 1988.

Library of Congress Cataloging-in-Publication Data

Janiak, Andrew, author.
  Newton / Andrew Janiak.
    pages   cm
  Summary: "This book takes a distinct angle on his life and work" – Provided by
publisher.
  Includes bibliographical references and index.
  ISBN 978-1-4051-8729-9 (hardback) – ISBN 978-1-4051-8728-2 (paper)   1. Newton,
Isaac, 1642–1727.   I. Title.
  B1299.N34J355 2015
  192–dc23

                                                    2014026819

A catalogue record for this book is available from the British Library.

Cover image: © GL Archive / Alamy

Set in 9/12pt Trump Mediaeval by SPi Publisher Services, Pondicherry, India

1   2015

I dedicate this book to my two philosophical sons
Isaac and Saul
who will never think an apple is just an apple

contents

acknowledgments

Since this book has been 7 years in the making, I have incurred many debts along the way. First and foremost, I thank Steve Nadler for his foresight and patience: foresight for asking me to write this text in my own way and patience for giving me plenty of time to figure out how to do so. Second, I thank Karen Detlefsen, Niccolò Guicciardini, Hylarie Kochiras, and Tad Schmaltz for reading an earlier draft, along with four anonymous referees for Wiley-Blackwell, all of whose comments made this a far better book. Third, over the past decade, many colleagues and friends have discussed Newton with me, including especially Zvi Biener, Katherine Brading, Patrick Connolly, Graciela DePierris, Rob DiSalle, Mary Domski, Lisa Downing, Steffen Ducheyne, Katherine Dunlop, Moti Feingold, Michael Friedman, Alan Gabbey, Dan Garber, Geoff Gorham, Bill Harper, Gary Hatfield, Nick Huggett, Michael Hunter, Sarah Hutton, Rob Iliffe, Dana Jalobeanu, Christian Johnson, Lynn Joy, Antonia LoLordo, Ted McGuire, Scott Mandelbrote, David Marshall Miller, Christia Mercer, Alan Nelson, Carla-Rita Palmerino, Marco Panza, Alex Rosenberg, Jim Ruffner, David Sanford, Eric Schliesser, Alison Simmons, Ed Slowik, Chris Smeenk, George Smith, Steve Snobelen, Marius Stan, Richard Stein, Karin Verelst, and Catherine Wilson. Over the years, I chatted about Newton, metaphysics, and many other topics with Fred Dretske and Iris Einheuser—I sorely miss them both.

I couldn't accomplish much of anything without the love and encouragement of Rebecca Stein, a true public intellectual.

I presented many of the ideas in this book to audiences at the Royal Society in London, the American Philosophical Association (Eastern and Western division meetings), Harvard University, the University of Pennsylvania, Ohio State University, the University of Notre Dame, the Rotman Institute at the University of Western Ontario, Hendrix College, Stanford University, the University of Ghent, Bergamo University, Leiden University, the University of King's College in Halifax, and the Max Planck Institüt for Wissenschaftsgeschichte in Berlin. Grants from the American Philosophical Society, the Josiah Charles Trent Memorial Foundation, and the Arts and Sciences Committee on Faculty Research at Duke University, funded the archival research for this book. I am grateful for their support.

preface

Why another book on Newton? There are innumerable works on his status as a leading mathematician of the past three hundred years, his work as a founder of modern physics, his intriguing biography, his experiments in alchemy, his deeply held religious beliefs, and also his role in fighting counterfeiters of the royal currency as Warden of the Mint. Newton fascinates us, and will continue to do so, for these and many other reasons. But this book takes a distinct angle on his life and work. Rather than placing him within the history of mathematics, the history of science, or even within modern British history generally, it places him instead within the history of modern philosophy, viewing him as a philosophical figure. Unlike his work in mathematics, physics, even alchemy and religion, thinking of Newton as a philosopher requires some explanation for the contemporary reader. In what sense was Newton a philosopher? Did he dabble in philosophy here and there, as perhaps any scientist can be expected to do, especially when scientific upheavals are prominent in his day? Or did he engage with philosophy in a more fundamental way?

Newton was not a systematic philosopher. He did not sit down one day to write a philosophical treatise, as Descartes wrote the *Meditations*, Spinoza the *Ethics*, or Locke the *Essay*. When he wrote a treatise, such as *Principia mathematica*, or the *Opticks*, it was not a treatise in systematic philosophy. He read and discussed many such works; but instead of adding to their number, he chose to engage with philosophical problems and topics primarily when his contemporaries challenged his ideas and methods. But as it turns out, Newton's mature intellectual life from 1672 until his death in 1727 was marked by constant challenges, controversies, and debates, and this surprises us most. To write the history of Newton the mathematician, or Newton the scientist, is to write of a triumphant figure—one whose ideas and contributions to numerous fields were warmly embraced by future generations of mathematicians and physicists. Indeed, Newton's profound influence on these fields was felt for two centuries. Thus the fact that Newton's work was met with skepticism, even derision, during his lifetime is difficult to square with our standard conception of him. But if we reconceive of him as a philosopher, and acknowledge that the history of modern philosophy is a history of profound debates and lasting controversies, then we can incorporate challenges and debates into our conception of Newton's intellectual life. All of the canonical philosophers of the modern period—from Descartes to Spinoza to Locke—engaged in philosophical disputes throughout their lives. And in that sense, Newton is in good company. He was not as systematic as these figures in his thinking, but he was just as philosophical.

The guiding thread of my narrative will therefore be the controversies throughout Newton's life, which generate his most important philosophical reflections. His first publications, which appeared in the *Philosophical Transactions* of the Royal Society in the early 1670s, were characteristic because they immediately caused a substantial and lasting dispute concerning the proper methodology within optics among some of Newton's most important contemporaries, especially Christaan Huygens in Holland and Robert Hooke in England. As Newton's thinking matured during the 1670s and 1680s, he engaged in a systematic debate with reigning Cartesian ideas in philosophy. This engagement eventually led him to embrace a new way of thinking about questions within the philosophy of nature in his magnum opus, *Principia mathematica*, which first appeared in 1687. Given the fact that "Newtonian mechanics" dominated thinking about nature for generations, today's readers may be surprised to learn that Newton's *Principia* was strongly challenged by many of the leading thinkers in his day, including Huygens and the talented young Continental mathematician Gottfried Wilhelm Leibniz. Since Leibniz and Newton co-discovered the calculus, it is difficult to grasp why they would have engaged in substantial and unresolvable philosophical disputes. But those disputes, which gathered steam a few years after *Principia mathematica* appeared, would eventually erupt into a major confrontation early in the new century, ending only with Leibniz's death in 1716. By then, Newton had developed a series of philosophical views in his attempt to defend and further the ideas and methods he had embraced many years earlier. The past decade of Newton's life would continue in the same vein. Although he had many supporters in England and, increasingly, in Continental Europe, during his final years, it would be many years after his death before his ideas and methods would garner widespread support throughout the intellectual community. In this book, we try to recapture a flavor of the many debates and controversies in which Newton engaged throughout his life. And these are what made him a philosopher.

life and times

I f one picks up a book about Isaac Newton, one expects to find a character conforming to the legend. One expects to encounter a mathematician who invented calculus and employed its great analytical power for understanding natural phenomena. One expects to find a scientist who ignored the philosophical and metaphysical preoccupations of his predecessors, focusing on experimental and mathematical questions that form the nucleus of modern physics. One expects to learn of a rational thinker who scorned the religious superstitions and practices of his day, portending a new secular age in which science would reign as the surest route to knowledge of the natural world. But historians of science have long since recognized the profound gap between Newton the legend and Newton the actual historical figure (Cohen and Smith 2002, 1–6). As biographers of Newton have often suggested, one reason for this gap is that Newton was actually much more exercised about religion, theology, philosophy, and even alchemy than one would expect (Dobbs 1975, Manuel 1968, Westfall 1980). There is, however, a deeper reason for the gap, one connected intimately to the proper methodology for studying the history of science and philosophy: Newton lived in an era that is profoundly different from our own in the way that it organized human knowledge. Like his contemporaries, Newton thought about science and religion, theology and philosophy, nature and God in ways that are strikingly peculiar to any twenty-first century reader. Indeed, his thinking was different enough that he lacked any such categories, as did his contemporaries: the early moderns organized human knowledge in a way that is profoundly foreign to us. It is always a struggle to come to understand the work of any genius. But in Newton's case, we have the additional challenge of coming to understand his age.

Newton lived in tumultuous times. When he was born on Christmas Day in 1642, the historically stable British monarchy with centuries of tradition underpinning it was in crisis. A civil war had broken out, one that would lead to fundamental political and social change within the next two decades.

Newton, First Edition. Andrew Janiak.
© 2015 Andrew Janiak. Published 2015 by John Wiley & Sons, Ltd.

By the time Newton was a young man, England had undergone not only civil war and a political revolution, but also the beheading of the King, the bloody rule of Oliver Cromwell, and the Restoration of the monarchy in 1660. These events had a deep impact on the most important philosophers working while Newton was a young man: in 1659, in a preface to one of his most important works on experiments with his air pump, Robert Boyle wrote of "the strange confusions of this unhappy nation" (Boyle 1999, vol. 1: 145). The revolution in politics and society was accompanied by equally profound developments in intellectual life. When Newton enrolled in Trinity College, Cambridge, in 1660, a traditional curriculum was still in place, but adventurous and talented students were directed to read the great *moderns* of the day, who were overthrowing the Scholastic tradition that had reigned for centuries in Europe's great universities. Many of the moderns were Newton's countrymen, including Thomas Hobbes, Robert Boyle, and Henry More, the latter being a friend of Newton's family and a key leader of the Cambridge Platonist movement in midcentury. Newton avidly read their works, along with the latest writings from philosophers on the Continent, especially Descartes and the Dutch mathematician Christiaan Huygens (McGuire and Tamny 1983). The political and intellectual spheres came together early in Newton's life with the founding of the Royal Society in London in 1662, which had the imprimatur of King Charles II. It would become the model for scientific societies throughout Europe in the next generation. Newton's career would parallel the rise of the Royal Society: he sent his earliest papers, on optics, to the Society for publication in its *Philosophical Transactions* in the 1670s; published his magnum opus, *Philosophiae Naturalis Principia Mathematica* (Mathematical Principles of Natural Philosophy) through the Society in 1687; and would eventually become its president in 1703. By the time of Newton's death in 1727, England and its political and intellectual life were fundamentally different than they were at the time of his youth, and Newton played as central a role in transforming the intellectual and cultural life of his country as any other figure. Although he is usually mentioned along with Robert Boyle and Charles Darwin as one of England's three greatest scientists, he might also be listed along with Milton and Shakespeare, for his impact on British intellectual life in the early modern period was deep and lasting. Scientists, philosophers, mathematicians and even theologians spent much of the eighteenth century digesting, furthering, and criticizing Newton's work. He played the kind of role that Kant played in nineteenth-century German-speaking philosophy: everyone worked in his wake.

Isaac Newton himself lived a somewhat tumultuous life. The tumult resulted from early tragedies in his family: his father died a few months before he was born and he spent much of his childhood away from his mother. Contradictions emerged later: an intensely private person who shunned public controversies from his earliest days, he was also a recognized public intellectual, a knight of the British Empire who not only presided over the Royal

Society but also sought a seat in Parliament (representing Cambridge) and served in London in the politically influential post of Warden of the Mint. A founder of what we now call modern mathematical physics, he was also a deeply religious man with numerous—often deeply heterodox—opinions on biblical chronology, the history of Christianity, and theological doctrine, including the nature and status of the Trinity.[1] Although anti-Trinitarianism was illegal due to the Blasphemy Act of 1648, Newton embraced it privately, providing hints to friends like the philosopher John Locke in the early 1690s and the philosopher–theologian Samuel Clarke in his later years. He agonized over finding the proper interpretation of scripture and of Christianity's most complex doctrines. Newton's *Nachlass*[2] includes not only hundreds of pages of work in mathematics, optics, and natural philosophy but also numerous manuscripts dealing with alchemical experiments and the history of alchemical thought and thousands of pages of theological materials from every decade of Newton's life[3]: a complex man, indeed.

Newton's immense impact on science and society, and his immensely complicated personality, transcends the capacity of any one volume to capture it. Blackwell Great Minds is devoted to the history of philosophy. If we employ the history of early modern philosophy as the lens through which to view Newton's work, what picture emerges? Newton was not a systematic philosopher: although he read a number of systematic philosophical treatises, including Descartes's *Meditations*, he never wrote one. But he did in fact develop and defend a wide range of philosophical views. He did so primarily in reaction to the many controversies that his publications, ideas, and methods generated from his earliest work in the 1670s until the end of his life in the first third of the eighteenth century. Hence, the focus in this book is on Newton's philosophical debates and discussions with other thinkers—including, especially, Descartes and his followers, Huygens, Locke, and finally Leibniz and his followers. The philosophically salient aspects of Newton's life can be broken into three stages for simplicity's sake: the early years, circa 1660–1680; the middle period, circa 1680–1700; and the late years, 1700–1727. Each of these periods involved substantial philosophical output in reaction to substantive debates.

The early period took place largely in Cambridge. After finishing his studies as an undergraduate at Trinity College, Cambridge in 1665, Newton did considerable work in mathematics (and other areas), rising to become the second Lucasian Professor of Mathematics at the University of Cambridge in 1669 (the first holder of the chair was his teacher, Isaac Barrow). His required course of lectures as Lucasian Professor includes some important reflections on mathematics and natural philosophy. During the 1670s, he also made lasting contributions to experimental optics that helped solidify his reputation in England and abroad. The debates about methodology prompted by his optical writings prefigured an important aspect of Newton's lifelong philosophical work, especially the issue of whether *hypotheses* or other kinds of speculation should be embraced in philosophy.

In the middle period, the 1680s–1690s, Newton made huge advances in natural philosophy, culminating in the publication of his magnum opus, *Principia Mathematica*, in 1687. During this period, Newton befriended John Locke and had several important philosophical exchanges with various figures, including G.W. Leibniz (the German philosopher and mathematician) and Richard Bentley (a London theologian and later the long-serving Master of Trinity College). By the turn of the new century, *Newtonianism* was a powerful intellectual force in England and was soon to be one on the Continent. But it remained highly controversial.

The final period of Newton's life was focused on developing his philosophy and on defending it against its numerous critics. The most dramatic moment in this period came in 1715, when Leibniz articulated several powerful philosophical objections to Newtonianism in a series of letters sent to Princess Caroline of Wales and through her to Samuel Clarke (who was then a member of Newton's circle in London). This ignited a major cross-Channel debate that precipitated the Leibniz–Clarke correspondence, perhaps the most influential philosophical exchange of the entire eighteenth century. Controversy did not subside with Newton's death: in the following decades, the Leibnizian and Newtonian systems had displaced Cartesianism as the major philosophical orientations of Europe and the debate between them continued throughout the rest of the century. Émilie du Châtelet wrote an important treatise, *Institutions de Physique* (1740), which attempted to mediate the dispute between Leibniz and Newton, and in his *Critique of Pure Reason* (1781), Immanuel Kant continued that general project with his groundbreaking work. The shadow of Isaac Newton was long indeed.

1.1 Background and Childhood

In a small town in Lincolnshire, England, Hannah Newton gave birth to her son Isaac early on Christmas morning in 1642.[4] The fact that he was born on Christmas obviously became the stuff of legend. Isaac was apparently in a very weak condition when he was born—it took a full week before he was baptized, on the first day of the New Year. Although he would eventually rise to become the world's greatest natural philosopher, his early years were marked by tragedy. Isaac's father and namesake had died while Hannah was 6 months pregnant, so the two never met. What kind of effect this fact had on Newton's upbringing has been the subject of intense speculation over the years.[5] It may have helped shape Isaac's lifelong inability to maintain friendships he had formed. Luckily for Hannah and the young Isaac, his father left a modest estate including a manor house and a flock of roughly 200 sheep, which was above average for this part of the English countryside. The Newtons therefore were far from wealthy, and were certainly not aristocracy, but the family was in a stable financial position during Isaac's youth. This stability, however, was soon torn by another event: when he was just 3, his mother, Hannah, remarried and left him in the care of his maternal grandmother. He would not live with his mother again until he was 11, so his formative years were spent without either of his parents. Nonetheless, Hannah was a resourceful person, for her second marriage, to the Reverend Barnabas Smith, greatly increased the family's wealth and helped to secure Isaac's future. We can only speculate about the challenge she faced in helping her family at the cost of living apart from her young son. For his part, the elder Newton recalled feeling great anger during his youth.

Despite Hannah's finances, it seems that few in her family had received any formal education. Indeed, it appears that Isaac's father could not write his own name.[6] But things would be different for the young Isaac. His mother arranged for him to attend the Grantham School, where the influential Cambridge Platonist Henry More had also gone as a boy (one of Newton's teachers was More's former student). He enrolled at age 12 and lived with the nearby apothecary—he thus lived apart from his mother again after just a year together. He presumably studied mostly Latin and almost certainly no mathematics at Grantham, and he would have devoted substantial time to Bible study. Although he learned no mathematics and no natural philosophy at this time, both of which were flourishing in England and on the Continent in this period, his knowledge of Latin and of scripture would serve him throughout the rest of his life. More immediately, they also prepared him for future university study. But he would not continue with his studies directly: when he graduated from Grantham at 17, his mother called him back to Woolsthorpe and tried to encourage him to engage with the upkeep of the family farm. Apparently, these efforts came to naught. Isaac was ill suited to farm life and did little to help with the daily work on his mother's land. Her small staff thought he was useless; one of them noted that he was fit "for nothing but the 'Versity.'" That turned out to be a prescient remark: in June 1660, when he was not yet 18, Isaac would set out on a journey for Cambridge. In a sense, he would never return.

On June 5, 1660, the young Isaac passed his entrance examination and enrolled in Trinity College. The colleges were technically separate from the University of Cambridge: students who sought degrees would enroll in the university as well. Newton did so 1 month after arriving in Cambridge. Although he had traveled just over a 100 kilometers, he had obviously entered a completely new world. The son of functionally illiterate parents, he was now a full-fledged member of one of the oldest institutions of learning in all of Europe.[7] He would eventually become one of its most famous graduates.

1.2 Early Years in Cambridge

The university as an institution had existed in England since the twelfth century, and in Newton's day, the curriculum at Cambridge's colleges had not changed substantially in many years. Indeed, it seems that much of the formal study at Trinity College—in fields such as logic, ethics, and rhetoric—had little influence on Newton's thinking and on his future work. But the curriculum was just one aspect of the flourishing intellectual community that the young Newton had joined, and it is this wider community that enables us to understand how Newton received his true education. There are two crucial features of the community that profoundly influenced Newton in his first years in Cambridge. First, he began to learn substantial amounts of mathematics, both through his own reading of texts like Euclid's *Elements* and van Schooten's extended Latin edition of Descartes's *Geometry* and especially through the instruction of Isaac Barrow, a Cambridge don who was the first person to hold the now famed Lucasian Professorship of Mathematics. Newton attended Barrow's lectures on mathematics and worked with him personally. It was Barrow more than any other figure at Cambridge who came to recognize Newton's intellectual gifts, not to say his genius, and who quickly facilitated his rapid rise at Trinity College. Given that the 17-year-old Newton knew little if any mathematics after his training at Grantham, it is astonishing that he would become the second holder of the Lucasian chair a mere 9 years after arriving in Cambridge, discovering the generalization of the binomial theorem and fundamental aspects of what we now call the integral and differential calculus in the intervening period. Such facts present us with the temptation to picture Newton as a lone genius, finding and solving complex mathematical and scientific problems completely on his own through sheer intelligence. Despite his undeniable and prodigious gifts, the young Newton did not exist in an intellectual vacuum: if it were not for Barrow's instruction and encouragement, we do not know what Newton might have accomplished on his own. Second, and just as importantly, although the curriculum was of little use to Newton, like many enterprising and talented young students, he was instructed to read the great *moderns* on his own. His notebook from his early years at Trinity College records his voluminous reading of More, Galileo, Descartes, Charleton (who passed on the views of Gassendi and of certain atomists), Hobbes, and Boyle, among others (McGuire and Tamny 1983). Because of these two facts, Newton quickly became aware of the very latest and most advanced work in both mathematics and natural philosophy. It would not be long before he himself had made major advancements in each of these areas.

Newton's early years are now the stuff of legend. As with many legends, some details are apparently apocryphal, but there may be a kernel of truth in them. For instance, during the great plague of the summer of 1665, Newton returned home to Woolsthorpe to stay with his mother, as Cambridge was evacuated. During his stay in the countryside, the famed episode of the falling apple is said to have happened. The story is compelling and fits with our conception of the lone genius grappling with a nearly unsolvable problem, like the question of how to understand free fall on earth and the motions of the planetary bodies in a unified way. But it simply is not true that Newton discovered his complete theory of universal gravity at this time: we can document the emergence of that theory during the period from 1684 to 1686, the time when Newton wrote successive drafts of a manuscript entitled *De motu corporum* (On the motion of bodies). This ultimately became *Principia Mathematica* (1687, first edition), but only after many drafts and many crucial developments. It also seems that Newton had not yet conceived of his crucial concept of impressed force (*vis impressa*), which sits at the center of his mature physics (Westfall 1980, 148). But 1664–1666 has been called Newton's *anni mirabiles*, or miracle years, for a good reason: he did make substantial advances in mathematics at this time; in particular, he claimed years later that he had worked out his fundamental conception of the calculus during these 2 years. This is obviously a remarkable feat for a young man who had just a few years of college under his belt, having had a rather paltry education before then, especially in the relevant areas. When Newton returned to Cambridge in 1667, Isaac Barrow eventually learned of these great leaps in mathematics and was wise to promote Newton to the Lucasian chair a mere 2 years later. Perhaps no embellished legend is needed: it is astonishing to think that basic aspects of the calculus—which remains so fundamental to modern science and mathematics to this day—were worked out by a young college student on a farm in the English countryside.[8]

Another legend of Newton's early years is that he worked in an intellectual vacuum, holed up for hours at his mother's house or in his room at Trinity College, a solitary figure single-handedly discovering many fundamental underpinnings of modern mathematical physics. The kernel of truth here, of course, is that Newton did in fact grow up largely on his own—at least without his parents—and his 2 years in Woolsthorpe during the plague were spent largely alone, at least intellectually speaking. His achievements during those years are obviously awesome by any measure. But as we have seen, Newton was not alone in Cambridge: he had the important influence of senior figures and his records from the time record celebrations with friends in the tavern when he received welcome academic news. So the legend must be tempered.

Newton's actual writings during his early years as Lucasian Professor indicate a prodigious output. In the period 1670–1675, Newton created a telescope, celebrated by the newly formed Royal Society, and made fundamental contributions to optics, which were published in the *Philosophical Transactions* (see Chapter 3). As it turned out, Newton's claim that he had used a prism in order to determine experimentally that ordinary sunlight contains a series of embedded rays of various colors and that the colors of the rainbow are not created through a modification of light embroiled him in a substantial controversy. Numerous important figures from this time, including the famous Continental mathematician Huygens and the London experimental philosopher Robert Hooke, objected to Newton's methodology. Newton found the ensuing extensive debate extremely taxing, and he developed a lifelong aversion to intellectual controversy. But his reputation, both in England and, increasingly, on the Continent, had been established. It was soon to increase dramatically.

1.3 Mature Years in Cambridge and London

Despite these early achievements, no one among Newton's contemporaries was prepared for his work in the next decade. In this period, the stuff of legend is not apocryphal: it is well documented. As has been told countless times, in August of 1684, Edmond Halley—for whom Halley's comet is named—came to visit Newton in Cambridge in order to discover his opinion about a subject of much dispute in celestial mechanics. At this time, many in the Royal Society and elsewhere were at work on a cluster of problems that might be described as follows: how can one take Kepler's Laws, which were then considered among the very best descriptions of the planetary orbits, and understand them in the context of dynamical or causal principles? What kind of cause—for some, what kind of *force*—would lead to planetary orbits of the kind described by Kepler? In particular, Halley asked Newton the following question: what kind of curve would a planet describe in its orbit around the sun if it were acted upon by an attractive force that was inversely proportional to the square of its distance from the sun? Newton immediately replied that the curve would be an ellipse, rather than a circle.[9] Halley was amazed that Newton had the answer at the ready. But Newton also said that he had mislaid the paper on which the relevant calculations had been made, so Halley left empty handed. He would not be disappointed for long. In November of that year, Newton sent Halley a nine-page paper, entitled *De Motu*, that presented the sought-after demonstration, along with several other advances in celestial mechanics. Halley was delighted, and immediately returned to Cambridge for further discussion. It was these events that precipitated the many drafts of *De Motu* that eventually became *Principia Mathematica*. It is shocking to think that if Halley had not visited Newton and then persisted in talking with him, one of the founding texts of what we now call modern science might not exist.[10]

While he was writing the text that was to become the *Principia*, Newton corresponded with Halley. One of his letters in particular indicates how Newton understood the discipline of natural philosophy, to which he intended to contribute with his new book, even while warning Halley of his aversion to intellectual debate. On June 20, 1686, he wrote to Halley as follows:

> I designed the whole to consist of three books.... The third I now design to suppress. Philosophy is such an impertinently litigious lady that a man had as good be engaged in law suits as have to do with her. I found it so formerly [he presumably means the 1670s optics disputes] & now I no sooner come near her again but she gives me warning. The two first books without the third will not so well bear the title of Philosophiae naturalis Principia Mathematica & therefore I had altered it to this De Motu corporum libri duo: but upon second thoughts I retain the former title. Twill help the sale of the book which I ought not to diminish now tis yours. (Correspondence II: 437)

This letter was sent in response to Halley, who had written to Newton 2 weeks earlier that he ought to include Book III because "the application of this mathematical part, to the system of the world; is what will render it acceptable to all naturalists, as well as mathematicians, and much advance the sale of the book" (*Correspondence* II: 434). Without the third book, in which Newton discusses what he calls "the system of the world," the first two books of *Principia Mathematica* could not very accurately be called natural philosophy; rather, they would be better described as "two books on the motion of bodies." For Newton, as for Halley, natural philosophy was not principally concerned with just any motion of bodies that was tractable through mathematical analysis; rather, it was concerned with the mathematical analysis of the actual motions of the bodies within our solar system—within nature as we perceive it in our vicinity of the universe. That coheres with a long tradition in natural philosophy. Newton's innovation is to provide a mathematical analysis of the motions of these bodies (Chapter 5 describes why this maneuver is innovative). It is no surprise that for Newton, as for many natural philosophers in this period, one of the great outstanding questions is how to understand the earth–sun system, including the question of whether the earth or the sun is at its center. Just a year after this letter, the first edition of what many would now regard as the first true text of modern mathematical physics appeared. For his part, Halley wrote an anonymous piece in the *Philosophical Transactions* announcing the arrival of the text: "it may be justly said, that so many and so Valuable *Philosophical Truths*, as are herein discovered and put past Dispute, were never yet owing to the Capacity and Industry of any one Man."[11] And so at the age of 44, Newton was quickly propelled into the first rank of mathematicians and philosophers in England.[12]

The decade of the 1690s brought Newton considerable attention for his magnum opus, along with several new and significant friendships. When John Locke returned from political exile in 1688, he made a point of meeting Newton soon after and the two struck up a friendship. Their correspondence indicates that they held similar unorthodox religious beliefs, each finding reason, for instance, to question the official Anglican doctrine of the Trinity. These beliefs were closely held by Newton throughout his adult life, and Locke may have been the first person to whom he revealed them. In the second edition of the *Principia* in 1713, Newton may have given some hints as to his real views, especially in the newly added General Scholium at the book's end, but he would never publish his anti-Trinitarian conceptions openly, as they would have landed him in considerable political (and perhaps legal) trouble. For his part, Locke took Newton's work very seriously: he wrote an anonymous, largely laudatory, review of the *Principia* (having famously asked Huygens to vouch for the mathematics he could not understand) in the *Bibliothèque Universelle*, mentioned Newton in the preface to his *Essay Concerning Human Understanding* (1690), and told Bishop Edward Stillingfleet that Newton's work had convinced him that his long-held mechanist understanding of natural change required revision (see Chapters 5 and 6).

During this same time, Newton quickly developed an intense and very close friendship with the Swiss mathematician Nicolas Fatio de Duillier, who reports being converted from Cartesianism to Newtonianism in the process (Westfall 1980, 493). Yet Newton's tumultuous personal life did not come to an end with these particular friendships: as his correspondence amply demonstrates, he often found himself passionately devoted to a friend, only to have a significant fight with him later. Some scholars have speculated that the constant tumult of Newton's life can be traced back to the absences of his childhood.

In the mid-1690s, the allure of Cambridge and its intellectual environment had begun to fade for Newton. The figures who had such an immense impact on his early years, especially Isaac Barrow and Henry More, had long since died, and in some ways, the intellectual life that Newton sought had shifted to London, where figures like Richard Bentley were then living, and where the Royal Society was located.[13] But Newton did not move to London merely to seek intellectual company, and the picture of Newton as the solitary scholar is difficult to square with his many years in the capital. In 1696, after 35 years in Cambridge, Newton decided to move permanently to London, taking up the post of Warden of the Mint as his new official position. Newton's time as Warden, focused on bureaucratic and logistical issues, especially the question of how to defeat counterfeiters of the currency, is of little interest philosophically, but it does indicate that the mature Newton was a political figure and far from being a solitary scholar. Newton's political position, however, did not end his philosophizing: it was during this period that he finally decided to publish what became his second great book, the *Opticks*. Newton's research in optics was largely in completed form long before he decided to publish his work, and the results of his numerous experiments, together in a single volume. In 1704, the first edition of the *Opticks*, which would lead to its own powerful tradition in the experimental aspects of natural philosophy in the eighteenth century, appeared after the death of Newton's old rival in optics, Robert Hooke. Newton's friend, Samuel Clarke, translated the *Opticks* into Latin in 1706, thereby making it available to a wide Continental audience. In subsequent editions, Newton would add a series of long *Queries* as appendices to the volume: these sections of the text, which presented some of Newton's more speculative views in natural philosophy, early chemistry, and even theology, would have a long afterlife. With Newton's two texts, he had made fundamental contributions to both the mathematical and the experimental sides of the program in natural philosophy that would forever be associated with his name.

Warden of the Mint was not Newton's most important official position during this period of his life. In 1703, the Royal Society elected him its President, a role for which he would forever be known, and he threw himself into its activities. The society, which had foundered for some time during the previous decade, began to flourish again under Newton's leadership. Some of the talents for administrative duties and details that he had shown during his time as Warden became evident when he was President. Newton was soon to reach the pinnacle of his political and institutional power: 2 years after becoming President, Queen Anne knighted him in a grand ceremony back in Cambridge. He would thereafter be known as Sir Isaac.

1.4 Final Years

Although Newton did not publish another major work during his last two decades, he did make substantial revisions and additions to both the *Opticks* and the *Principia*. Many of these changes were prompted by the serious criticisms leveled against his views by leading mathematicians and philosophers on the Continent, especially Huygens and Leibniz. Indeed, the last two decades of Newton's life are marked by an intriguing contrast: on the one hand, Newton was at the height of his intellectual and institutional power and prominence, and he held an unquestioned position as the leading intellectual figure in England at that time; on the other hand, despite his numerous followers throughout his native land, including Bentley and Clarke, his views in natural philosophy and in theology (to the extent that they were known) were the subject of vigorous debate and deep controversy throughout the Continent. Numerous figures in Europe in the early eighteenth century were still convinced of the basic truth of Cartesianism, and therefore spent considerable energy attempting to undermine Newton's views. For those who had come to dispense with Cartesian ideas, however, there remained a powerful and influential alternative to Newton, namely, the philosophical orientation of Leibniz (Chapter 6). In the 1690s, Leibniz had published a number of important papers—in the *Acta Eruditorum* and elsewhere—that were critical of Descartes's views in natural philosophy and metaphysics, and many figures in the early eighteenth century saw him as the leading metaphysician of the day.[14] An extensive debate between Leibniz and his followers and Newton and his followers would erupt during this period, focused both on substantive philosophical, theological, and mathematical issues and on nonsubstantive issues connected with the political and nationalist implications of the calculus priority dispute. The many denunciations issued by both sides in the dispute over which mathematician first discovered the calculus, which became extremely heated in the 1710s and ended only with Leibniz's death in 1716, should not overshadow the genuine and genuinely interesting philosophical issues debated by both sides.

Leibniz and Newton had briefly and cordially corresponded with one another in 1693 (Newton 2014, 141–145). Although brief, we do see a glimmer of their future disagreement concerning the best understanding of gravity: Leibniz insisted that the action of gravity, both terrestrially and celestially, be reduced to contact action in some fashion, perhaps owing to interactions with a fluid vortex in the heavens, but Newton resisted this maneuver (Chapter 6).

They would never agree on this issue, and as the calculus priority dispute heated up in the beginning of the next century, their philosophical differences deepened. In 1711 and 1712, Leibniz made it known to various correspondents and colleagues that he remained unconvinced by Newton's theory of gravity, especially its deviation from the norms for causal explanation established by the so-called mechanical philosophy. He also fundamentally rejected the conception of space, time, and motion that Newton articulated in the famous opening Scholium of the *Principia*, contending that it violated the principle of sufficient reason, which Leibniz took to be a bedrock principle with which every physical theory must cohere. When Newton was revising the *Principia* in 1713 with the help of the new general editor, Roger Cotes, a fellow of Trinity College and himself a promising young philosopher, he certainly had his eye on these disputes with the Leibnizians. Hence, the second edition of the text contained numerous remarks—in various parts of the main text, in Cotes's long editor's preface, and in the new final appendix, the General Scholium—concerning the methods of Newton's philosophy designed to rebut the criticisms of Leibniz and others.

Yet this debate did not subside with the new edition of the text. In 1715, Leibniz sent a scathing criticism of Newtonian ideas to one of the most prominent political figures in England at the time, Princess Caroline of Wales. Her role as a mediator, and perhaps instigator, of a broad philosophical debate between the two camps was crucial (Bertoloni Meli 1999, 2002). She ensured that the circle around Newton saw the letter, and it was decided that the theologian Samuel Clarke, a close friend of Newton's at this time and his parish priest in London, would reply to Leibniz on Sir Isaac's behalf. Although Newton had corresponded with Leibniz before, his well-known and nearly lifelong aversion to controversy may have led him to choose Clarke instead of responding himself. In addition, Leibniz raised theological and metaphysical objections against Newtonianism in his first letter to Princess Caroline, and since Newton had never developed a systematic philosophical conception of the world, as Clarke had done in his *Demonstration of the Being and Attributes of God* (1704), it was wise to choose a systematic philosopher and theologian like Clarke to reply to Leibniz's charges. What ensued was an extensive, increasingly detailed, and increasingly acrimonious, but nonetheless substantive, philosophical debate that touched on all the major topics of the day: the nature of space and time, the proper method of natural philosophy, the uses of experiment, the nature of miracles, and God's relationship to the creation, including the possible inscrutability of the divine will. The correspondence was hugely influential throughout the eighteenth century. In France, led by figures like Émilie du Châtelet, and in German-speaking Prussia, led by Immanuel Kant, the debate between the Leibnizians and the Newtonians became the centerpiece of much work in theoretical philosophy and metaphysics.[15] Descartes had been decisively eclipsed by his two greatest critics of the late seventeenth century.

Despite his frailty at birth, Newton outlived Leibniz and many of his other critics and friends.[16] He spent the last years of his life in declining health. A third edition of the *Principia* appeared in 1726, just a year before he died, but it did not differ substantially from the second edition.[17] And as might be natural, Newton spent his last few years reminiscing about his past and telling stories to his friends and acquaintances. It is apparently from these days that the story of the apple originated (Westfall 1980, 862). Despite his declining health, however, Newton continued to preside over the Royal Society. And the Society's influence continued to be felt: on Newton's last meeting, in March of 1727, a letter from the newly formed Academy of Science in St. Petersburg was read. Just 3 weeks later, Sir Isaac died at the age of 85. The Royal Society canceled its next meeting in the wake of his death. By the end of that month, he had been interred in Westminster Abbey, at the center of London and indeed of British politics and culture, where his crypt remains to this day.

Newton's ideas did not die with him. His most profound impact on the future was probably the orientation toward solving problems outlined in the *Principia*. Although he chose to employ complex geometrical methods and future work would be done in the language of the calculus (which of course Newton himself discovered), there is no doubt that it is accurate to call the physics of the late eighteenth and early nineteenth century *Newtonian*.[18] Just as profoundly, although Einstein's revolutionary work in 1905–1915 helped to establish a new orientation toward physics with the special and general theories of relativity, it remains the case that even from the new perspective, Newton's theory is *approximately* true. Engineers still use Newtonian ideas to this day. This means that Newton made a lasting contribution to our understanding of the natural world. He also had a profound impact on the subsequent history of philosophy. For many philosophers—one might mention a crowd as diverse as John Locke and David Hume in England, Émilie du Châtelet and Voltaire in France, and Immanuel Kant in Prussia—Newton's science could be understood as replacing geometry as a fundamental epistemological model for knowledge-seeking endeavors. It could also be seen as providing a picture of the natural world, and of the laws that govern it, that any philosophically serious perspective must confront. It is no exaggeration to say that the main philosophical debates, projects, and preoccupations of the eighteenth century can be understood only in the light of Newton's work and influence.

notes

1 There are numerous biographies of Newton stretching back for roughly two centuries, along with various fictionalized accounts of his life and work. The most comprehensive account remains the classic biography (Westfall 1980).

2 In the early modern period, it was common for correspondence between two individuals, and the unpublished manuscripts of one author, to circulate among various intellectual circles. Hence, I include correspondence and some of Newton's manuscripts to be part of the canon of the *public Newton*. For instance, manuscripts such as *De Gravitatione* and the famous *De Motu* drafts from 1685, which connect very closely with Newton's published work in the *Principia* and his correspondence with various individuals, would count as part of this canon. As we will see, there is also evidence that John Locke knew about the ideas of *De Gravitatione*, if not the text itself. But his manuscripts in alchemy and biblical chronology are not continuous with any published works and therefore have a more private status. This is of course a rough methodological distinction that bears further thought.

3 Betty Jo Teeter Dobbs did foundational scholarship on Newton's work in the alchemical tradition—see especially Dobbs (1975, 1991). For a discussion of more recent work, see Figala (2002) and William Newman's extensive research, which is represented at "The Chymistry of Isaac Newton" (http://webapp1.dlib.indiana.edu/newton/).

4 Throughout this text, I use the dates of the new calendar, unless otherwise noted (as in this case). For perhaps obvious reasons, it was important to Newton later in his life that his birthday be expressed using the old calendar, since he was born on Christmas by it (not to mention the year of Galileo's death) but in 1643 by the new calendar in use on the Continent.

5 See especially the influential and controversial account in Manuel (1968).

6 Hannah Newton seems to have been semiliterate: there is apparently a single surviving letter from Hannah to her son; in it, she expressed her love for him and indicates that she prays to God for him. It was sent in May of 1665, after Newton had been in Cambridge for 5 years, but the original is torn and therefore incomplete (see Westfall 1980, 141)

7 The University of Cambridge was founded in the early thirteenth century—legend has it that the university was founded by intellectuals who had grown weary of the new university in Oxford. Henry the VIII founded Trinity College in 1546.

8 It is now accepted that G.W. Leibniz developed his own version of the calculus independently of Newton. The debate over the calculus priority dispute raged ferociously among Newton and Leibniz's circles in the early eighteenth century, but historians put little stock in the debate today. See especially Hall (1980) and Bertoloni Meli (1993).

9 Although astronomers for centuries had thought that the planetary orbits must be circular, for various important reasons, Kepler had argued that they are in fact elliptical (although this is consistent with the idea, which became important in later contexts, that the orbits are *nearly* circular). This innovation proved to be crucial for later work in celestial mechanics. Ellipses are figures in which a straight line from the center to any arbitrary point on the figure does not constitute a single radius that is equal to all other radii. For that reason, astronomers in antiquity may have considered them less than perfect.

10 On Halley's role in printing the *Principia*, see Cohen (1971, 130–142).

11 See *Philosophical Transactions* 16 (1686–1687): 291–297.

12 This fact does not mean that Newton's contemporaries endorsed his new ideas and methods; rather, even his fiercest critics, such as Leibniz and Huygens, quickly recognized his genius and stated so publically.

13 Bentley was an important theologian. He had been chosen to deliver the first Boyle Lectures in London in 1692; the lecture series was endowed by Robert Boyle in his will for the promotion of reasonable interpretations of Christianity and the establishment of harmony between religion and natural philosophy. Bentley corresponded with Newton in 1693 to seek his advice concerning the religious implications of his *Principia*, and for some time, Newton thought that Bentley might edit the second edition of the text (as it turned out, however, it would be many more years before the second edition was published, under the editorship of the young astronomer Roger Cotes).

14 This was certainly the case in many areas of the Continent, although (for obvious reasons) it took longer for Leibniz's views to be accepted in French regions, where Cartesianism continued to flourish for the first few decades of the eighteenth century. However, by the 1730s and 1740s, it had come under significant attack by figures like Voltaire, who wrote extensively about the superiority of Newton's views, and by figures like Émilie du Châtelet, who argued that the views of Leibniz—and of his prolific follower Christian Wolff—were superior to those of Descartes. Indeed, for influential figures like Châtelet, even more so than for Voltaire, the great philosophical struggle of the eighteenth century would be between Leibnizian and Newtonian ideas.

15 Émilie du Châtelet's work, *Institutions de physique*, first published in Paris in 1740 and again in revised edition in Amsterdam in 1742, attempted to mediate the dispute between the two camps by establishing a Leibnizian metaphysical foundation for Newtonian physics. Although it was immediately translated into German and Italian and had a major influence on French Enlightenment thought, the *Institutions* was never translated into English and has unfortunately been ignored by many histories of eighteenth-century philosophy. Intriguingly, working in Prussia a generation later, Immanuel Kant (who cited some of Châtelet's work) also determined that his fundamental problem was to reconcile the leading (Leibnizian) metaphysics of his day with the leading (Newtonian) physics. This problem animated both his so-called precritical work and also the *Critique of Pure Reason* (1781). On Châtelet, see Hutton (2004) and Detlefsen (2013); on Kant, see especially Friedman (1992, 2012).

16 Leibniz died in November of 1716, which abruptly ended his correspondence with Clarke. Although Clarke himself outlived Newton by 2 years, others in Newton's circle died earlier, including John Locke (who died in 1704) and Roger Cotes (who died very young in 1716—he was just 5 years old when the first edition of the *Principia* appeared). Although he was not sentimental, Newton did mourn the loss of these friends: in the case of Cotes, he was reported to have said, with typical understatement, "if Cotes had lived, we may have learned something."

17 Philosophically speaking, one of the most important additions was the new Rule Four in the *Regulae philosophandi* section of Book 3.

18 By the end of the century, the various disputes among Cartesians, Leibnizians, and Newtonians had died out, at least as far as physics itself was concerned. This reflects, in part, the fact that physics was becoming separated from philosophy; or more accurately, it reflects the fact that the natural philosophy practiced by figures like Descartes and even Newton was separating into two distinct fields, as I discuss in Chapter 2. For a detailed and illuminating account of Newton's influence on physics as a discipline, see Smith (2012).

was newton a scientist?

What was Isaac Newton? A mathematician: along with his eventual rival, the German figure G.W. Leibniz, he codiscovered calculus and made many other lasting contributions to the development of modern mathematics. A scientist: he discovered not only the three laws of motion that became the underpinning of physics in the modern era but also the law of universal gravitation, which pointed the way toward a unified treatment of terrestrial and celestial phenomena within a single physical theory of nature. As if that were not enough, he also made fundamental contributions to experimental optics in the late seventeenth century in the *Philosophical Transactions* of the Royal Society and in the early eighteenth century in his *Opticks*. Indeed, Newton is remarkable for the fact that his work as a theoretician is matched by his work as an experimentalist—either aspect of his oeuvre would be sufficient to secure his place in the canon of modern science. So in the popular imagination and in the history books, Newton is seen as one of the greatest scientists of the past three centuries, on a par with few others, perhaps just Darwin and Einstein. This is surely the view that will dominate our understanding of Newton in the twenty-first century and well beyond. And for many purposes, this view *ought* to remain the standard. This is what Newton means to us.

But what if our question is not, what does Newton mean to us? What if our question is, how was Newton understood during his own lifetime? Alternatively, how did Newton understand what he was doing? These are the kinds of question that animate historical research in general and scholarship in the history of philosophy in particular. It is not as if the popular view of Newton is *false*; he did in fact accomplish everything attributed to him, if not considerably more (taking various unpublished manuscripts and correspondence into account). The problem is that the view is not *precise*: there are important historical reasons for concluding that although we may wish to view Newton as a scientist, it would be more *accurate* to think of him in another, slightly different, way.[1] The simplest of these historical reasons is that no such category existed during Newton's day. The category of the

Newton, First Edition. Andrew Janiak.
© 2015 Andrew Janiak. Published 2015 by John Wiley & Sons, Ltd.

scientist—along with that word in English—is actually a nineteenth-century invention. Unlike many inventions, whose exact origins remain murky, we can say precisely when this category arose: at a meeting of the British Association for the Advancement of Science in June 1833, the Cambridge philosopher William Whewell coined the word *scientist* to capture a new category of intellectual. At the meeting, Whewell said that just as the practitioners of art are called *artists*, the practitioners of science ought to be called *scientists*, indicating that they should no longer be called *philosophers*. Whewell was responding to Samuel Taylor Coleridge's plea that the members of the British Association stop calling themselves *natural philosophers*, for the scope of their research had narrowed considerably in recent years (Cannon 1978, 201– 202, Schaffer 1986, Snyder 2011, 1–7).[2] The first time that *scientist* was used in print was a year later, when Whewell discussed the outcome of the British Association meeting in his (anonymous) review of Mary Somerville's book, *On the Connexion of the Physical Sciences* (Whewell 1834, 59).

Now one might object that since Whewell said that the practitioners of *science* ought now to be referred to as *scientists*, then this implies that *science* was a category before this episode. Indeed, the French academy, founded after the Royal Society, was called the *Académie Royale des Sciences*, and in various texts, Newton sometimes writes of *scientiae naturalis*, or what we might translate as *natural science*, rather than of "*philosophiae naturalis*."[3] These facts would seem to mitigate my argument.

It is true that the word *science*, which derives from the Latin term *scientia*, has been in continuous use in numerous contexts since the fourteenth century; and it is also true that figures before and after Newton often discussed *scientiae naturalis* in their texts. However, this is misleading—before and during Newton's day, these terms in Latin and in English had a much broader significance, meaning roughly *knowledge*. So *scientiae naturalis* meant *natural knowledge*. The terms did not obtain their modern meaning until the midto late nineteenth century: thus, the new meaning of *science*, referring to the natural sciences specifically and allowing us to distinguish between, for example, the sciences and the humanities, arose roughly at the time that the word *scientist* was coined.[4] So for good reason, before the middle of the nineteenth century, people like Newton were called *philosophers* or, more specifically, *natural philosophers* (referring to those philosophers studying nature). But is this still largely semantics? What is in a name?

In this specific case, names matter: the words *physics* and *natural science* pick out something distinct from the words *natural philosophy*. During the seventeenth century, and well into the eighteenth, figures like Newton worked within the well-established tradition of natural philosophy.[5] The modern discipline of physics, like those of chemistry and biology, was not formed until the beginning of the nineteenth century.[6] Seventeenth-century philosophers who studied nature investigated such things as planetary motions, the nature of matter, causal relations, and the possibility of a vacuum, but they also discussed many aspects of human beings, including the human psyche or the soul, and also how nature reflects its divine creator (Hatfield 1996). Discussions of God were especially prominent in seventeenth-century natural philosophy (Funkenstein 1986). As the title of Newton's magnum opus, *Mathematical Principles of Natural Philosophy* (1687), suggests, he intended his work to be in dialogue with Descartes's *Principles of Philosophy* (1644), a complex text that includes discussions of everything from the laws of nature to the nature of God's causal influence on the world. Just as Descartes had sought to replace Aristotelian or Scholastic methods and doctrines in natural philosophy, Newton sought his work to replace Descartes's. Newton famously wrote in the second edition (1713) of the *Principia*, in the General Scholium to the text, "Enough concerning God; to treat of God from phenomena certainly belongs to natural philosophy" ["*Et haec de deo, de quo utique ex phaenomenis differere, ad philosophiam naturalem pertinet*"], as I discuss in depth in Chapter 7. If we are not historically precise in our interpretation of words and concepts, then this proclamation in Newton's magnum opus will seem especially odd.

One might object here that placing Newton within the old tradition of natural philosophy ignores the fact that his work was a transformational aspect of what has longed been called the scientific revolution. It is certainly true that medieval natural philosophy had a very different character than the discipline practiced by figures such as Descartes and Newton. In the Aristotelian traditions of the thirteenth through the sixteenth centuries, philosophers often focused on analyzing Aristotle's ideas about the natural world, especially within the Christianized context of the medieval period (Murdoch 1982). Philosophers studying nature were often actually studying texts—such as Aristotle's *Physics* or commentaries on Aristotle—rather than conducting experiments or engaging in observations, and they often did not employ mathematical techniques. Traditionally, natural philosophy in Aristotelian circles was not conceived of as a mathematical discipline (unlike, say, optics or astronomy); instead, it focused especially on the natures of objects and on causation. In the seventeenth century, natural philosophers like Galileo, Boyle, Descartes, and Newton began to reject not only the doctrines of the Aristotelians but their techniques as well, developing a number of new mathematical, conceptual, and experimental methods. Of course, these developments have often been regarded as central to the scientific revolution. Despite the centrality of these changes during the seventeenth century, however, the *scope* of natural philosophy had not dramatically changed.[7] Natural philosophers like Newton expended considerable energy trying to understand, for example, the nature of motion, but they regarded that endeavor as a component of an overarching enterprise that also included an analysis of the divine being, just as Aristotelian-influenced philosophers studying nature in a Christian context had done. For that reason, it seems wise to regard Newton as a natural philosopher working within a well-established, if fundamentally evolving, intellectual tradition.

Yet the idea that Newton is best understood as a natural philosopher, rather than as a scientist or a physicist, continues to be controversial, even among prominent scholars of Newton's work.[8] For instance, the influential historian of medieval and early modern science Edward Grant has recently made the following argument:

> In judging what Newton was really doing in his *Mathematical Principles of Natural Philosophy*, we should not be misled by the title. Newton might have used either of two medieval and early modern synonyms for natural philosophy, namely, "natural science" (*scientia naturalis*) or "physics" (*physica*), to produce, respectively, the titles "Mathematical Principles of Natural Science," and "Mathematical Principles of Physics." Whatever he might have named his treatise, Newton was mathematizing natural philosophy and, depending on the subject matter, also was producing particular sciences. Whatever terms he may have used in his title, a glance at the approximately 530 pages of the *Principia* can leave no doubt that Newton was doing mathematical physics. We need not engage in mental gymnastics about the real meaning of the expression "natural philosophy." And we should not be misled by the fact that because the term "scientist" was only introduced in the nineteenth century, therefore no activity we would want to call science could have occurred before that century simply because "scientists" may have been called by another name: natural philosophers. (Grant 2007, 314)

Grant's perspective seems perfectly reasonable: surely, it is not linguistic facts and developments that should be taken to determine Newton's intellectual status; it is conceptual facts that matter. As Grant suggests, there is also considerable historical evidence to suggest that terms such as *physica* were used interchangeably with *natural philosophy*. To take one prominent example, Jacques Rohault's famous Cartesian textbook was first published in French in 1671 under the title *Traité de Physique*; after accruing many Newtonian notes to the text written by Samuel Clarke, it eventually appeared in English in 1723 as *System of Natural Philosophy*. The text itself, leaving aside Clarke's notes, had not fundamentally changed. However, I argue in the following that despite these historical and linguistic facts, conceptual facts count against Grant's view.

Similarly, in their influential account in the *Cambridge Companion to Newton*—part of a series of companions to philosophers and therefore a text that demands an answer to the question of Newton's intellectual status—the famous Newton scholars I. Bernard Cohen and George Smith provide several powerful objections to the idea that Newton was a philosopher in any meaningful sense. First and foremost, they argue that Newton's *Principia* had such a profound effect on future intellectual endeavors that it undermined the old idea of natural philosophy, fomenting a modern split between science and philosophy:

> It is a comment on the radical split between science and philosophy that because of Newton's *Principia* we no longer read Descartes's *Principia* as central to his philosophy, viewing it instead as Descartes's science. Correspondingly, to say that Newton's *Principia* is a work in philosophy is to use this term in a way that it rendered obsolete. (Cohen and Smith 2002, 2)

There is much to be said for this point of view. It is certainly true that Newton's work, in the *Principia* and elsewhere, helped to foment an eventual split between science and philosophy. Alternatively put, the work of Newton began a long historical process whose eventual outcome was a recognizably modern distinction between experimental and theoretical science, especially physics, on the one hand, and philosophy, especially metaphysics and epistemology, on the other. And secondly, if we use the word *philosophy* in its twenty-first century sense, then it is obviously mistaken to regard the *Principia* as a contribution to that discipline. No history of modern philosophy course in the world, so far as I know, has students read Newton's *Principia* cover to cover, as they would read Descartes's *Meditations*, Spinoza's *Ethics*, or Locke's *Essay*.

But students in history of modern philosophy courses might very well read Descartes's *Principles of Philosophy*, for it contains discussions of his understanding of substances; of God; of space, time, and matter; and of our knowledge of these things (metaphysics and epistemology were not sharply distinguished in this period (Stein 2002, 256–257)). This is the first clue that Cohen and Smith have adopted a somewhat anachronistic attitude in their argument. Indeed, the first part of Descartes's *Principles*—entitled "On the Principles of Human Knowledge" and comprising roughly 36 pages in the original Latin edition—recounts the very metaphysical and epistemological principles made famous in the *Meditations*, first published 3 years earlier (1641). It does so because Descartes explicitly regarded metaphysics as forming the foundation for investigations into the natural world (see Chapter 4). And the second part of the work—entitled "On the principles of material things," and comprising roughly 40 pages—discusses related topics such as God's attributes, the nature of matter, and the character of motion. The third and fourth parts, on the visible world and the earth, respectively, contain what Cohen and Smith would probably call Descartes's *science*, presenting, as they do, such classic topics as Descartes's vortex theory of planetary motion. But these are interrelated aspects of a single text, and so the view that the text is a work in science—one that contains a great deal of what we would *now* call theology, metaphysics, and epistemology—makes little historical sense, even if it accords with our categorization of the intellectual landscape. That fact is evident from a well-known aspect of Descartes's view: he *derives* the first two laws of nature—which, as we will see in Chapter 4, express the modern principle of inertia rather well— from the nature of God's immutability as the fundamental cause of all motion in the world (a view that was later associated with *occasionalism*). Thus, it is best to conceive of Descartes's work as it would have been conceived of at the time and, as his title suggests, this is a work in philosophy.[9]

It seems to me, however, that there is a more important reason to think of Newton as a philosopher, one that transcends the semantic and conceptual issues debated by scholars like Grant, Cohen, and Smith. Since Thomas Kuhn's work, *The Structure of Scientific Revolutions* (1962), became famous, historians, philosophers, and sociologists analyzing science have been especially aware of the importance of historical developments in the sciences but also of the sense in which a science is the joint intellectual endeavor of a community of practitioners (historically understood). To be a scientist, in Kuhn's image, is to be a member of a community characterized by certain kinds of basic *agreement* regarding facts about the world, techniques of observation, mathematical methods, and much else besides (originally referred to as a *paradigm*). In this way, it would make little sense to speak of a lone scientist studying the world according to her own idiosyncratic methods and techniques. These two aspects of Kuhn's transformational analysis of past science intersect in intriguing ways, as his discussion of the history of optics before Newton indicates:

> At various times all these schools made significant contributions to the body of concepts, phenomena, and techniques from which Newton drew the first nearly uniformly accepted paradigm for physical optics. Any definition of the scientist that excludes at least the more creative members of these various schools will exclude their modern successors as well. Those men were scientists. Yet anyone examining a survey of physical optics before Newton may well conclude that, though the field's practitioners were scientists, the net result of all their activity was something less than science. Being able to take no common body of belief for granted, each writer on physical optics felt forced to build his field anew from its foundations. (Kuhn 1962, 13)

Kuhn is struggling in this passage to convince his readers that we must not ignore the false theories of the past by implicitly reserving the concept of *scientist* only for those figures whose work is continuous with current theory (or considered true by today's standards). Hence, history has a crucial role to play in illuminating contemporary science. But if we grant Kuhn the importance of history, then it seems we find a tension between the use of *scientist* and the use of *science*, for Kuhn also shows convincingly that previous works in, for example, optics each had to begin anew from the foundations because no body of facts or belief could be taken for granted. They were not engaged in a modern scientific field because they lacked fundamental agreement. My own suggestion is that we use *scientist* to track that key feature of a field, which is consistent with an important strand in Kuhn's thinking.

So the question becomes, was Newton's community characterized by fundamental agreement concerning facts, data, techniques, methods, and the like? Newton was actually a member of at least two intellectual communities in the course of his long life: Cambridge University and the Royal Society. Newton did not work in a vacuum: René Descartes, Isaac Barrow, and John Wallis in mathematics; Henry More in theology; Christiaan Huygens in natural philosophy; Robert Boyle and Robert Hooke in experimental philosophy; Edmond Halley in astronomy; and John Locke in philosophy—these figures (and others) formed intellectual communities of which Newton was an active member. What Newton's communities *lacked*, however, was precisely the kind of fundamental agreement about facts, techniques, and methods that characterize what Kuhn called *normal science*, the day-to-day experiments, theorizing, calculations, and data collection that form the basis of modern scientific fields. This was not due to the fact that figures like Huygens, Boyle, Hooke, and Newton were not engaged in experimentation, theorizing, calculating, and data collection, for they devoted much of their lives to such activities. Rather, it was due to the fact that among these figures, there were long-standing, massive disagreements about facts, the use of mathematics, the proper methodologies to follow in obtaining experimental and observational results, the relation between theories of natural phenomena and basic metaphysical principles, and much else besides (see Chapters 3–6).

It is often said that the Royal Society of London was the first major scientific society in early modern Europe (with the Académie Royale des Sciences following closely on its heels in 1666). But this point should not obscure the fact that fundamental disagreements were prevalent even among the fellows of the Royal Society. For instance, toward the beginning of Newton's life, in 1672, he fomented a debate about the proper methodology of optics with other members of the Society: Robert Hooke and Christiaan Huygens fundamentally rejected his approach to understanding light (Chapter 3). For another example, from the late 1680s until the second decade of the next century, Newton was engaged in a debate with Society fellows such as Huygens[10] and Leibniz concerning his theory of gravity (Chapter 6). This dispute did not concern empirical data or a particular mathematical innovation used by Newton; instead, these leading figures debated such issues as what counts as an intelligible explanation of gravity and what kinds of explanatory constraints the mechanical philosophy places on theories of nature. They never agreed. Newton was not a member of a community of scientists, then, because there was no *science in our sense*: that is, there was no intellectual endeavor characterized by the sorts of background agreement concerning facts, techniques, and methods highlighted by Kuhn as essential to the scientific enterprise.

Ironically, if there was *any* candidate for what we might call the *paradigm* of natural philosophy between, say, 1672 and 1727, the heyday of Newton's intellectual work, it was certainly the *mechanical philosophy* (Boas 1952, Osler 2010, 77–78). Every leading thinker in this period—including Robert Boyle in protochemistry, or *chymistry*, and in experimental philosophy; Robert Hooke in microscopy, optics, celestial mechanics, and early geology; Christiaan Huygens and Gottfried Leibniz in mathematics and the theory of motion; and John Locke in philosophy—endorsed the fundamental mechanist idea that natural phenomena should be understood and explained solely in terms of matter and motion. This was sometimes called *corpuscularianism*, sometimes the mechanical philosophy, and sometimes more simply *the new philosophy*. It was influential precisely because many figures before 1672, most prominently Galileo in Italy, Mersenne in France, Descartes in Holland, and Hobbes in England, had already endorsed this concept as the leading alternative to the Aristotelian ideas of the schools. But as we will see in depth in Chapters 3, 5, and 6, consensus proved elusive: perhaps the greatest of all these natural philosophers, Isaac Newton himself, refused throughout his long career to endorse the fundamental tenets of the mechanist approach to understanding nature (Janiak 2008, 87–129; cf. Machamer *et al.* 2012). And indeed, his peers and interlocutors constantly proclaimed that he had deviated from their mechanist consensus, from the very beginning of his career until its very end.

This feature of Newton's work is perhaps most evident in his relationship with his famous rival, Leibniz. Were they scientists working together in an intellectual community? A bit of historical knowledge would appear to suggest that the answer *must* be "yes." Each was a member of the Royal Society early on in his career, corresponding with its early secretary, Henry Oldenburg, and other members; each was a leading mathematician, eventually codiscovering what we now call calculus, which has obviously been essential to the development and growth of the modern sciences; each developed highly sophisticated and complex theories of planetary motion; each was critical of the methods and ideas of the Cartesians; and so on. However, these commonalities mask a key fact: beginning roughly in 1690, and continuing unabated until Leibniz's death in 1716, these two figures expended considerable energy engaging in fundamental disputes concerning the proper methods of studying nature. It is not as if Leibniz thought that Newton's theory of universal gravity had failed to account for certain astronomical data, or recent observations of comet paths through the solar system, or the like; he rejected the most basic aspects of Newton's approach to thinking about the potential causes of the planetary orbits. Newton had argued that when natural philosophers search for the causes of the motions of the planets, they should use the concept of a centripetal force, which itself is one kind of impressed force (see Chapter 4). He eventually (and famously) concluded in the first seven propositions of Book III of the *Principia* that the force of gravity on earth, which accounts for free fall, also accounts for the planetary orbits and the lunar orbit—hence the idea of *universal* gravity. It is not that Leibniz regarded this conclusion as *false*; he rejected the idea that the force of gravity—or indeed, any centripetal force that does not involve physical contact between material bodies—was even a *candidate* for being the cause of the planetary motions. Newton's idea of the forces of nature is at the very center of his project in the *Principia*: to reject those forces as being unintelligible, as being inadmissible even as possible causes of the planetary motions, just is to reject Newton's project *per se*. And that was what Leibniz did.

Imagine an analogue from today's science: would we call someone a biologist who claimed, not simply that her colleague's theory could not explain, for example, how a moth's grey wings were adaptive in a particular forest environment, but who claimed that there simply is no such thing as evolution by natural selection?[11] What if our imaginary biologist did not merely doubt, for example, that a particular mouse's DNA had a certain influence on the proteins in its blood, but denied the existence of DNA altogether or, better, denied that DNA even made sense as a possible physical system, claiming that it was verging on nonsense to postulate a double helix of strands of molecules with a certain character? That was the kind of maneuver that Leibniz made: he did not merely doubt Newton's theory of gravity; he denied that there was any such thing as the forces of nature in Newton's sense at all. He thought that philosophers should completely jettison the very idea of a Newtonian force of nature, for the Newtonians had unwittingly revived exactly the kind of Scholastic *occult* powers that many seventeenth-century authors had spent their careers undermining. In fact, there is a respect in which Leibniz's objection to Newtonian natural philosophy was even deeper: as he made especially clear in his celebrated correspondence with the Newtonian philosopher and theologian Samuel Clarke, who represented Newton and his followers in England, Leibniz believed that Newtonian ideas about space, time, matter, and forces violated the most fundamental principle of metaphysics, namely, the principle of sufficient reason (Clarke and Leibniz 1717). He argued, for instance, that the Newtonian conception of space as an infinite Euclidean magnitude that is independent of all the objects (and object relations) in nature is incompatible with the requirement that every state of affairs and event in nature must have a sufficient reason why it is so (and not otherwise). For Leibniz, one can know on this basis alone—that is, one can know *a priori*, independently of any empirical evidence at all—that Newton's basic ideas about space, time, motion, matter, and force are fundamentally mistaken. In tandem, Newton simply rejected the importance of the principle of sufficient reason; that is, the very basis for all of Leibniz's reasoning about nature (in his own opinion) was never accepted by Newton.[12] In this precise sense, *there was no science of physics in 1690*: the disagreements among the leading figures of the day were simply too deep. Hence, the linguistic facts are just as irrelevant as Grant says: it is the lack of a community formed by deep methodological, theoretical, and factual agreement that is decisive. If we were to follow Grant and call Newton's work *mathematical physics*, then we would require a distinct concept (and term or phrase) to characterize the discipline in Newton's future that was marked by fundamental *agreement*. Today's scientists cannot work in a research community if their colleagues insist that their basic conclusions violate fundamental *metaphysical* principles![13]

Kuhn's *Structure* helpfully emphasizes the role of the textbook in disseminating scientific knowledge, and in particular, its role in communicating the facts, methods, and ideas commonly accepted within a scientific discipline to its next generation of practitioners. (It is illuminating that there are no textbooks as such in philosophy.)[14] Could Leibniz and Newton have written a textbook together? Certainly, they agreed on many fundamental mathematical ideas: Newton's discovery of the generalization of the binomial theorem, and their joint discovery of what we now call the integral and differential calculus, would certainly form the heart of the textbook. They might also agree on the importance of certain technologies for the study of nature: Newton invented an important telescope and Leibniz was fascinated by the new microscopes of their day (Wilson 1995). But their deep agreement in mathematics and in experimental technology serves to highlight how deep their disagreements in natural philosophy really were. Leibniz would begin his textbook with the principles of contradiction (for truths in mathematics) and the principle of sufficient reason (for truths about nature), arguing that all philosophizing must be consistent with them. Newton rarely spoke of the first principle, and would regard the second as irrelevant. The next chapter of the textbook would be equally contentious: whereas Leibniz would require that any explanations of natural phenomena refer to laws of nature that are consistent with a mechanist conception of body, Newton would reject that stricture, arguing that we ought to consider explanations that involve force laws and a concept of force that is *abstract*, without any tie to mechanical models (see Chapter 5); Leibniz would insist on attributing the planetary orbits to the motions of vortices, and Newton would reject the vortex theory (see Chapter 6); and so on. If the members of a community cannot agree on what to include in their textbook, then they lack a modern scientific discipline.

The debates that animated natural philosophy within Newton's lifetime are intimately connected with his persona as a philosopher. There is no doubt at all that Newton was not a systematic philosopher (Cohen and Smith 2002, 1–4). Newton never wrote a systematic treatise like Descartes's *Meditations*, Spinoza's *Ethics*, or Locke's *Essay*, although he read many of them. He was not systematic, but rather adventitious: he engaged in philosophical reasoning precisely when he was challenged by a figure like Hooke or Huygens or Leibniz, finding ways of explicating and defending his methodology; his views of space, time, and matter; his understanding of force; his concepts of substance and of infinity; and his beliefs about God. This is as true of his posthumously published anti-Cartesian tract *De Gravitatione* as it is of the second edition of his magnum opus; it is as true of his unpublished correspondence as it is of the queries to his other great work, the *Opticks*. This is why I will focus on the controversies and debates that animated Newton's life, for it is precisely in those contexts that he chose to delve into traditional and pressing philosophical topics. Each chapter that follows will deal with some debate or controversy in Newton's life.

There is another—related but distinct—conceptual reason to consider Newton's work *natural philosophy*: whereas the modern sciences are characterized by fundamental agreement, as Kuhn indicates, natural philosophy has long been characterized by fundamental *disagreement*. In that sense, *natural philosophy is like philosophy itself*. It is a major theme of philosophy in the modern period that it is marked by fundamental debates about what philosophy is, what its proper methods are, what kind of knowledge it can achieve (if any), and so on. Famous descriptions of this situation in modern philosophy abound (see Kant's statement quoted in the following). In tandem, between 1600 and 1750, philosophers studying nature exhibited a vast array of opinions concerning the proper methods in their field. Despite their agreement that the Aristotelian worldview must be reformed, if not simply rejected, figures such as Bacon, Galileo, Descartes, Hobbes, Hooke, Boyle, Leibniz, and Newton agreed on little else. Whereas Bacon was famously enamored of obtaining observational and empirical data when studying nature, Descartes provided an *a priori* derivation of the basic laws of nature from an analysis of the divine being; whereas Cartesian physics was largely a qualitative investigation into natural phenomena, Newton insisted on employing advanced geometrical methods throughout his work; just as Descartes thought Galileo's work lacked a proper metaphysical foundation, Leibniz would assert the same of Newton's; and so on. A consensus on basic facts about the world, on the proper mathematical methods to use when studying the world, and on the kinds of causes that can be found for phenomena in the world would be elusive for at least 150 years. Fundamental disagreement was widespread in natural philosophy throughout the entire period of the so-called scientific revolution.

This fact about modern natural philosophy is evident if we focus on the difference between the state of Newton's field in 1700—during the height of his fame and influence—and its state in 1800, long after his death in 1727. Partly due to Henry More's influence, Cartesianism was extremely popular in Cambridge during the second half of the seventeenth century: it was not until at least 1700 that the curriculum focused on Newtonian ideas (Gascoigne 1985). But even if there was a Newtonian consensus in that (albeit significant) part of England, Cartesianism remained fundamentally important on the Continent through most of the first half of the eighteenth century. Even as Cartesianism waned, however, there was no Baconian-cum-Newtonian consensus in this period: whereas a figure like Voltaire was promoting what we might regard as a purely Newtonian orientation toward studying nature (Voltaire 1738), other figures in France, such as Émilie du Châtelet, were convinced that Leibnizian ideas were also crucial to creating a true picture of the natural world (Châtelet 1740, 1742). Similarly, vortex theories of planetary motion, which had been anathema to Newton, remained extremely popular on the Continent until at least 1750, when the great mathematician Euler began to revise his views (Aiton 1972). Even in the mid- to late eighteenth century, substantive, even fundamental, differences among various natural philosophers remained evident.[15] By 1800, roughly speaking, it may be fair to say that with figures such as Laplace and Lagrange, what we now call *Newtonian mechanics* had become the dominant strain of thinking about nature throughout much of Europe; Cartesianism had died out, as had most of Leibniz's ideas concerning the physical world.[16] By this time, then, we might acknowledge the emergence of a community of physicists working together on the basis of agreements on facts, techniques, and methods. It is no surprise, therefore, that within a few decades, figures like Whewell recognized this situation, arguing that a new concept, and a new term, was needed to characterize the activities of his community.[17] By this time, one might say, there was no longer any such thing as natural philosophy: its animating debates about fundamental principles concerning the study of nature had ended as basic agreements had been forged. The point is not that Whewell simply wanted a new word; he wanted to mark the fact that the activities of his community were fundamentally distinct from those of the past.

We are now in a position to render the distinction between what we might call the contextual and the decontextual conceptions of the scientist a bit more precise. According to the decontextual conception, presented by Grant and Cohen and Smith, a person is a scientist if she meets two criteria: (1) she engages in certain kinds of intellectual and practical activities, including observational and experimental activities, mathematical reasoning and calculation, and theorizing that employs the latter while being sensitive to the former[18], and (2) the kinds of work mentioned in (1) is continuous in certain respects with contemporary scientific thought and practice. There is no doubt at all that Newton was a scientist in *this* sense. In my view, however, we should endorse (1) but replace (2) with (2'), which is contextual: (2') one is a scientist if she is a member of a community characterized by fundamental agreement concerning the most basic intellectual and practical activities to be employed in the study of nature. This idea has two consequences: first, a lone figure engaging in various intellectual and practical activities cannot be a scientist on her own if she lacks communal support[19], and, second, a figure in a community characterized by widespread, and fundamental, *disagreement* also cannot be considered a scientist.[20] Of course, we may want to reply: but Newton engaged in precisely those intellectual and practical activities that *would become* essential to modern physics, and in that sense, he is part of *our* scientific community. He agrees with *us*. That is obviously true but decontextual.

The emphasis placed here on fundamental communal agreement not only reflects Kuhn's influential scholarship on the history of modern science, but also, and just as importantly, the basis for our modern distinction between science and philosophy. Since at least the late eighteenth century, philosophers have noted that whereas the modern natural sciences are characterized by fundamental agreement on basic principles, modern metaphysics and epistemology sorely lack such agreement. For instance, after describing some developments during the seventeenth century involving Galileo and his followers, Kant remarks in the preface to the second edition of the *Critique of Pure Reason* (1787, B xiv–xv):

> In metaphysics one must reverse course innumerable times because one discovers that it does not lead where we want to go, and it is so far from reaching unanimity in the assertions of its adherents that it is much more a battlefield, and indeed one that appears to be especially determined for testing one's skills in mock combat on it; no fighter has ever gained the least bit of ground, nor has any been able to base any lasting possession on his victory. Thus there is no doubt that up to now the procedure of metaphysics has been a mere fumbling, and what is worse, a fumbling among mere concepts.

Of course, Kant sought to rectify this situation, placing metaphysics once and for all on the "secure path of a science." But this was not to happen: although Kant helped to set the stage for nineteenth-century philosophy in a fundamental way, philosophers did not all become Kantians; the basic agreement that leads to progress in the sciences continued to elude philosophy.

Kant's dream of making philosophy *wissenschaftliche* through a philosophical revolution animated much of the development of the discipline during the first half of the twentieth century. Perhaps the most influential version of the idea in the English-speaking world hails from Quine's work: as part of his attempt to undermine the famous analytic/synthetic distinction, itself a remnant (but not a precise reflection) of Kant's views, he argued that philosophy was in fact an aspect of the natural sciences, continuous with—and indistinguishable from—them (Quine 1951). For Quine, philosophy does not embrace any special method, nor does it have special content or beliefs or facts associated with it: it is simply one part of the whole of science (the whole of which meets the "tribunal of experience" together, rather than proposition by proposition, as earlier thinkers like Carnap had argued). Hence, we get "empiricism without the dogmas." But if anything is clear about English-speaking philosophy in the past 50 years, it is that widespread and fundamental agreement about its basic principles continues to be elusive.[21] And in that precise sense, Quine's holistic, often compelling, conception of the unified intellectual activity of investigating the natural world cannot hide the fact that some intellectual communities agree on a wide range of basic principles, facts, and ideas, while others do not. Thus, even if we grant Quine his view that science and philosophy cannot be distinguished by methods or beliefs or ideas, we retain a systematic means of distinguishing the two enterprises from one another, and indeed, we retain the very same means that confronted Kant two centuries ago.

In the modern period, then, despite the best efforts of some of our most influential philosophers, the discipline of philosophy has always been characterized by fundamental—principled, deep, unresolvable—disagreement. Since that is precisely the intellectual situation that Newton faced throughout his entire career—from at least 1672 until his death in 1727—it makes good historical sense to regard Newton as a philosopher among philosophers. The great irony here is that Newton always exhibited a profound distaste, a deep aversion, to intellectual debate and controversy; he sought a community characterized by deep agreement. But his ideas generated endless debates. If we allow a harmless anachronism: Newton *wanted* to be a scientist, but he was always a philosopher.

Newton was a natural philosopher among other natural philosophers, engaging in the kinds of debate that such thinkers had always engaged in. But Newton's *influence* extended well beyond the confines of philosophers studying nature, encompassing numerous figures and traditions in Britain, on the Continent, and even in the new world over the course of the eighteenth century.[22] Newton's influence has at least two salient aspects. First, his achievement in the *Opticks* and in the *Principia* was understood to be of such philosophical import that few philosophers in the eighteenth century ignored it. Most of the canonical philosophers in this period sought to interpret many of Newton's epistemic claims within the terms of their own systems, and many saw the coherence of their own views with those of Newton as a criterion of philosophical excellence. Early in the century, Berkeley grappled with

Newton's work on calculus in *The Analyst* and with his dynamics in *De Motu*, and he even mentioned gravity, the paradigmatic Newtonian force, in his popular work *Three Dialogues between Hylas and Philonous* (1713). When Berkeley lists what philosophers take to be the so-called primary qualities of material bodies in the *Three Dialogues*, he remarkably adds *gravity* to the more familiar list of size, shape, motion, and solidity, thereby suggesting that the received view of material bodies had already changed before the second edition of the *Principia* had circulated widely. Hume interpreted Newtonian natural philosophy in an empiricist vein and noted some of its broader implications in his *Treatise of Human Nature* (1739) and *Enquiry Concerning Human Understanding* (1750). Newton's work also served as the impetus for the extremely influential correspondence between Leibniz and the Newtonian Samuel Clarke early in the century, a correspondence that proved significant even for thinkers writing toward the century's end. Unlike the *vis viva* controversy and other disputes between the Cartesians and the Leibnizians, which died out by the middle of the century, the debate between the Leibnizians and the Newtonians remained philosophically salient for decades, serving as the impetus for Châtelet's influential work during the French Enlightenment, *Foundations of Physics* (1740), and also as one of the driving forces behind Kant's development of the *critical* philosophy during the 1770s, culminating in the *Critique of Pure Reason* (1781). In addition, Newton's work spawned an immense commentarial literature in English, French, and Latin, including John Keill's *Introduction to Natural Philosophy* (1726); Henry Pemberton's *A View of Sir Isaac Newton's Philosophy* (1728); Voltaire's *Elements of the Philosophy of Newton* (1738); Willem s' Gravesande's *Mathematical Elements of Natural Philosophy* (1747); Colin MacLaurin's *An Account of Sir Isaac Newton's Philosophical Discoveries* (1748), which probably influenced Hume; and Du Châtelet's and Clairaut's commentary on Newton's *Principia* (1759). These and other commentaries were printed in various editions, were translated into various languages, and were often influential.

A second aspect of Newton's influence involves thinkers who attempted in one way or another to articulate, follow, or extend the Newtonian *method* in natural philosophy when treating issues and questions that Newton ignored. Euclidean geometry and its methods were seen as a fundamental epistemic model for much of seventeenth-century philosophy—Descartes' *Meditations* attempts to achieve a type of certainty he likens to that found in geometry, and Spinoza wrote his *Ethics* according to the *geometrical method*. Propositions deduced from theorems in Euclidean geometry were seen as paradigm cases of knowledge. We might see Newton's work as providing eighteenth-century philosophy with one of its primary models, and with a series of epistemic exemplars as well, but part of philosophy's task was to articulate precisely what the new Newtonian method involved. David Hume is perhaps clearest about this aspect of Newton's influence. His *Treatise* of 1739 has the subtitle, "An Attempt to Introduce the Experimental Method of Reasoning into Moral Subjects," and many philosophers have argued that he meant (at least in part) the method of the *Opticks* and the *Principia* (DePierris 2012). Indeed, as Hume's text makes abundantly clear, various eighteenth-century philosophers, including not only Hume in Scotland but Jean-Jacques Rousseau on the Continent, were taken to be, or attempted to become, "the Newton of the mind."[23] For Hume, this meant following what he took to be an empirical method by providing the proper description of the relevant natural phenomena and then finding the most general principles that account for them (of course, one aspect of Hume's work is to provide an analysis of the concept of causation that is far more extensive than anything found in Newton, which influences what counts as an *account* of a phenomenon). This method would allow us to achieve the highest level of knowledge attainable in the realm of what Hume calls *matters of fact*.[24]

Despite the influence of Newton's *method* on eighteenth-century philosophy, it is obvious that the *Principia*'s greater impact on the eighteenth century is to have helped effect a branching within natural philosophy that led to the development of mathematical physics, on the one hand, and modern philosophy, on the other. And yet to achieve an understanding of how Newton himself approached natural philosophy, as I have argued, we must carefully bracket such historical developments. Indeed, if we resist the temptation to understand Newton as working within a well-established discipline called mathematical physics, if we see him instead as a philosopher studying nature, his achievement is far more impressive, for instead of contributing to a well-founded field of physics, as someone such as Einstein did, he had to *begin* a process that would eventually lead aspects of natural philosophy to be transformed into a new field of study. This transformation took many decades, involving a series of methodological and foundational debates about the proper means for obtaining knowledge about nature. Newton himself not only engaged in these debates throughout his mature life, his work in both optics and in the *Principia* generated some of the most significant methodological and philosophical controversies in the entire eighteenth century.

There is one burden that my interpretation of Newton's field must confront, a burden that the conception of him as a scientist can evade. If Newton is really doing natural philosophy, just as Descartes was, then his field is, at least from our point of view, a bizarre mélange. Natural philosophy between 1600 and 1750 encompassed what we would consider to be fundamentally distinct intellectual endeavors, including what *we* would call: philosophy—especially what we now call *metaphysics* and *epistemology*; the natural sciences—especially physics, perhaps along with some chemistry; and, theology—especially questions about God's role as the creator of the natural world, but usually excluding Scriptural interpretation.[25] Employing the category of natural philosophy represents a Pyrrhic victory if we conceive of it as comprising a series of distinct intellectual projects characterized by our current categories of metaphysics, epistemology, physics, and theology. It can certainly be tempting to believe that if a text in natural philosophy—such as Descartes's, or Newton's, *Principia*—mentions God or the divine, then that field must therefore have included theological issues. Similarly, if Descartes or Newton discusses the distinction between space and body, or the essence of matter, it is tempting to conclude that natural philosophy must have included metaphysical issues. But this is misleading. Despite their numerous disagreements—many of which animate the development of natural philosophy throughout the century—Cartesians and Newtonians agreed that natural philosophy is *distinct* from both theology and metaphysics. In this period, it is common to speak of the two great books—the book of nature and the Bible—and each was seen as the work of God. The theologian's discussion of the divine is often guided by faith and by an interpretation of scripture. In contrast, the natural philosopher's discussion of the divine is centered on the book of nature; hence he will interpret nature as the work of a creator, employing it as his sole guide (Newton writes: "treating of God from phenomena...").[26] Metaphysics in the seventeenth century was understood in disparate ways: it might be an analysis of *being qua being* (à la Aristotle); it might be thought of as *first philosophy*, a philosophical inquiry that is (logically) prior to any other (à la Descartes); or it might be regarded as focusing on the analysis and employment of basic principles of reasoning (à la Leibniz). But however it was conceived, it was distinguished from natural philosophy, with its focus on nature and *natural* beings, like rocks, planets, and of course human beings, along with their creator. This means, of course, that we cannot employ *our* concept of nature to understand *their* project: early modern philosophers studying nature all presupposed that it included not only the human being, including the mind or the will, but also an ineliminable link to the creator. For us to understand their project, we must confront this question: why did philosophers like Descartes or Newton think that a mathematical analysis of a planetary orbit, or an experimental investigation of heat, or a discussion of the possibility of a vacuum, could be connected in some way to a study of the creator of the world? That question will help to animate this book.

notes

1 This kind of distinction reflects one of Newton's most important contributions to epistemic debates: we should dispense with insisting that propositions are either true or false, instead conceiving of some propositions as approximately true, with the proviso that under some conditions, such as the discovery of further empirical evidence, we can make them more exact.

2 The report issued from the first meeting of the British Association for the Advancement of Science in September of 1831 stated their goal: "to promote the intercourse of the cultivations of science with one another, and with foreign philosophers," cited in Cannon (1978, 202).

3 I wish to thank an anonymous referee for raising these objections. For his use of "scientiae naturalis," see Newton's optical lectures from the early 1670s (1984, vol. 1: 86*ff*).

4 Indeed, the Oxford English Dictionary has the new meaning of *science* first appearing in 1867, namely, in the generation after Whewell's invention.

5 For differing understanding of the history of natural philosophy, see French and Cunningham (1996) and Grant (2007). Cunningham and Grant had an extended debate that involved, among other things, the question of how to interpret Newton's relation to the tradition of natural philosophy, and their debate sparked other reflections as well: see, for example, Cunningham (1988, 1991, 2000) and Grant (2000, 2007). For an influential interpretation of Newton's work in natural philosophy, see Stein (2002); see also Domski (2010), Ducheyne (2012), and Janiak (2008).

6 Contemporary scholarship in the history of modern science locates the emergence of physics, biology, and chemistry, involving both linguistic and conceptual shifts, near the beginning of the nineteenth century (certainly not before that time). Whereas Buchwald and Hong argue that physics was established by roughly the first third of the nineteenth century (2003, 167), Cannon contends that it emerged specifically in France between 1810 and 1830 with the work of Ampere, Carnot, Fresnel, and Fourier. Bensaude-Vincent notes that most historians would locate chemistry's emergence in the early nineteenth century, following Lavoisier's work at the end of the last century and Dalton's atomic hypothesis in 1808; she adds that it would be decades before some of their basic ideas and methods were widely accepted throughout the community (2003, 196–198), which might argue for a later periodization. For his part, Richards contends that biology had both a *linguistic* and a *conceptual* birth circa 1800 (2003, 16–18). Cantor argues that optics emerged in its recognizably modern form in roughly 1830, when it became part of mathematical physics (1983, 18). In this way, there is considerable agreement concerning the fall of natural philosophy and the rise of numerous modern scientific disciplines. Hakfoort, who writes of eighteenth-century *natural philosophers* like Euler working in optics, advocates a historical periodization that seems consistent with Cantor's approach (Hakfoort 1995, 180–185). He helpfully describes and criticizes what he calls *presentism* in the historiography of optics, arguing more generally that natural philosophy came to an end sometime in the late eighteenth century, possibly the early nineteenth (1995, 182).

7 As Hakfoort writes in his history of optics: "In medieval times important subjects that nowadays are treated in the physical sciences were part of Aristotelian natural philosophy, which in its turn was closely linked to metaphysics. The goal of natural philosophy was to provide a complete account of nature. This account was considered well established because it was based on metaphysical and empirical certainties. This *ideal* of a complete, certain, and partly a priori picture of the natural world did not die when the *contents* of Aristotelian natural philosophy were rejected in the Scientific Revolution" (1995, 181).

8 For instance, see the strong criticisms of the approach in Cohen and Smith (2002, vol. 1–4: 19), and Grant (2007, 313–316). Grant provides an especially detailed rejection of the view I endorse in this chapter. To be clear, my argument is that it is more accurate to consider Newton a natural philosopher rather than a scientist. This argument does not entail that it is more accurate to consider Newton a natural philosopher than a mathematician, an alchemist, a religious man, a politician, and so on. Newton had many personas. Each of these categories must be analyzed historically and contextually. Moreover, Kuhn's argument

in *Structure* concerns the history of science: whether, for example, mathematics, alchemy, religion, or politics is somehow predicated on fundamental agreement concerning facts, methods, and principles is an intriguing but separate issue. Many of Kuhn's readers in the 1960s and 1970s asserted that their own disciplines—from art history to dance to sociology—exhibited *paradigms* of the kind that Kuhn had singled out as crucial for understanding science's history, but this extension of his analysis was always controversial. The same would be true in the cases of categories expressing Newton's other personas, at least without substantial argument. Thanks to an anonymous referee for pressing this point.

9   Cohen and Smith make another point—did Newton's *Principia* render the idea that it is a work in philosophy *obsolete*? They are surely correct in one sense: it would be odd to think of *Philosophiae Naturalis Principia Mathematica* as part of the tradition that includes such works as the *Ethics* or the *Essay*, not least because the former is a work containing hundreds of pages of highly sophisticated mathematics (as Grant emphasizes) and the latter are certainly not. So it is not a work in philosophy. Yet it remains the case that it is a work in what was then called *natural philosophy*, a category for an intellectual enterprise that no longer exists.

10 The debate was among perceived equals. Newton clearly believed that Huygens was a fantastic mathematician and philosopher: he told Leibniz in 1693 that Huygens's remarks on his discoveries were *brilliant*; Newton was typically short on praise. Huygens employed a number of mathematical and physical methods that met with Newton's approval. As he tells the theologian (and later Newtonian) Richard Bentley in famous exchange in 1691, one of the best preparations for reading the *Principia* is working one's way through Huygens's *Horollogium Oscillatorum* (1673). But after the publication of the *Principia*, Huygens (along with Leibniz) criticized some of Newton's ideas and methods on very general grounds, arguing in particular that his theory of gravity did not produce an intelligible explanation of the planetary orbits and of the free fall of bodies on earth, because of its failure to adhere to the explanatory standards of the mechanical philosophy.

11 Here I am thinking of the famous article "Nothing in biology makes sense except in light of evolution" (Dobzhansky 1973).

12 For his part, Clarke did accept a *voluntarist*, rather than a *rationalist*, version of the principle of sufficient reason, but his version lacked most of the consequences that Leibniz's version clearly had. For the intriguing details of Leibniz's complex argument against the Newtonian view of space and for Clarke's reply to it, see Chapter 6.

13 It is not as if Newton disagreed fundamentally with *everyone* in his community. He had substantial agreement with some prominent figures in his day— Halley and Flamsteed in astronomy come to mind, as does Clarke in theology. But we must be careful not to beg the question by choosing members of his community on the basis of their agreement with him, and if we leave Hooke, Huygens and Leibniz out, then we are leaving out some of the most important figures of his day.

14 There are textbooks in logic, where agreement is deep and widespread. But in the rest of philosophy, textbooks are either anthologies of articles and excerpts—many of which are explicitly intended to present debates in the

field—or representations of some school's or individual's perspective. There are no textbooks in the classic sense because philosophers make their careers disagreeing with one another.

15 Buchwald and Hong write: "The magnitude of the change can best be appreciated by considering the situation in the mid-eighteenth century. Physics, or, more precisely, natural philosophy, was then neither confined to specialized institutions nor dominated by self-conscious professionals who spoke primarily to one another. There were of course scientific societies, such as the Royal Society of London and the Academie des Sciences in Paris, but discussions were also conducted in salons and coffeehouses. Moreover, boundaries between the professional and the amateur were neither well defined nor strongly policed. Also, there were substantial differences between the kinds of natural philosophy done at different places, for theories and experimental practice were often highly localized. The physics carried out by Cambridge Newtonians, for example, had little in common with the Newtonianism of Joseph Priestley, let alone that of French Newtonians in the Academie. And only a small portion of natural philosophy was quantitative or tied to exacting experiment" (Buchwald and Hong 2003, 164).

16 For details, see Fox (1974), who argues that what he calls *Laplacean physics* had its greatest success from 1805 until 1815. Perhaps already by the middle of the eighteenth century in France, *physique generale* was taken to refer to Newtonian mechanics, and *physique particuliere* referred to experimental investigations of electricity and magnetism, heat, and other phenomena (Buchwald and Hong 2003, 168). A very safe and conservative estimate, then, might be that physics emerged not earlier than 1750 and no later than the first few decades of the nineteenth century.

17 Consider this remark: "We suggest that physics as a separate discipline with distinctive methods—exact, quantitative, and experimental—can be reasonably well discerned by the end of the first third of the nineteenth century" (Buchwald and Hong 2003, 165). This would place the emergence of physics precisely at the moment of Whewell's famous pronouncement.

18 As will become clear, this aspect of the analysis that I propose here is not in dispute among the figures whose views I consider in this chapter, so it need not be much more precise than I have made it. Of course, many historians, sociologists and philosophers of science throughout the twentieth century have spilled much ink attempting to render this characterization more precise. This condition alone, of course, would rule out lots of seventeenth-century figures right off the bat: no one debates whether John Milton was a scientist, and for good reason.

19 Karen Detlefsen and Hylarie Kochiras raised an intriguing objection to this point: what if there is a lone figure whose ideas, methods and practices are actually continuous with those in a larger community but who is, as a matter of fact, shunned by the members of that community on sexist, racist or other grounds? (There are many examples of just such unjust and irrational exclusion throughout the history of modern science.) This is a key question that requires a much deeper analysis than I can provide here. But part of the answer might be this: if an individual is shunned by, or excluded from, a community on what are essentially noncognitive or irrational grounds, then from our analytical point of view, she is in fact a rightful member of that community in the

only sense that matters for understanding science's history. That is, if her rejection is irrational, then that is the key element for our analysis; that is why I have stressed the importance of recovering the *rationality* of various objections to Boyle's and Newton's ideas and methods in Chapters 3 and 5, indicating the rational basis for deep disagreement during the early modern period.

20 It may be helpful to regard this analysis as analogous (in certain respects) to the famous idea in biology that if scientists found a creature on Alpha Centauri that was morphologically indistinct from a contemporary German Shepard, that would not itself entail that they had found a canine, because the specimen in question would lack the proper historical relations to other canines. The concept of a species might be historical in a way that's analogous to the concept of a scientist.

21 Finding a means of overcoming fundamental disagreements—for instance, among realists and idealists who cannot agree on basic topics, such as whether physical objects like tables are real in some relevant sense—is also an animating feature of the ideas of Quine's rival, namely Rudolf Carnap. See especially the argument in Carnap (1950).

22 For recent accounts, see Domski (2012), which contains details of Newton's connections to figures such as Descartes, Spinoza, Wolff, and Kant. For a broader perspective on Newton's influence on the eighteenth century, see Snobelen (2009). Cohen (1956) provides a classic account of the fate of the Newtonian method in America, focusing on Benjamin Franklin's work.

23 Surprisingly, Kant declared that Rousseau was *the Newton of the mind*—for discussion, see Neiman (1997).

24 A proposition expressing a matter of fact cannot be known to be true without appeal to experience because, unlike in the case of *relations of ideas*, the negation of the proposition is not contradictory. For discussion of Hume's relation to Newton, with citations to the voluminous literature on that topic, cf. De Pierris (2012) and Schliesser (2007) for different approaches.

25 On the idea of natural philosophy, see section 2 of Hatfield (1996), and Funkenstein (1986).

26 For an influential pre-Newtonian conception, see the Cartesian treatise by Rohault, *System of Natural Philosophy*, vol. I: 20–21 (first published in 1671). Rohault is especially concerned to indicate that natural philosophy analyzes objects within their natural state, where the contrast class is not the quasi-Aristotelian *violent* state of a thing, but rather some state that God creates against the ordinary course of nature. Hence, Rohault explicitly brackets miracles and what he calls *the mysteries of faith*.

making philosophy experimental: boyle and hobbes and hooke and newton

Most students enrolled in a course in the history of modern philosophy learn that the seventeenth and eighteenth centuries were animated by a grand struggle between the proponents of Continental Rationalism, especially Descartes, Spinoza, and Leibniz, and the defenders of British Empiricism, especially Locke, Berkeley, and Hume. It has traditionally been useful to employ these two philosophical categories, for they divide the historical landscape neatly into two camps marked not only by intellectual differences but clear geographical ones as well. There certainly are some crucial differences between a philosopher who contends that the primary source of knowledge is a priori reasoning (call her a rationalist) and one who insists that the primary source must be our sensory experience of the world (call her an empiricist). The theory of ideas expounded by the so-called empiricists is another useful way of distinguishing their orientation toward philosophical problems from that of their Continental predecessors. One cannot doubt that Leibniz's attitudes toward philosophy differ markedly from Locke's, as Leibniz was the first to indicate in his response to Locke's magnum opus, *New Essays Concerning Human Understanding*. Other differences abound. Indeed, the grand narrative involving empiricism and rationalism would not have captured the imaginations of generations of philosophers if it lacked such significant and substantive foundations to its various slogans.

Alas, this grand narrative, useful and compelling as it may be, is anachronistic, much like the use of *scientist*. There was no such thing as *empiricism* in the early modern period.[1] Figures such as Locke, Berkeley, and Hume did not call themselves, nor did others call them, *empiricists* in their own day. Instead, they were proponents of what was then called the *experimental philosophy* or, as Hume called it in 1739 in the subtitle to his *Treatise*, the *experimental method*

Newton, First Edition. Andrew Janiak.
© 2015 Andrew Janiak. Published 2015 by John Wiley & Sons, Ltd.

of reasoning. Without any unified camp called *empiricism*, it makes little sense to postulate its *rationalist* opponent, not least because, as we will see, opposition to the experimental method or its uses in philosophy was not a particularly unifying element for the members of that camp. Many self-styled experimental philosophers expended considerable energy criticizing the views of Descartes in natural philosophy, but none more so than Leibniz, who built his early career on his detailed and vociferous analysis of Cartesian *errors*. Ironically, the distinction between rationalism and empiricism began to enter the philosophical lexicon when Kant published the *Critique of Pure Reason* (1781, first edition) in an attempt to transcend the seemingly intractable debate between these two camps through his new orientation toward metaphysics, *transcendental idealism*. It was especially useful to Kant to postulate two camps engaged in a fundamental disagreement precisely to show how his *Copernican revolution* in philosophy could overcome this problem by splitting the difference between these two views and setting his discipline on the secure path of a science for the first time.

But if we leave aside the general desire to achieve historical and linguistic accuracy, why does this point matter? Why should readers in the twenty-first century be particularly sensitive to the fact that a seventeenth-century philosopher may have called his work *experimental* rather than *empiricist*? Surely, these amount to the same thing.

They do not amount to the same thing (see Roux, 2014). The most significant difference between thinking of the history of philosophy through the concept of *empiricism* rather than that of the *experimental philosophy* connects directly with the discussion in Chapter 2: historically, only canonical philosophers such as Locke or Berkeley have been considered empiricists, but a much wider cast of characters, including Hooke, Boyle, and, of course, Newton, have been characterized as proponents of the experimental philosophy. Rightly so. Newton was clearly a self-styled proponent of the experimental philosophy, but he was not an empiricist.[2] Unlike empiricism, which is typically understood as a movement within what we would now call epistemology—and indeed, in this guise, it continues to garner support to this day, although it is far from achieving consensus—defenders and proponents of experimental methods were typically working within the tradition of natural philosophy discussed previously. Some philosophers argued that experimentation, including observation and careful measurement of various features of natural phenomena, is the best means of obtaining knowledge of nature; but others denied that natural philosophy ought to include experimental methods at all. The fact that philosophers studying nature ever debated the usefulness of experiments seems peculiar to modern readers: how could anyone studying the natural world ever have doubted that experiments, observations, and sensory perception were essential to obtaining knowledge? How *else* would anyone achieve knowledge of the natural world? Sitting in the proverbial armchair is useless in that regard. One task of this chapter is to address this issue. But even before we have its answer, we can immediately recognize that the experimental philosophy is a useful historical category to employ when studying the early modern period, for this reason: unlike in philosophy where such things as empiricism, realism, and antirealism are continually debated, in contemporary science, there simply is no debate about whether experiments are useful. Of course, the setup or the results of a particular experiment are subject to debate; but no serious scientist today would argue that science itself should have nothing to do with experiments. That issue has obviously long since been settled.

One might therefore say that studying the history of the experimental philosophy is more difficult than studying the history of empiricism: we must use our historical knowledge to recover the basic reasoning behind the (now defunct) contention that experiments are useless for obtaining knowledge of nature. The ideas of a Locke or of a Hume may in certain respects seem quaint or old fashioned to modern readers, but empiricism as a philosophical doctrine remains an ongoing concern. In contrast, the ideas of the experimental philosophy's opponents, such as Hobbes, can at times seem nothing short of bizarre. This difference reflects the basis for the modern distinction between science and philosophy. Once the modern sciences of biology, chemistry, and physics emerged in the late eighteenth or early nineteenth century (see Chapter 2), continuing work in those areas was predicated on basic agreements concerning such things as the essential roles of experiment and observation; any historical figure who questioned such roles is seen, from our point of view, as reactionary or confused. Since philosophy has never been predicated on that kind of fundamental agreement, historical (or contemporary) figures who question some argument or view are not difficult to understand: they are merely doing precisely what philosophers have always done. The best way to understand why some historical figures rejected the experimental philosophy is to uncover the historical context of their work by studying all the senses in which natural philosophy in the early modern era was *not yet* characterized by fundamental agreement. The task of this chapter, in part, is to address this problem directly, uncovering the reasons that someone like Hobbes would have had for opposing experiment so strongly. Part of the story has to do with the history of natural philosophy in the seventeenth century and the profound transformation that it underwent at the hands of figures like Boyle, Hooke, and Newton.

This chapter explores two fascinating episodes concerning the experimental philosophy involving four of the most significant philosophers in mid-seventeenth-century Britain. In the first episode, involving the natural philosopher Robert Boyle—for whom Boyle's Law, known to chemistry students everywhere, was later named—and the moral and political philosopher Thomas Hobbes, a great debate erupted about the role of experiment and of experimental knowledge. In 1661–1662, Hobbes and Boyle debated in particular what the bounds of natural philosophy, especially in its experimental guise, might be and what the concomitant bounds of metaphysical speculation might be. Whereas Hobbes defended a self-consciously traditionalist conception of natural philosophy and its methods for discovering truths about nature, Boyle argued that Hobbes was largely dabbling in speculative or metaphysical issues that were not tractable through the use of experimental methods or the analysis of experimental evidence. Boyle sought to reorient natural philosophy precisely toward those questions that were tractable through experimental methods and experimental analysis.

In a certain sense, the second episode grew out of the first. It illustrates a curious fact: fundamental debates about the role of experiments in natural philosophy did not occur solely between proponents and critics of the experimental philosophy; such debates occurred even among its strongest expositors and defenders. The young Robert Hooke was an assistant to Boyle before his dispute with Hobbes; he would go on to become the official *curator of experiments* for the Royal Society of London (founded in 1660 and given its royal imprimatur in 1662). Hooke's *Micrographia* (1665) is one of the great neglected works of the scientific revolution: it is replete with fascinating experimental and observational discussions. By the time that Hooke was an established figure in London, a young Isaac Newton, working from his rooms in Trinity College, Cambridge, began to publish his experimental findings in optics in the official organ of the Royal Society, the *Philosophical Transactions*. When Newton's work on the effects which prisms have on sunlight appeared in the *Philosophical Transactions* in 1672, they caused an immediate stir among many philosophers, especially Hooke. From Hooke's point of view, Newton had advocated a corpuscular theory of light, contending that his experiments had indicated that ordinary sunlight consists of a stream of minute particles that cannot be perceived as such in ordinary perceptual circumstances. In response, Hooke defended the wave theory of light, arguing that all of Newton's experimental data were consistent with that theory as well. But Newton's reply was surprising: instead of trying to show that his data were in fact consistent only with the corpuscular theory of light, or even that they tilted toward that theory, which he preferred, he insisted that he was not really advocating that theory at all. Instead, his goal was to draw a few experimentally sound conclusions regarding sunlight and colors. Hooke seemed to believe that this approach made little sense: a theory of light should tell us whether it is a wave or a stream of particles. Like Boyle and Hobbes, then, Hooke and Newton were debating the question of how experimental methods could be used by philosophers to draw conclusions about nature. Unlike the Boyle–Hobbes debate, however, the Hooke–Newton debate occurred between two strong proponents of the experimental philosophy.

Each of these two episodes illustrates an important point for our study. The first episode helps to set the stage for the emergence of Newton's special brand of philosophizing about nature. It indicates how the greatest experimentalist in the generation before Newton—namely, Boyle—faced stiff resistance to his suggestions about how to ask questions concerning nature that experimental and empirical information can answer. It also shows that the experimental tradition in natural philosophy that would eventually be strongly identified with British intellectual life, especially by the early eighteenth century, experienced significant birth pangs even within Britain itself. There simply was no *Baconian* consensus. The status of experiment and of empirical information about natural phenomena was still very much in dispute when Newton began to publish his findings in the *Philosophical Transactions*, and it would continue to be in dispute throughout the rest of the century. The second episode helps to illustrate the extent to which Newton's views and positions emerged through extensive philosophical—by which I mean, foundational or fundamental—disputes with numerous influential interlocutors. Even when presenting his basic experimental results, Newton was always engaged in philosophy.

The two episodes also help to indicate how elusive philosophical consensus in the midcentury proved to be, even among figures working within England. There is a certain irony to this situation. Whereas Boyle and Hobbes were both anti-Aristotelian in orientation, and more importantly, strong proponents and defenders of the new mechanist thinking about nature, they disagreed profoundly on the use of experimental methods in philosophy. In a way, the inverse is true of our other pair. Whereas Hooke and Newton were anti-Aristotelian in orientation and, more importantly, strong proponents and defenders of the new experimental philosophy, they disagreed profoundly on the importance of mechanistic thinking within optics (or so I will argue in the following). Debates about the fundamentals persisted.

Moreover, the two episodes have an intriguing intersection. An animating feature of Boyle's debate with Hobbes is this: what is the value of formulating questions about natural phenomena—such as concerns about the nature or weight of atmospheric air—that can be answered through obtaining experimental results? In 1660–1662, Hobbes doubts that this approach has any real value. A decade later, Newton's debate with Hooke and Huygens had a related animating feature: what counts as a question about natural phenomena—such as concerns about sunlight's heterogeneous features—that can be answered through experimental results? One might think that once Boyle had convinced a wide community of philosophers that Hobbes was wrong, that there was indeed a substantial value to formulating questions that are subject to empirical answers, the debate was over. But in fact, over the course of the next decade, the debate merely shifted. As Boyle's former experimental colleague and as the curator of experiments, Hooke was as convinced as anyone in England of the value of the experimental approach to philosophy. And yet once Newton presented his theory of the heterogeneity of light, along with a corresponding conception of color, Hooke doubted that Newton had formulated questions that were subject to empirical answers. He insisted that some of the propositions that Newton regarded as supported by strong empirical evidence were mere conjectures, mere *hypotheses*. A lengthy and at times acrimonious dispute concerning the correct conception of the distinction between mere conjectures and empirically supported propositions ensued.

3.1   Boyle's Debate with Hobbes

It is difficult for a twenty-first century reader to place herself within the intellectual context of England in the 1660s. Figures such as Boyle and Hooke and Newton and Huygens were part of a broad philosophical movement that stood for a few basic propositions: first, to understand the motions of objects through the world, whether on earth or in the heavens, one needs to employ various kinds of mathematical techniques (especially various kinds of geometrical and analytical reasoning); second, observation of objects, events, and phenomena is a key guide to describing them; third, when studying natural phenomena, one ought to formulate and run experiments to obtain data that can then be used to understand, and perhaps eventually to explain, those phenomena; and fourth, since many facts about the natural world cannot be discovered by unaided human perception, natural philosophers ought to develop, build, test, and calibrate various kinds of instruments, especially telescopes and microscopes but also pendulums and other devices, in order to probe nature. A contemporary reader might say: of course! The task of any historically sensitive account of the development of natural philosophy in the 1660s and 1670s, then, is clear: one must characterize the intellectual and historical context in such a way that today's readers can understand why some of the leading philosophers of that time would have opposed all of these (seemingly obvious) ideas with great vigor. And one must provide that characterization without falling into a trap: it is always easy to portray figures in the past as heroes who were rejecting the central dogmas of their discipline—one thinks of stories about Galileo's conflict with the Catholic Church over the earth's motion (for which see Chapter 7)—by challenging the institutional and intellectual authorities of their day. Hence, one might simply say that Scholastic and Aristotelian philosophers in places like Oxford or Cambridge or Paris in the mid-seventeenth-century were committed to what we now regard as an outmoded methodology for the study of nature and figures such as Boyle and Hooke challenged their dominant views. But that is too easy. The debates in the 1660s and 1670s concerning the new experimental philosophy that occurred between Boyle and Hobbes and Hooke and Newton lacked that feature, for all of these figures were great defenders of the *modern*, anti-Scholastic point of view. Indeed, Hobbes was one of the most important moderns of his time, a great critic of Aristotelian ideas, and a proponent of the latest thinking about the mechanical philosophy.[3] And yet he vigorously opposed Boyle's ideas about experiments. Why?

One piece of background methodology informing my historical analysis may help to set the stage. The goal of my analysis is not to presuppose that we can understand Hobbes's opposition to Boyle by somehow construing his views as *true* (or his arguments as sound). The point is rather that we can see him as *rational*: even if he was mistaken in way one or another from our perspective, that does not entail that he was irrational. But rationality, in my view, is historically specific, at least in one relevant sense. Nowadays, it would clearly be irrational to present a systematic opposition to the use of experiments in natural science. So a presentation of the historical and intellectual context can enable us to understand that in the 1660s, it was perfectly rational to debate this issue: experimental methods were just then being developed; there was no long-standing tradition of running experiments in natural philosophy that opponents would have to grasp or explain. Hence, opposition of Hobbes's kind is understandable to us in that light.

The basic features of seventeenth-century natural philosophy outlined in Chapter 2 are especially pertinent here, for they serve as a crucial historical background for Hobbes's famous criticisms of Boyle's use of the air pump. As we have seen, Hobbes was no Aristotelian: he was a thoroughgoing, if not an *arch*, mechanist, contending that all changes within nature were due to the impacts of material bodies with sizes, shapes, and motions on one another, not to mention a committed materialist. As he argues in his *Elements of Philosophy*, what the *writers of metaphysics*—by which he obviously means various kinds of Aristotelian—call formal and final causes are in fact just *efficient* causes (Hobbes 1839, part II, chap. 10, §7). In a sense, he was even more committed to the mechanical philosophy than one of its principal founders, Descartes, because Hobbes rejected the very idea of immaterial substance, which meant that human beings lacked any aspect that exceeded the reach of mechanistic explanations, at least in principle (Henry 2013, 121). But he did retain a crucial—Aristotelian-inspired—conception of natural philosophy's *aims*, arguing that the goal of the philosopher studying nature is to provide causal explanations of the phenomena in question. Hobbes's causal explanations would make reference solely to mechanical processes involving interactions among material objects (and their constituent particles), rather than to the classic four Aristotelian *aitiai*. Yet they were causal explanations for all that, and they were central to his philosophizing about nature: he was deeply skeptical of any account of a natural phenomenon that was not explanatory. He found it difficult, if not impossible, to regard experimental results as anything but irrelevant to the explanatory task of the philosopher. He also insisted that natural philosophy be a demonstrative discipline, one that issues in demonstrative knowledge of nature (Shapin and Schaffer 1985, 19). Unlike natural history, which involves the collections of various curious facts, natural philosophy provides rational knowledge of nature in the strongest sense. In that way, the experimental focus of the newly formed Royal Society, which was itself associated strongly with Boyle and with Hooke, was rejected by Hobbes, who never became a member (Martinich 1999, 296–299).

Although Hobbes is obviously known primarily as a political and moral philosopher—his *Leviathan* having long been a part of the canon—he did extensive work in natural philosophy as well, and that work serves as a key part of the background to his debate with Boyle (made famous by Shapin and Schaffer (1985)). Indeed, long before he had read about Boyle's experiments, Hobbes had already developed a very detailed and extensive conception of nature and of the proper philosophical methods for studying it. This conception, along with the depth of Hobbes's commitment to mechanist thinking, is laid out in great detail in the first book of *The Elements of Philosophy* (1655), entitled "Concerning Body."[4] He argues in this text, first of all, that philosophy provides us with knowledge through its two most fundamental methods: (1) by arguing from causes to effects and (2) by arguing from effects to causes. This familiar idea is given an intriguingly antiexperimental twist from the start: Hobbes argues, second of all, that these arguments proceed solely by *ratiocination* (or what he calls *computation*) and not through sensory experience (Hobbes 1839, part I, chap. 1, §2). He then notes, third of all, that philosophy is divisible into natural and civil foci, where the former is concerned solely with bodies that are *generated*—hence, it does not include discussions of God (because the divine is not created), aspects of history (because this involves experience rather than ratiocination), or issues of faith (because this is distinct from reason). Hence, the natural philosopher analyzes causal relations among physical bodies through reason and without relying essentially on experience. From the start, then, it is clear that Hobbes already had reason to be skeptical of the experimental philosophy's methodological presuppositions, at least when causal reasoning was at issue.

Hobbes also defended several substantive views concerning nature that would eventually place him specifically at odds with Boyle's approach. For instance, Hobbes distinguishes between two conceptions of space: first, *imaginary space* is the *phantasm* or imaginative representation of some body existing without the mind, one in which we represent only the extension of that body; and second, *real space* is the extension of a body, one that is independent of our thought (unlike our representations) and coincident or coextended with some part of space (Hobbes 1839, part II, chap. 8, §4). To illustrate, an apple on my desk in my office has a certain extension (it occupies three spatial dimensions), which Hobbes calls a *real space*; but when I look at my apple and then close my eyes and imagine it, I am dealing with an *imaginary space*. Here is the kicker: since real space is identical to the extension of bodies, there can be no such thing as empty space (Hobbes 1839, part II, chap. 7, §2). Of course, we can *imagine* empty space—that is where we obtain imaginary space—because we can imagine the extension of a body considered independently of that body and its other features (*accidents*), but such a represented empty space is merely a representation. For instance, I can see my apple, imagine it, and then imagine that all its features—its redness, its smell, etc.—other than its extension disappear, and then I am left with the *place* of the apple, which Hobbes identifies with imaginary space (1839, part II, chap. 8, §5). Unlike the apple itself, the place of the apple is not part of the world around me; it is just a phantasm or representation. So empty space is not a contradictory notion—it is not logically impossible—but since it is merely something that we can imagine, rather than something that can exist, it is not a feature of nature.[5]

Lest there be any doubt that Hobbes intends to reject the possibility of a vacuum in his *Elements of Philosophy*, he explicitly tackles that issue in part four of his text by providing his own arguments and by criticizing the arguments of others, including Lucretius, who accepted the vacuum. From our point of view, the most significant aspect of his analysis involves what he (intriguingly) calls an *experiment*, by which he means a *gedankenexperiment* that is designed to illustrate the fact that a vacuum is not possible in nature (even if it is logically possible). Hobbes explains that if we take a vessel AB, which has little holes at its bottom, B, and a large hole at its top, A, and if we fill it with water, we find that the water will not flow through the holes at B unless the hole at A is open (Figure 3.1).

This is counterintuitive, says Hobbes, because "the natural motion of the water" as a heavy body would be toward the ground, but my covering the hole

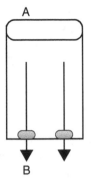

Figure 3.1

at A hinders this motion. Why is that so? Hobbes explains that the water cannot flow through the holes at B unless the air adjacent to them has been displaced and that displacement cannot happen, in turn, unless the opening of the hole at A allows air to flow into the vessel (part IV, chap. 26, §2). Hobbes clearly endorses a plenist view in his causal explanation of this phenomenon. Moreover, he apparently presupposes a mechanist conception of causal relations—one articulated explicitly earlier in the text (part II, chap. 9, §7)—when he assumes that the only way that my covering the hole at A, which is spatially separated from the holes at B, could prevent water flowing through those holes is if the air acts as an intermediary by blocking the water flow, for the air adjacent to B is contiguous with air near the middle of the exterior of the vessel, which is contiguous, in turn, with the air adjacent to A. His mechanist view earlier in the text takes this form: there can be no cause of motion in any body except in a contiguous body (part II, chap. 9, §7). Thus, Hobbes's mechanical view of causation would prevent him from endorsing any explanation of this phenomenon that violates his prohibition against noncontiguous causation among bodies.

Hobbes's argument can be read as having several basic steps: first, if there were a vacuum adjacent to B, then there would be nothing there to prevent the water from following its *natural motion* through the holes; second, the air adjacent to B prevents the water from flowing; third, the only way that the air at B can be displaced to make room for the water to flow is if something contiguous to the air causes it to move; and fourth, an event at A, like removing the cover over the hole, could influence the air at B only if the two phenomena are contiguous to one another, in this case through the intermediary air surrounding the vessel on all sides. Think of the fourth point roughly as follows: removing the covering at A allows some air particles to push on the water in the vessel; their displacement allows adjacent air particles to take their place; and so on, until there is room for the water at B to take the place of the air particles formerly located there. In a vacuum, the water at B would flow regardless of what is done at A, since the two are spatially separated. Of course, as Hobbes admits, this argument presupposes that the water has a natural motion toward the ground, by which he means at least that our goal is to explain why the water does *not* fall.[6]

In his *New Experiments Physico-Mechanicall* of 1660, Boyle presents 43 experiments involving what he called his *pneumatical engine*, which was designed and operated with Hooke's assistance. He indicates in his note to the reader that his goal is to study "the nature of the air" with his experiments, and to further his "grand design of promoting experimental and useful philosophy" with them (Boyle 1999, vol. 1: 143). Before describing any of the 43 experiments, Boyle undertakes a long description of the apparatus that Hooke designed, referring in great detail to its various parts as outlined in a figure that opens the work. He then tackles the philosophical heart of the matter at the outset: there may be certain leaks in the glass vessel and the attached air pump, which has an intriguing consequence for a long-standing philosophical question. He writes: "even at a very small leak there may enough get in, to make the *vacuum* soon lose that name; by which I here declare once for all, that I understand not a space wherein there is no body at all, but such as is either altogether, or almost totally devoid of air" (Boyle 1999, vol. 1: 163). Thus, Boyle indicates that he will take the old philosophical (and contested) concept of the vacuum (Grant 1981) to apply only to some space in which there is no air, or very little, rather than to a space that is empty of body altogether. The reason is clear: Boyle was perfectly well aware that many philosophers, including Descartes and Hobbes, had argued strenuously against the physical possibility of a vacuum in the latter sense, and so he chose to remain silent on that question. Yet he insisted that although he may never have achieved a vacuum even in his restricted—if you like, in his experimental or operational—sense, nonetheless, he came close enough in his experiments to have discovered "hitherto unobserved *Phaenomena* of nature" (Boyle 1999, vol. 1: 164).

Boyle wastes no time in explaining to his reader what he takes his experiments to have shown. After describing the basic workings of his engine in one paragraph, he then immediately presents his principal discovery:

> For the more easy understanding of the experiments tryable by our engine, I thought it not superfluous, nor unseasonable in the recital of this first of them, to insinuate that notion by which it seems likely that most, if not all, of them will prove explicable. Your Lordship will easily suppose, that the notion I speak of is, that there is a spring, or elastical power in the air we live in. By which ελατης [driver] or spring in the air, that which I mean is this: that our air either consists of, or at least abounds with, parts of such a nature, that in case they be bent or compressed by the weight of the incumbent part of the atmosphere, or by any other body, they do endeavor, as much as in them lies, to free themselves from that pressure, by bearing against the contiguous bodies that keep them bent; and, as soon as those bodies are removed or reduced to give them way, by presently unbending and stretching out themselves, either quite, or so far forth as the contiguous bodies that resist them will permit, and thereby expanding the whole parcel of air, these elastical bodies compose. (Boyle 1999, vol. 1: 165)

Boyle thinks that his experiments have enabled him to discover this *hitherto unobserved* feature of ordinary air, its *springiness*, which in this period he seems to think is distinct from weight and possibly from pressure. One can explicate his experimental results if one postulates this feature of the air, although of course the feature itself remains imperceptible through any direct means.

But Boyle does not end his discussion with a description of this newly uncovered feature of atmospheric air. In a clear foreshadowing of a crucial Newtonian distinction (as we will see),[7] Boyle then calls his claim about the spring of the air his *doctrine* (1999, vol. 1: 167), a view that he distinguishes from two *hypotheses* which are each taken to be explanations of the new feature of the air propounded in the *doctrine*. The hypotheses differ from one another in a fascinating respect. The first hypothesis, which Boyle clearly favors, *explicates* the spring of the air by postulating that the air consists of little bodies that bear this feature of springiness; that is, like a little ball of wool, each microscopic body that constitutes air bears a capability of being compressed. Since the microscopic constituents of the air bear this power or feature, it can be regarded as a fundamental feature, one that is not reduced away to distinct features of microlevel bodies. The second hypothesis, which Boyle attributes broadly to Descartes, would explicate the spring of the air by the action of the ether that pervades the earth's atmosphere. According to this hypothesis, we need not attribute any power of compression to the particles that constitute the air—the spring of the air can be reduced to the behavior of the ether itself (Boyle 1999, vol. 1: 166–167). Boyle then insists that although he favors the first hypothesis, he need not choose between them: he clearly believes that his experiments are not predicated on either hypothesis and that his doctrine does not entail the truth of either hypothesis. Hence, his readers might accept his doctrine on the basis of his experiments, even while rejecting his hypothesis (and perhaps the Cartesian hypothesis as well). As we will see, Boyle's distinction between the *doctrine* that he takes to be supported by his experimental results and the *hypotheses* that he takes to be possible explanations of a natural phenomenon postulated in that doctrine is central to Newton's own experimental methodology.

But Hobbes did not focus primarily on Boyle's attempt to distinguish between a doctrine that had a solid empirical basis and a set of hypothetical explanations of a natural phenomenon described in that doctrine. He was not principally interested in challenging Boyle's methodology. Perhaps he concluded that Boyle's work was marred by a far more serious deficiency. Having already committed himself to a plenist and a mechanist conception of nature, Hobbes took the time to write a lengthy critique of Boyle's *New Experiments Physico-Mechanicall* a year after its publication, in 1661; he entitled the critique *Dialogus Physicus*, or *Physical Dialogue*.[8] Hobbes begins his dialogue with a note to the reader indicating his view of what he calls *physics*[9]: it is the "science of natural causes." This is no surprise to readers of *The Elements of Philosophy*. From Hobbes's point of view, as the dialogue makes clear, Boyle's experiments with the air pump are aimed at tackling two principal issues: first, the question of whether a vacuum is possible and, second, the *nature* of air. Hobbes argues that the latter is logically prior to the former: one cannot determine whether a vacuum in nature is genuinely possible unless one first determines the nature of the air itself. In particular, an experiment with an air pump cannot determine the possibility of a vacuum until that nature is established (for reasons I indicate in the following). He then argues for the following conception of the air's nature: air is a continuous fluid quantity; it is both infinitely divisible and subtle. That is, if one takes any part of the air—say, the amount of air in a small enclosed space like an ordinary light bulb—one can always conceive of that quantity as being divided by some process. So any quantity of air is divisible into half that quantity. Hence, the air is infinitely divisible. Hobbes immediately argues for the irrelevance of the air pump on this basis: one can contend that the air pump creates a vacuum when the pump sucks all the air out of an otherwise sealed cylinder, but the experiment can never prove this result, because the air can flow into any space, however small. Thus, when the mechanism supposedly sucks air out of the cylinder, in fact, air continues to flow into it through even the smallest pores within the glass cylinder (or another part of the apparatus). If you like, the nature of air itself prevents Boyle from constructing an airtight apparatus. Clearly, it might appear to ordinary observers as if the air is evacuated, but the subtle nature and infinite divisibility of air means that it cannot be truly airtight. Hence, by the end of the fifth page of the dialogue, Hobbes has already presented one argument with the conclusion that experiments are irrelevant if one wishes to investigate the possibility of a vacuum, itself a classic topic within natural philosophy.

Hobbes has another kind of argument up his sleeve, one that indicates an aspect of how he distinguishes knowledge of the air that derives from sense perception and knowledge that derives from reason, another reflection of his views in *The Elements of Philosophy*. He notes, first of all, that ordinary people are not *ridiculous* to believe that when, for example, I look across a field to see a squirrel eating a nut, I am able to perceive the distant squirrel through empty space. This is not ridiculous because the beliefs of ordinary people are guided by sense perception, and of course I do not perceive the air between the squirrel and me at all—I merely see the squirrel. But this just means that sense perception cannot be our guide here: instead, we must use reason to determine whether perception could operate through empty space, that is, through a vacuum. As Shapin and Schaffer indicate (1985, 366, note 30), Hobbes makes this point clearly near the very end of *The Elements of Philosophy*:

It is not therefore a thing so very ridiculous for ordinary people to think all that space empty, in which we say is air; it being the work of reason to make us conceive that the air is anything. For by which of our senses is it, that we take notice of the air, seeing we neither see, nor hear, nor taste, nor small, nor feel it to be anything? When we feel heat, we do not impute it to the air, but to the fire: nor do we say the air is cold, but we ourselves are cold; and when we feel the wing, we rather think something is coming, than that any thing is already come. Also, we do not at all feel the weight of water in water, much less of air in air. That we come to know that to be a body, which we call air, it is by reasoning;

but it is from one reason only, namely, because it is impossible for remote bodies to work upon our organs of sense but by the help of bodies intermediate, without which we could have no sense of them, till they come to be contiguous. Wherefore, from the senses alone, without reasoning from effects, we cannot have sufficient evidence of the nature of bodies (part IV, chap. 30, §14).

So for Hobbes, if we take a vacuum to mean an absolute absence of body, that is, a completely empty space, rather than a space that is empty of anything perceivable or empty of some particular kind of body, but not necessarily of all kinds of body, then we could not perceive an object through a vacuum. As he writes in the *Physical Dialogue*: "Do not your colleagues grant that vision is produced by a continuous action from the object to the eye? Do they not also consider all action to be motion, and all motion to be of a body? So how could the motion be derived from the object ... to your eyes, through a vacuum, that is, through a nonbody?" (366). Being an arch mechanist, as we have seen, Hobbes is convinced that noncontiguous causation is impossible: a remote body cannot have a causal impact on me, whether on my *organs of sense* or any other aspect of me, without impacting upon me or causally interacting with something else that impacts upon me. And perception is obviously a causal process. It would also seem to follow from these points that if the glass air pump actually contained a vacuum, we could see the outer front edge facing us, because that would interact with the air, but not its inner back edge, because that would interact with no body (because of the supposed vacuum inside it). And yet we do see both edges of the vessel. In this way, Hobbes cleverly appeals to a basic mechanist principle here, one that would certainly have been accepted by Boyle and his supporters.

In criticizing Boyle, Hobbes was relying on a very long tradition of studying nature by providing causal explanations of natural phenomena as the key avenue to understanding them. He maintained this traditional view by separating it from the Aristotelian ideas that had dominated natural philosophy for generations, presenting his version of an experiment to illustrate how a causal explanation of a phenomenon ought to proceed. It was Boyle who broke even more sharply with the natural philosophical tradition, focusing on experiments and the information they provide about natural phenomena, while ignoring the widely accepted notion that the philosopher can grasp a phenomenon in nature only by providing a causal explanation of it. With tradition and a long-standing consensus on his side, Hobbes seems perfectly rational, even if history sides with Boyle.

3.2 Hooke's Debate with Newton

Philosophers have long known about various aspects of Newton's work that are salient for understanding debates in the early modern period: his views of space and time, for instance, have been the subject of philosophical controversy since their very first appearance. This fact partly reflects contemporary interests. But in Newton's own day, debates within natural philosophy concerning the proper role for experimentation and observation were heated. In at least three relevant respects, Newton's early work in optics, which was published in the *Philosophical Transactions* of the Royal Society beginning in 1672, set the stage for the principal themes of his long career in natural philosophy (he remained active well into his seventies). Firstly, Newton's letter to the Society's secretary, Henry Oldenburg, often called the "New theory about light and colors," generated an immediate, extensive, and protracted debate that eventually involved important philosophers such as Robert Hooke in Britain and Christiaan Huygens, G.W. Leibniz, and Ignatius Pardies on the Continent. Newton consistently regarded these figures not merely as disagreeing with his views, but as misinterpreting them. This experience helped to shape Newton's famous and lifelong aversion to intellectual controversy, a feature of his personality that he often mentioned in letters, and one that he would never outgrow. Secondly, because Newton regarded himself as misinterpreted by his critics, he had recourse to metalevel or methodological discussions of the practice of optics and of the kinds of knowledge that philosophers can obtain when engaging in experiments with light. The novelty and power of Newton's work in the *Principia* years later would eventually generate strikingly similar controversies that led him to analogous kinds of methodological discussions of his experimental practice within natural philosophy and of the kinds of knowledge that one can obtain in that field using either experimental or mathematical techniques. From *our* point of view, Newton's science was unusually philosophical for these reasons. Thirdly and finally, in his earliest optical work, Newton began to formulate a distinction that would remain salient throughout his long intellectual career, contending that a philosopher must distinguish between a claim about some feature of nature that is derived from experimental or observational evidence, expressed in a *doctrine*, and a claim that is a mere *hypothesis*, a kind of speculation about nature that is not, or not *yet*, so derived. Newton's much later proclamation in the second edition of the *Principia* (1713), "*Hypotheses non fingo*," or "I feign no hypotheses," would infuriate his critics just as much as it would prod his followers into making the pronouncement a central component of a newly emerging Newtonian method.

In "New theory about light and colors," published in the *Philosophical Transactions* in 1672, Newton presented a number of (now famous) experiments in which sunlight was allowed to pass through one or two prisms in order to probe some of its basic features. The paper recounts a number of experiments that Newton says he had conducted several years earlier. A contemporary reader might think that the subject of this paper—light and colors—is pretty obvious, but in fact, seventeenth-century optics was fundamentally different from today's discipline,[10] and like many fields, it underwent a substantial evolution through the early modern period. The field of optics has its origins in the Ancient Greek period, when figures like Euclid and Ptolemy wrote works on the subject, but they often focused primarily on the science of vision, analyzing, for example, the visual rays that were sometimes thought to extrude from the eye, enabling it to perceive distant physical objects. In the early modern period, Kepler and Descartes each made fundamental contributions to the field, including the discovery of the inversion of the retinal image (in the former case) and an explanation of refraction (in the latter case). Newton's work helped to shift the focus of optics from an analysis of vision to an investigation of light. That investigation had at least two aspects: first, there was the physical question of whether light consisted of waves or particles, a question that obviously continued to have relevance into the twentieth century, when wave–particle duality was discovered, and, second, the question of what features rays of light exhibit under certain experimental conditions, such as passing through a particular medium (like air, water, or glass). It may seem obvious that these are distinct questions: one can study rays of sunlight passing through water, or through a prism, assessing such things as indices of refraction, without addressing the basic question of the physical nature of light. Newton himself seemed to regard this distinction as reasonably obvious. But Newton's interlocutors in the early 1670s—including luminaries such as Hooke and Huygens—found it difficult to make the distinction, at least in the way that Newton intended. Indeed, the celebrated debate among Newton, Hooke, Huygens, and Pardies centered on the question of whether one can in fact systematically distinguish between these two kinds of investigation. To understand the debate, the contemporary reader must strive to recapture the conception of optics behind Hooke and Huygens's skepticism about Newton's *new theory*.

Like Newton's discussion of light, his treatment of colors can confuse the contemporary reader. It may seem straightforward to us to conceive of what is at stake in providing a theory of color, but in fact it demands an articulation of the historical context in which Newton performed his experiments and reached his conclusions. In particular, colors are analogous to light: philosophical theories of color underwent a profound transformation during the struggle between Aristotelian or Scholastic conceptions and mechanist conceptions in the seventeenth century (Shapiro 1993, 5–7). The standard historical narrative is roughly as follows: the Aristotelians of the sixteenth and seventeenth centuries regarded colors as intrinsic, or at least basic (if extrinsic), features of bodies that were revealed to human perceivers by the presence of light. Mechanical philosophers such as Galileo, in the *Assayer* of 1623, and Descartes, in the *Meditations* and *Principles* (1641 and 1644, respectively), argued in contrast that colors are actually ideas or sensations within perceivers themselves, and not intrinsic (or perhaps even extrinsic) features of material objects. Robert Boyle's celebrated distinction between *primary* and *secondary* qualities, which enabled him to articulate this broadly mechanist conception of colors, was rendered famous by Locke's articulation of the view in his *Essay* (first published in 1690 but written years earlier). Like sounds and smells, colors are *secondary qualities*, that is, they are ideas or sensations caused by an interaction between the material objects, which consist of microscopic particles with size, shape, and mobility (these are *primary qualities*), and the human perceiver. Newton was clearly influenced by these mechanistic challenges to Aristotelian views (Shapiro 1993,

8–9), but he insisted on a distinct point: his experiments had indicated that colors are in fact features of light itself and, indeed, that each color is a separable aspect of a ray of sunlight (one that exhibits a particular index of refraction). His theory said little about sensations and nothing about ideas. It is unclear, then, whether Newton had provided a model of colors that was consistent with the mechanical philosophy. As Hooke and especially Huygens continually insisted, Newton may have actually deviated, deliberately or inadvertently, from the emerging mechanist consensus concerning the proper method for asking and answering questions about natural phenomena.

The basic details of Newton's experiments with the prism are roughly as follows. Newton indicates at the outset that he wishes to investigate what he calls "the celebrated *Phenomena of Colours*." Newton's various prism experiments, which he describes in considerable depth, suggested to him a *doctrine* that he expresses in thirteen consecutive numbered propositions. Included in these propositions are the following claims about features of rays of light: first, the rays of light that emerge when sunlight passes through a prism exhibit various colors, such as red, blue, and violet; second, these colors differ in their *degrees of refrangibility*, which means that they exhibit and retain an index of refraction, even when they are passed through a second prism; third, in particular, red rays are refracted the least by the prism, violet rays the most, and the other colors are intermediate; fourth, these colors—or colorful rays—are not the result of modifications of sunlight, but rather are "*original* and *connate properties*" of it; and, fifth, these facts mean that although ordinary sunlight appears white, or perhaps colorless, to our perception, it actually contains numerous colors within it, a feature of it that can be experimentally revealed.

One cannot overstate the controversy that these points generated. As James Gregory (nephew of David) remarked to John Collins in a letter of April 1672: "I was exceedingly surprised with these experiments of Mr. Newton; they will cause great changes throughout all the body of natural philosophy, by all appearance, if the matter of fact be true, which I have no ground to question. I would gladly see what Mr. Hooke can say against the doctrine raised upon them" (Newton 1959–, vol. 1: 120). First and foremost, the contention that ordinary sunlight contains colors within it (*connately*) struck many readers as preposterous. To an Aristotelian, it might be obvious not only that colors are features of material bodies, but just as importantly, that they are *perceptible* features. The notion of a hidden—or more pointedly, of an invisible—color that requires physical manipulation to appear to our perception is a considerable stretch. Similarly, although a mechanist would reject the basic features of the Aristotelian view, she would agree that colors are perceptible: after all, if the redness of my notebook is actually a sensation of redness that I have, rather than a feature of the book, then it is a paradigm case of something perceptible. The idea of a hidden—or invisible or imperceptible—sensation makes little sense, unless one develops a complex theory of unconscious perception. So in that sense, Newton is using the concept of a color in an odd way, for his colors are actually *imperceptible* under all normal perceiving conditions—they appear only after the sunlight has passed through the prism! This became a centerpiece of Newton's debate with Hooke, as we will see in the following.

To make matters worse, Newton could not help but add an additional argument to his paper, one involving what he regarded as a reasonable inference—if not actually a *demonstrative* argument—from the fact that ordinary sunlight contains within it blue, red, and violet rays. That fact, if it can be called such, was highly controversial per se, as we have seen. It was rendered even more controversial by Newton's inference: light itself is likely a stream of particles, rather than a wave. This contention would become a crucial issue for several reasons, including most prominently the fact that Newton himself proclaimed that he wished to remain *neutral* on this difficult question, and therefore wished to present experimental results that would not be predicated on or intertwined with the corpuscular conception of light. Newton presents his inference in the following passage, which follows the *doctrine* expressed in thirteen propositions:

> These things being so, it can be no longer disputed, whether there be colours in the dark, nor whether they be the qualities of the objects we see, no nor perhaps, whether Light be a Body. For, since Colours are the *qualities* of Light, having its Rays for their entire and immediate subject, how can we think those Rays *qualities* also, unless one quality may be the subject of and sustain another; which in effect is to call it *substance*. We should not know Bodies for substances, were it not for their sensible qualities, and the Principal of those being now found due to something else, we have as good reason to believe that to be a substance also. (Correspondence, 1: 100)

Newton seems to be arguing as follows here: since rays of light have colors as basic features, we should regard these colors as qualities or properties of the rays, despite the fact that these properties are imperceptible under any ordinary circumstance; but doing so requires us to think of the rays as bearers of qualities, which is to say, as substances in their own right. And if rays of light are substances, this means that we cannot also think of them as qualities or properties of anything else. Newton's neutrality on the wave–particle question might be thought to hinge on his use of "perhaps" in the previous paragraph, but that word was insufficient for his readers. As Hooke wrote in June of that year, he noticed the "perhaps" in Newton's paper, but many of his readers thought, nonetheless, that Newton was presenting a strongly held view in that paragraph (*Correspondence* 1: 199). They saw the care with which he presented the argument in the paragraph as a clear indication of the depth of his commitment to the corpuscular conception. Newton may have been deliberately echoing Boyle's distinction in the *New Experiments* between an experimentally established *doctrine* and the possible *hypotheses* that the philosopher might endorse, but which are not regarded as experimentally supported themselves. He even borrows Boyle's terminology.

Newton's argument is especially significant because of the way in which it illustrates his employment of two classic philosophical categories—*substance* and *quality*—to reach a conclusion that involves an interpretation of an experimental result. In particular, as Newton's readers would have immediately recognized, his argument is predicated on a widely accepted notion of a substance at the time, one easily found in Descartes,[11] namely, that substances are those items that are the subjects of properties but not properties of anything else. His interpretation of his experimental result is this: if we study the results of the prism experiments, we find that the colors of rays of light are fundamental qualities of those rays, for the color of a ray cannot be altered (even by letting it pass through a second prism) and it constantly maintains its specific index of refraction. Philosophy does the rest: if a ray of light is a bearer of a fundamental quality, then it must be the subject of that quality—otherwise put, it must be a substance in its own right. But if rays are substances, it follows that we cannot think them as properties or qualities; and that fact, in turn, suggests that they are not waves, for waves are features of some medium (think of waves on the ocean). Newton concludes: light is a stream of particles (a *body*). Without the experimental results, Newton cannot claim that colors are fundamental features of rays of light—indeed, ordinary perception would suggest otherwise. But without the philosophical concepts, Newton could not conclude that light is a *body*. As Hooke was quick to argue, there appears to be no experimental evidence suggesting that light is a body.[12]

Newton's inference became one of the centerpieces of the debate that his paper generated. Just days after Newton's paper was read at the Royal Society, Robert Hooke responded with a detailed letter to Oldenburg. In the first few sentences, Hooke indicates that from his point of view, Newton's "Hypothesis of saving the phenomena of colours" essentially involves the contention that rays of light are particulate, rather than wavelike.[13] Hooke argues, in contrast, that light "is nothing but a pulse or motion propagated through an homogeneous, uniform and transparent medium;" that is, he argues that light is wavelike. He makes it perfectly clear, moreover, that his hypothesis—the name did not carry a negative connotation in his work—can save the phenomena of colors just as well as Newton's, which is to say, his hypothesis is compatible with the experimental evidence Newton gathers. Evidently, the line of argument in the passage quoted previously caught Hooke's eye. Among philosophers, he was not alone. In a letter to Huygens explaining Newton's theory of light, Leibniz writes that Newton takes light to be a *body* propelled from the sun to the earth which, according to Leibniz, Newton takes to explain both the differential refrangibility of rays of light and the phenomena of colors.[14]

Newton and his interlocutors clearly embraced two distinct interpretations of his argument: first, Newton's own view, as we have seen, is that his experimental results, plus some philosophical argumentation, suggest the conclusion that light must be a body; second, Hooke's view, and possibly Leibniz and Huygens's as well, is that Newton took his corpuscular *hypothesis* to *explain* his experimental results. For Newton, the key is to recognize that although the *doctrine* connected with the experimental results—plus the philosophy—imply the corpuscular theory, the former are not predicated on the latter. Hence, the *doctrine* ought to be accepted even by wave theorists (assuming the experiments themselves lack problems). But Hooke had a distinct view: since he interpreted Newton as arguing that the corpuscular theory explains the experimental results, there would appear to be little sense in taking the results themselves as significant. Their point is to serve as the focus of an explanatory corpuscular theory. The fact that Hooke interpreted Newton in this way is evident from his immediate response to Newton's paper: the wave theory of light, according to Hooke, is equally capable of explaining the experimental results in question. Since the results are neutral—again, according to Hooke—on this crucial debate concerning the physical character of light, they remain uninteresting per se.

This debate about the usefulness of hypotheses would appear to represent a rock bottom dispute between Hooke and Newton, a feature it shares with the Hobbes–Boyle dispute. In an unpublished letter intended for the President of the Royal Society at the time, Lord Brouncker, Hooke not only defends his attitude toward hypotheses against Newton's criticism, he raises the stakes by indicating its importance for philosophy generally. Newton had claimed that "it was besides the business in hand to dispute about hypotheses" in their debate. Hooke fundamentally disagrees, citing Bacon's authority to bolster his point (Newton 1959, vol. 1: 202): "I judge there is nothing [that] conduces so much to the advancement of philosophy as the examining of hypotheses by experiments and the inquiry into experiments by hypotheses. And I have the authority of the incomparable Verulam to warrant me." Whereas Hooke avowedly follows Bacon in his method, it should be clear that Newton follows Boyle's method from 1660, going so far as to use his precise terminology. Whereas Newton insists that he must remain neutral on various hypotheses concerning, for example, the nature of light and the physical character of colors (more on which later), Hooke places the assessment of hypotheses through experimental results at the very heart of his philosophical methodology. Hooke and Newton each conducted fundamentally important experiments in optics in this era, but adopted fundamentally opposed methodologies for the study of light.[15]

Hooke was not alone. For instance, Christiaan Huygens, who was probably the leading mathematical philosopher in continental Europe at that time, published a very brief criticism of Newton's paper in the *Philosophical Transactions*, arguing that Newton's experimental results per se are essentially insignificant independently of any hypothesis explaining them. He writes:

> For my part, I believe that an *hypothesis* that should explain mechanically and by the nature of motion the colors *yellow* and *blue*, would be sufficient for all the rest, in regard that those others, being only more deeply charged (as appears by the prisms of Mr. Hooke) do produce the dark or deep-red and blue; and that of these four all the other colors may be compounded. Neither do I see, why Mr. Newton doth not content himself with the two colors, yellow and blue; for it will be much more easy to find an *hypothesis* by motion, that may explicate these two differences, than for so many diversities as there are of other colors. And till he hath found this *hypothesis*, he hath not taught us,

what it is wherein consists the nature and difference of colors, but only this accident (which certainly is very considerable) of their *different refrangibility.* (Newton 1958, 136)

Huygens is uninterested in Newton's experimental results per se—he wishes to see them folded into a theory (*hypothesis*) that provides a mechanical explanation of what colors are. Contending that colors, or colored rays, compose ordinary sunlight and are differentially refrangible does not explain what colors really are; for that, we require a mechanical explanation, one that makes use of a conception of motion—presumably, either the motion of a wave through a medium, or the motion of basic particles through space. For Huygens, Newton's task as a philosopher studying light is to explain the nature of colors, a task that philosophers had readily tackled since antiquity. But Newton tries to avoid that task altogether: he presents experimental results concerning colors without saying what colors really are.

One potential way of viewing this disagreement between Newton on the one hand and Hooke and Huygens on the other involves the contemporary distinction between data and evidence (Smith 2012). The distinction is roughly as follows: whereas data can be obtained from running experiments independently of considering any particular theory, we require a theory in order to turn those data into evidence for (or against) some theory. Independently of any theory, data cannot serve as evidence. We might then say that whereas Newton's self-avowed attitude was to present data from his prism experiments without considering various optical theories (e.g., mechanical corpuscular or mechanical wave theories), Hooke and Huygens insisted that the data per se are not especially significant, for their interest arises only if they can serve as evidence for a particular theory (*hypothesis*) in optics. Huygens makes this point explicit without using this contemporary distinction. And Hooke implies the point when he repeatedly insists that (in our terminology) the data obtained by Newton cannot serve as evidence for his theory, since Hooke's theory is just as compatible with them. Data that are not evidence for a theory are basically moot. Newton's doctrine provided a trove of data, but no evidence in the relevant sense (or so we might say on Hooke's behalf).

As scholars have long understood, one of the most salient aspects of this debate is what we would now call its epistemological feature: Newton, Hooke, and Huygens disagreed on the epistemic status of the various elements within Newton's paper. From Newton's point of view, it was crucial to understand that what he called his *doctrine*, probably following Boyle, was limited to his basic claims about the differential refrangibility of the colored rays of sunlight, the latter of which is heterogeneous in character. He insisted that these experimental results could not be questioned on theoretical grounds—they could not be questioned on the basis of preconceived notions about sunlight, for instance, or on the grounds that they are inconsistent with some overarching conception of light's physical character—and must therefore be accepted, unless contrary experimental results were found. Hence, his philosophy in this paper was experimental rather than speculative. Experiments suggested *doctrines*; speculation involved entertaining *hypotheses*. But Newton's interlocutors did not respect this point: Pardies immediately called Newton's doctrine (or theory) his *hypothesis*, and Hooke used *theory* and *hypothesis* interchangeably. For this reason, their debate did not center on analyzing the prism experiments, their setup, the data they generated, and so on; it largely focused on the question of precisely where experiment ends and speculation begins (a feature found in Boyle's debate with Hobbes a decade earlier). Newton's inference regarding the physical nature of light did not help to clarify matters.

But there is another aspect to the debate, one that illuminates what would become Newton's lifelong vexed relationship with the philosophical consensus of his day, namely, mechanical approaches to studying, understanding, and explaining natural phenomena. (As we will see, the vexed nature of that relationship only intensified with the publication of the *Principia* in 1687, and with the appearance of its second edition in 1713.) Intriguingly, this feature of Newton's relation with his most important predecessors and interlocutors—including Descartes, Boyle, Hooke, Leibniz, and Huygens—is evident in this episode from an analysis of Newton's experimentally based doctrine of light itself, rather than from the debate about the distinction between such a doctrine and the *speculative* conceptions of light's nature also at issue. This aspect of the debate is evident in Huygens's remark that Newton ought to have found a hypothesis that "should explain mechanically and by the nature of motion" the phenomena of colors. As we have seen, Newton's doctrine included the contention that ordinary sunlight contains within it blue and red rays (these are *connate* properties of sunlight). If one ignores the question of whether this contention is experimental or speculative, one finds the origin of one of Hooke's criticisms of Newton. Hooke insists, first of all, that there is no *necessity* of concluding from the prism experiments that sunlight is heterogeneous in this way—that aspect of the debate is well known. But second of all, he suggests that colors themselves are not features of sunlight at all because they are nothing but sensations or ideas that are caused by motions. He does not think that it is empirically inaccurate to contend that colors are features of sunlight; he thinks it makes little sense. For Hooke, colors and other optical phenomena all involve the motions of waves through some kind of medium. The prism is a new medium for the sunlight: it refracts the ray of sunlight in the sense that it changes the motion of the ray, which causes us to have sensations of red and blue. Hence, for Hooke, the idea that colors are present within a ray of sunlight ought to be interpreted as the idea that there are motions present within the ray before it hits the prism. In a way, to say that colors are present within the ray before it enters the prism is akin to saying that the vibration of a guitar string is present within the string before I pluck it. One *could* think of guitar strings in that way, Hooke suggests, but it does not make much sense, and it certainly is not required by any experimental results.

Newton sent his reply to Hooke's criticisms to Oldenburg in June 1672; it is voluminous, containing numerous complex arguments. But one of them is surprising: Newton professes his neutrality not only on the difficult wave–particle question but also on the question of whether the idea that red and blue rays are *connate* properties of sunlight must itself be interpreted within the mechanist framework. For Huygens, if it is not interpreted within the mechanist framework, if Newton fails to give a mechanical account of what colors really are, he has failed at his task as a philosopher. For Hooke, since sunlight is a wave phenomenon, involving the motion of pulses propagating through a medium, Newton's claim about colored rays should be interpreted as a claim about motions within sunlight itself. He also seems committed to the idea that if we grant Newton his particulate conception of light, the claim about red and blue rays amounts to the idea that red and blue particles are somehow contained within ordinary sunlight. So Hooke at least implicitly seeks from Newton the kind of mechanical account called for explicitly by Huygens. But Newton professes neutrality on the mechanist assumptions undergirding Hooke's (and Huygens's) interpretation of his paper: Newton wishes to claim that his conception of blue and red rays need not be understood either as the claim that certain wavelike phenomena are contained within the sunlight, nor the opposing claim that particulate phenomena are so contained. We can simply bracket the question of what the colored rays really are, and determine experimentally that such rays are contained within sunlight. Huygens remarks: if you do so, Newton, then you have discovered a mere *accident* about colors.

It is easy to miss this second aspect of Newton's professed neutrality, because he presents it most clearly in a passage in his June 1672 reply to Hooke that is focused mostly on the better-known issue of what counts as a *hypothesis*. Newton begins the passage: "Tis true that from my theory I argue the corporeity of light, but I do it without any absolute positiveness, as the word *perhaps* intimates, and make it at most but a very plausible consequence of the doctrine, and not a fundamental supposition, nor so much as a part of it, which was wholly comprehended in the precedent propositions [the 13 propositions that constitute his 'doctrine' in his original paper]" (173). He then adds:

> But I knew that the properties which I declared of light were in some measure capable of being explicated not only by that [corporeal view], but by many other mechanical hypotheses. And therefore I chose to decline them all, and speak of light in general terms, considering it abstractedly as something or other propagated every way in straight lines from luminous bodies, without determining what that thing is, whether a confused mixture of difform qualities, or modes of bodies, or of bodies themselves, or of any virtues power or beings whatsoever. And for the same reason I chose to speak of colors according to the information of our senses, as if they were qualities of light without us. Whereas by that hypothesis I must have considered them rather as modes of sensation excited in the mind by various motions figures or sizes of the corpuscles of light making various mechanical impressions on the organs of sense, as I expressed it in that place where I spoke of the corporeity of light. (174)

From Newton's perspective, both the wave and the particle views of light are *mechanical hypotheses*, so they are both the kinds of hypotheses on which he wished to remain neutral. Since he brackets these hypotheses—in part by ensuring that neither influences his experimental setup or results—he must not presuppose that sunlight consists of blue and red rays in the sense that it contains particles that cause us to have blue and red sensations. It must contain blue and red rays in a neutral sense: we must think of colors as qualities of light that exist independently of perception (*without us*) without ipso facto regarding them as causal effects of the motion of particles (or as wavelike phenomena, for that matter). Hence, Newton wishes to remain neutral not only on waves and particles but also on the mechanical philosophy. Whereas the *hypotheses* he brackets are *mechanical*, the *doctrine* he presents is not. The doctrine is neutral on the mechanical philosophy itself. For Huygens, that kind of neutrality leaves Newton with the presentation of some experimental results, some data, that are simply uninteresting, and not up to the task of the philosopher.

This second aspect of Newton's attempted neutrality poses an intriguing question: what would his interlocutors take the idea that one can treat colors "as if they were qualities of light without us" to mean? If it does not mean what any of the mechanists would mean—if it does not mean that blue or red sensations (or ideas or perceptions) are caused by the motions of particles, or waves, or something else—then the most obvious interpretation in this era would be that some kind of Scholastic or Aristotelian view would tell us what it means. That would indicate that the colors were considered as real or genuine qualities of the light itself, for that is precisely what the Aristotelians say about the colors of ordinary objects. If I have a blue notebook, its blueness is a real feature of it, just like its weight, length, and width. More precisely: that is precisely the kind of view that the mechanists attributed to their Scholastic and Aristotelian predecessors and interlocutors (regardless of the actual complexities of their views). So for someone like Hooke, Newton's supposed neutrality might very well amount to the claim that colors like red and blue are real qualities of rays of sunlight. This interpretation of what Newton was really doing, moreover, would have been bolstered by the typical view in this era that Scholastic and Aristotelian ideas cohere nicely with common sense, for Newton says explicitly that he was following the *information* accorded to us by our senses, unaided by any complex speculative view of light (such as the *mechanical hypotheses* favored by various authors). And of course, if there was any consensus in this era among Newton's principal predecessors and interlocutors, it was that this generally Scholastic perspective on real qualities was outmoded, or worse, unintelligible. Newton never helped his case by articulating an alternative conception according to which colors were qualities *without us*, but not in any Scholastic or Aristotelian sense. He seemed to evade the fact that if he was going to convince Hooke and others of his neutrality, he would have to provide them with an acceptable interpretation of what his claim about colors means.[16]

Looking back to the theme of Chapter 2, the great irony of this important episode in Newton's carly intellectual career is that the emerging consensus among philosophers that some version of a mechanical conception of nature must be adopted was actually disrupted by Newton himself. For he had insisted that he could treat colors as if they were qualities of sunlight itself, without endorsing any potential mechanical understanding of what that notion means. It seemed to some of his interlocutors that he was thereby violating the emerging consensus about mechanism, leaving room for Aristotelian and Scholastic ideas to be taken seriously again within natural philosophy. Looking ahead to a theme of Chapter 5, the intellectual dynamic and controversy in which Newton became embroiled did not end with his optical research in the 1670s, for precisely the same kind of dynamic, and the same kind of controversy, emerged again with his treatment of universal gravity in Book III of *Principia Mathematica* a decade later. As Leibniz and Huygens made particularly clear in their criticisms, Newton's new theory had unwittingly revived precisely the kind of reliance on obscure notions of real physical properties—often called *occult qualities*—that had enlivened Scholastic and Aristotelian conceptions of nature in previous generations. By refusing to accept the idea that mechanist conceptions of nature must establish the range of possible understandings and explanations of all physical phenomena, in both optics and in natural philosophy more generally, Newton broke an emerging consensus. He also failed to convince his interlocutors that a new consensus, expressing his kind of neutrality on basic questions about natural phenomena, should form. As we have already seen, it would be roughly another century before a new consensus would emerge on such questions, and by that time, natural philosophy had become an outmoded discipline, replaced by much more specific and focused disciplines such as chemistry and physics. Newton did not live to see these developments.

notes

1 Peter Anstey and his former research group in Otago, including Alberto Vanza and Kirsten Walsh, did considerable work on this question—see their many blog posts at https://blogs.otago.ac.nz/emxphi. See also Shapiro (2004).

2 Of course, Newton was a British philosopher who achieved fame in the early eighteenth century and who was a personal friend of Locke and a genuine influence on later figures such as Hume, so his views are important to what we would now call the history of empiricism. Some have attempted more specifically to link his views to those of Locke (Rogers 1978), an approach that can be traced back at least to Voltaire, and others have argued that he adopted a broadly empiricist approach to many questions in natural philosophy (Stein 2002). But Newton never articulated a broad philosophical program in metaphysics or epistemology that would now be called empiricist, and some of his most important views—concerning space, time, and motion, for instance, but also concerning the use of mathematics in general and calculus in particular—came in for extensive criticisms by canonical *empiricists* such as Berkeley.

3 Hobbes's "Epistle Dedicatory" to the first part of his *Elements of Philosophy*, written to the Earl of Devonshire, exhibits his status as a modern thinker, proclaiming

the motion of the earth (indicated by Copernicus) and the importance of studying motion after the fashion of Galileo. Before Copernicus, Galileo, and Harvey, who discovered the motion of the blood, "there was nothing certain in natural philosophy" (Hobbes 1839, vol. 1: viii). Lest his allegiance to the moderns be in any doubt, he adds a brief history of philosophy, proclaiming that when the thinkers of the early Church began to incorporate ideas from pagan philosophers into their work, they encountered many "foolish and false" ideas from the "physics and metaphysics of Aristotle" (vol. 1: x).

4   Newton read and discussed this work as an undergraduate at Trinity College (see Newton 1983, 450); cf. also 219–221 for McGuire and Tamny's analysis of Hobbes's influence on the young Newton's thinking).

5   Nowadays, we would probably say that for Hobbes, empty space is a logical possibility but not a metaphysical one, since he considers real space to be identical with the extension of a body: without a body present, we have no extension of that body, and therefore we have no real space that isn't identical to some body's extension.

6   This is complex: as a good anti-Aristotelian, Hobbes explicitly rejects the notion of a natural place on the grounds that it's inconsistent with (what we would call) the principle of inertia and with gravity, which he thinks is due to an attraction of the earth. As for the latter, he indicates that no one has ever explained that attraction. He does not indicate how he conceives of the relation between his mechanist commitments and his endorsement of attraction.

7   Boyle's influence on Newton's earliest thinking about topics in natural philosophy is clear. For instance, in his Trinity notebook, Newton refers explicitly to Boyle's *New Experiments* of 1660 and shows wide familiarity with its experiments and results (Newton 1983, 370, 372, 390, 400, 426). Boyle's influence on Newton's thinking in optics more broadly is discussed in Hall (1993, 13–14) and Shapiro (1993, 88–89, 118–119).

8   Hobbes's mathematical dispute with Wallis, focused on "squaring the circle," had already become heated, and so Hobbes added some work from that dispute to the 1661 *Dialogus Physicus* (Jesseph 1999, 13). We will encounter one aspect of the Hobbes–Wallis dispute in Chapter 5.

9   The word should not mislead us. Hobbes describes contemporary (probably Scholastic) books in that field as follows: "In physics books, many things present themselves which cannot be grasped, such as those things said of rarefaction and condensation, of immaterial substances, of essences and many other things" (Shapin and Schaffer 1985, 349). This is obviously what is meant by natural philosophy.

10 The historian of science Alan Shapiro describes Newton's optical theories in this way: "these theories are formulated in ways that are foreign to the modern sensibility. To appreciate them, we have to enter into seventeenth-century scientific methodology and Newton's philosophy of science" (1993, 3).

11 Newton would have been familiar with the discussion of substances in Descartes, *Principles of Philosophy*, part I: §§51–53, but also with the discussion in the second replies, which seems more relevant here (AT VII: 161). Newton owned the 1656 Elzevier (Amsterdam) text *Renati Des-Cartes Opera Philosophica editio tertia*, which contained the *Meditations* and all the objections and replies. In his copy, now at Trinity College Library, he carefully wrote the origins of each set of objections. Thanks to Tad Schmaltz for discussion of this point.

12 It is intriguing to ponder the question, what overall conception of *sensible qualities* does Newton presuppose in this piece? If a ray of sunlight passes through my window, the fact that it appears perfectly white to me does not undermine Newton's view (or so he thinks) that the ray actually contains a series of colors as its *qualities*. Are these qualities *sensible* if their presence can be detected only through the use of one or more prisms and never through the inspection of the sunlight through ordinary means (unaided perception, glasses, a magnifying glass, etc.)? These are apt to strike us as canonical philosophical problems.

13 See Hooke to Oldenburg, February 15, 1671/1672, *Correspondence* 1: 113. In recounting Newton's theory, Hooke does mention the points about refrangibility and heterogeneity, but he thinks that Newton's *first proposition* is "that light is a body" and that differently colored rays of light are in fact "several sorts of bodies." I take this to represent Hooke's interpretation of how Newton can account for the experimental results with the theory that light consists of particles. As Newton knew, Hooke had already articulated his own theory of colors and of light's nature as a wave in Observations IX and X in his *Micrographia* (Hooke 1665).

14 See Huygens (1888–1950, vol. 10: 602). Ignatius Pardies, another of Newton's interlocutors, similarly found it difficult to differentiate the claim about the corporeal nature of light from Newton's ideas concerning refrangibility and heterogeneity. See his two letters to the Royal Society concerning Newton's work, both of which are reprinted in Newton 1978; cf. the discussion of Pardies in Sabra (1981, 264–267). Like Newton, Pardies was especially interested in the Cartesian theory of motion—see Pardies (1670), which Newton had in his personal library (Harrison 1978, 210)—and this may have influenced his views in optics.

15 As Michael Hunter convinced me, my claim earlier does not entail that Hooke himself rejected Boyle's methods; rather, he may have endorsed them strongly but interpreted them differently than Newton. Similarly, my claim should not be understood to imply that Newton rejected Bacon's methods; indeed, to my knowledge, he was silent on them. It is nonetheless intriguing to ponder why Hooke cites Bacon as he does, while Newton parrots Boyle.

16 My argument here has important similarities with the interpretation presented by Westfall (1962); Sabra (1981, 232–233) criticizes this view. See also the illuminating points made in Harper and Smith (1995, 123).

newton's struggle with descartes

4.1 Setting the Historical Stage

Descartes's *Principia Philosophiae* (1644) forms the essential background to Newton's development of his mature conception of space, time, and motion in *Principia Mathematica* 43 years later. Newton took Descartes's *Principia* to be the central text in natural philosophy worth interpreting, criticizing, and, eventually, overthrowing. This is surprising to contemporary audiences for two reasons: first, space, time, and motion are not particularly important concepts in Descartes's philosophy; and second, it would seem that Descartes's views were not especially important in the seventeenth-century debate about space, time, and motion. What is more, the overwhelming importance of the Leibniz–Clarke correspondence for establishing the canonical conceptions of space and time in the eighteenth century (see Chapter 6) obscured Descartes's historically significant role for many years. Indeed, philosophers of science spent much of the twentieth century debating whether space is absolute or relational, which reflects the deep sense in which Leibniz and Clarke reset the terms of the debate about space, time, and motion (DiSalle 2006, Earman 1989, Sklar 1974). But when Newton began thinking about such topics as a young undergraduate at Trinity College, Leibniz had not yet entered the philosophical scene, so he focused much of his attention on Descartes. Indeed, Newton and many philosophers in England regarded Descartes as having finally replaced the orientation toward questions in natural philosophy found in the various neo-Aristotelian thinkers of the early modern period.[1]

Our understanding of Newton's relation to Descartes was greatly enhanced with the first publication of Newton's now famous anti-Cartesian tract *De Gravitatione* by Marie and Rupert Hall (1962), for this text provides an extensive analysis and criticism of Cartesian natural philosophy, never mentioning Leibniz.[2] The text discusses and criticizes many passages from Descartes's *Principles*. Indeed, Newton read the *Meditations* and the *Geometry* as a young man, but for him, Descartes was the Descartes of the *Principles* first and

Newton, First Edition. Andrew Janiak.
© 2015 Andrew Janiak. Published 2015 by John Wiley & Sons, Ltd.

foremost. Newton even titled his *magnum opus* to suggest that it ought to replace Descartes's *Principles*, and on occasion, Newton referred to *Principia Mathematica* as *his "Principia Philosophiae."* Newton's critical focus on Descartes was typical of English philosophers in the late seventeenth century (Henry 2013, 124, 135–138). Also typical among Newton's English cohort was the impression that Descartes and his followers represent a *speculative* or *hypothetical* philosophy in contrast to the experimental focus favored by figures such as Boyle and Hooke (Clarke 1989, Shapiro 2004).

What was the origin of Descartes's *Principles*, a text published near the end of his life (he died in 1650)? As we will see in more depth in Chapter 7, the Galileo affair played a key role: Descartes had originally intended to publish a major work in natural philosophy, *Le Monde* (*The World*), in 1633, but he told Mersenne that after the Vatican placed Galileo under house arrest that summer, he decided that he must suppress this work, since it included clear signs that he endorsed a Copernican view of the solar system. So Descartes reworked his thoughts about space, time, and motion, including his ideas about the earth's motion, publishing them in their canonical form only 11 years later in his *Principles*. He had decided that his views about space, time, and motion ought to be given a new metaphysical foundation, one that reflects many of the ideas he had characterized and defended in the intervening years in his *Meditations on First Philosophy* of 1641. These historical details set the stage for two well-known aspects of Descartes's importance for interpretations of Newton. First and foremost, Descartes's view of space, time, and motion in its canonical formulation in the *Principles* leads Newton to develop an extensive internal critique of the Cartesian system, one that eventually issues in Newton's own mature system in the *Principia*. Second, Newton also takes great pains to reject Descartes's attempt to ground natural philosophy in metaphysical conceptions of God, space, and matter.

4.2 Descartes's Metaphysical Foundation for Natural Philosophy

Descartes's *Meditations* is obviously known to students around the world. But his *Principles* remains a somewhat more obscure text, perhaps because its version of modern natural philosophy was so strongly overshadowed by the achievements of other figures, including those, like Christiaan Huygens, who were originally sympathetic to aspects of the Cartesian program, and those, like Newton, who were not. In the preface to the French edition of the *Principles*—which was published 3 years after the original, in 1647, under Descartes's guidance—we read that the system of human knowledge resembles a tree.[3] The roots of the tree of knowledge are metaphysics, the trunk is physics (or natural philosophy), and the branches are disciplines such as medicine and mechanics. This replaces Descartes's typical architectural metaphors—known to all students of the *Meditations*—by giving us a slightly new construal to the notion that metaphysics must serve as the foundation for physics. But what does any such metaphor mean? Does it mean that Cartesian physicists must endorse various metaphysical principles directly? Does it mean that physical theory must presuppose the truth of some metaphysical principle? Or does it perhaps mean that a metaphysical principle itself will entail some physical principle? In Descartes's system, the physical principles that we learn, such as the laws of nature, are very intimately connected with metaphysical ideas, such as conceptions of the nature of God; their relation is so intimate that we might indeed wish to conceive of them as forming a single organism.

Two aspects of Cartesian metaphysics are particularly salient for understanding the elements of Cartesian physics that engaged Newton. As we know from the *Meditations*, Descartes thought he had discovered the true metaphysics of extension, of the physical world, and the true metaphysics of God, an actually infinite—indeed, the unique actually infinite—substance whose continuing causal activity is a fundamental component of all causal interactions within nature.[4] More specifically, he thought that extension is a property, and as such, must be borne by some substance; this entails that empty space, or extension devoid of substances, is impossible, because it must be borne by a substance (Hobbes would echo this idea in his *Elements*). Hence, he took the world to be a plenum: space is identical to extended substance, so at every level, whether the microscopic level of molecules or the macroscopic level of stars, any given place within space must be numerically identical to some substance at that location (or numerically identical to some part of some substance). Empty space is metaphysically impossible. This obviously has consequences for how a physicist might understand motion and causation. He also thought that God decrees three laws of nature—the first two of which, as we will see, provide one of the very first modern formulations of the law of inertia (Descartes was scooped by Gassendi in 1641)—and that we can derive these laws from God's property of immutability and from the metaphysics of extension. (The details of that derivation will not detain us here.) The first two laws concern motion, and so they, too, will have obvious consequences for how a philosopher studying nature might conceive of motion. These two aspects of Cartesian metaphysics, then, set the stage for the introduction of the Cartesian conception of space, time, and motion.

Cartesian metaphysics obviously indicates that the philosopher cannot discover through empirical investigation that space is empty. Since there cannot be any empty space, any conception of motion endorsed by a Cartesian physicist must jettison the very idea. But Descartes knew that ordinary people do in fact tend to think of space as empty, or as locally empty, or as possibly empty. When they see birds fly through the sky, for instance, they tend to think of the birds as traversing an empty space. Of course, they know that the birds are flying through the air, but since they cannot perceive the air, they tend to ignore it. In this way, Descartes endorsed a view that Newton also found attractive: ordinary people think about space, time, and motion primarily through the lens of ordinary perception, that is, their thinking about such things as whether a particular space is empty tends to be guided by facts about what they can perceive under ordinary circumstances. In addition, since their thinking about space, time, and motion is guided primarily by ordinary sense perception, they tend to think about motion in terms of a body's changing relationship with its environment, as that environment is perceived. The way that Descartes understood this last idea in particular is as follows: he thought that ordinary people would think of motion as involving a change of place, because they think they can perceive when a place is empty, and can see a body coming to rest in that place, having passed other bodies along the way. A bird flies from one tree to another, traversing the empty places in between, passing branches and maybe some falling leaves along the way.

To acknowledge these points, Descartes makes an important maneuver in his thinking about space, time, and motion, one that, as we will see, is also absolutely central to Newton's thinking in this area. Descartes distinguishes in his *Principles* between the *vulgar* or ordinary and the *proper* or philosophical conception of motion. Descartes tells us (Latin: AT VIII-1: 53 | French: AT IX-2: 75) that motion in the ordinary sense is "nothing other than *the action by which a body passes from one place to another*."[5] Hence, we might say that the birds are moving in the sense that at first they were *over there*, in that maple tree, and then they acted by flapping their wings and ended up *over here*, in this pine tree next to the house. As far as ordinary, practical issues are concerned, this vulgar conception of motion would appear to be perfectly adequate: the birds' action moved them from one place to another. However, Descartes apparently views this ordinary understanding of motion as problematic from a philosophical point of view because it would appear to conflict with the true metaphysics: it uses a notion of *place* that may presuppose the possibility of empty space. Just as importantly, it treats motion as the *action* by which a body is transferred from place to place, which may conflict in some ways with the principle of inertia, and which certainly conflicts with his metaphysical view that motion is a mode of a moving body.[6]

In the next section of the text, Descartes jettisons the problematic notions of *place* and *action*, defining motion properly as follows:

> If, on the other hand, we consider what should be understood by *motion*, not in common usage but in accordance with the truth of the matter, and if our aim is to assign a determinate nature to it, we may say that *motion is the transfer of one piece of matter, or one body, from the vicinity of the others which immediately touch it, and which we consider to be at rest, to the vicinity of others* [*ex vicinia eorum corporum, quoe illud immediate contingent & tanquam quiescentia spectantur, in viciniam aliorum*]. (AT VIII-1: 53–54)

This conception of motion obviously reflects the metaphysics of extension. Since nature is a plenum, any travel from place to place will necessarily involve a change in the traveling body's relation to other bodies, and any body will necessarily be surrounded by other bodies—its *vicinity*—at every instant of its existence. If you like, these are not empirical claims, but rather are demanded by Descartes's metaphysics. Now, of course, they do not entail that we must conceive of proper motion as Descartes does. But they do entail that we cannot regard proper motion as motion within empty space, that we must at least acknowledge the fact that every body does have a vicinity of other bodies that surround it, and that (presumably) for any body to move, it must ipso facto change its relations to other bodies. That last claim does not itself entail that motion consists in a change of relations between the moving body and other bodies. But that is indeed Descartes's view. And it does connect with—even if it is not entailed by—his metaphysics. This helps to indicate how we might think of metaphysics and physics as part of a single Cartesian organism: the roots of our tree do not uniquely determine what trunk grows out of them, but they do form a coherent whole.

For its part, the metaphysics of God enables us to discover the three laws of motion that help form the heart of Descartes's natural philosophy. God decrees the laws of nature, of course, but in addition, our knowledge of God's nature—in particular our knowledge of the immutability of God's ordinary *concursus*—enables us to derive at least the first two of the three laws of nature.[7] Descartes's first two laws are as follows (part two, §§37–39; AT VIII-1: 62–63):

> The first law of nature [*lex naturae*]: that each and every thing, in so far as it can [*quantum in se est*], always perseveres in the same state, and thus what is once in motion always continues to move.... The second law of nature: that all motion is in itself rectilinear; and hence any body moving in a circle tends always to move away from the center of the circle it describes.[8]

Because he was overshadowed by figures like Galileo, Boyle, and Newton, Descartes has been given short shrift in the history of science. In the Scholium following corollary six to the laws, Newton himself cites Galileo: "By means of the first two laws and the first two corollaries Galileo found that the descent of heavy bodies is in the squared ratio of the time and that the motion of projectiles occurs in a parabola, as experiment confirms, except insofar as these motions are somewhat retarded by the resistance of the air" (*Principia* 424). Even if Newton is right in attributing this discovery to Galileo, it is not accurate to attribute the first two laws to him, since the Italian philosopher did not think in terms of this kind of generality when discussing motion and its causes (Cohen 1999, 113, Miller, forthcoming) and also takes circular motion to be inertial in an important sense. Moreover, Descartes's articulation of his first two laws of nature is of fundamental importance, and Newton was perfectly well aware of that fact: in an early manuscript (the "Wastebook"), he restates Descartes's first two laws (Herivel 1965, 141). Indeed, Descartes was one of the very first moderns to contend that the laws of nature govern all motion throughout the universe. That is, he rejected the Aristotelian notion that we must provide separate analyses of the sublunary and superlunary spheres: he provided a single analysis of nature following these two laws. It is therefore no surprise that Newton and company would have regarded Descartes, rather than any Aristotelian or, indeed, any other modern, as the philosopher to confront when thinking about space, time, and motion.

What do Descartes's two laws tell us about motion? They obviously do not indicate *what motion is*. Rather, they simply employ that concept. That is perfectly harmless per se, since as we have seen, Descartes provides a proper definition of motion separately. But what the laws do is this: they indicate certain fundamental features of motion by indicating certain basic facts about moving bodies. Taken together, they tell us specifically that if any body is moving rectilinearly, it will continue to do so unless caused to alter its course; if any body is moving in a curvilinear fashion, however, that body will not continue to do so, but rather will tend to move rectilinearly (or, *will move rectilinearly*) unless caused to alter *that* course. This does not tell us what it means to say that a body is moving, but it does tell us certain basic facts about what will happen to any moving body.

How, then, do these two laws of motion intersect with the two concepts of motion broached by Descartes? The laws would appear to conflict with the ordinary concept of motion. If motion is the action whereby a body passes from one place to another, then this may imply that an action is required for the maintenance of some motion. But the laws obviously indicate that a body moving rectilinearly will continue doing so without any action at all, that is, without any causal interaction between the moving body and anything else. No action is required for this motion to continue. That, of course, is the clear consequence of one aspect of the principle of inertia, and as Descartes knew perfectly well, this consequence can seem counterintuitive to the untrained observer relying on ordinary sense perception for her beliefs about motion. So just as the ordinary conception of motion may involve a concept—that of a place—that conflicts with the Cartesian metaphysical prohibition against empty space, it may also involve a concept—that of the action involved in any motion—that conflicts with the Cartesian laws of nature. At least prima facie, then, we can see that the ordinary concept is problematic.

One might immediately infer that Descartes developed the proper concept of motion in part to have an analysis of motion that was consistent with his laws of nature, or perhaps even to express some fact about motion that is implicitly or explicitly contained within the laws. That would be a sensible maneuver for him to make. Moreover, it would indicate that the laws have a kind of priority over our ordinary notions of the motion of bodies. And just as the laws must reflect Cartesian metaphysics in various ways, one might think that the proper concept of motion must also do so. Since the laws are derived from a key element of Cartesian metaphysics, namely, God, these points indicate a substantive way in which the Cartesian program can be seen as a unified whole, as Descartes intended. Alas, this story is flawed. As Newton never tired of showing through complex and creative argumentation, the Cartesian system was not a unified whole in this way. Perhaps surprisingly, it turns out that the laws of motion conflict not only with the ordinary concept of motion, as we might expect, but also with the *proper* concept of motion. And it is precisely the latter conflict, in turn, that helped Newton to develop his mature conception of space, time, and motion.

4.3 Newton's New Natural Philosophy: From *De Gravitatione* to the *Principia*

When Marie Boas Hall and Rupert Hall published their translations of various manuscripts from the Newton archives in 1962, it had a major impact on our conception of Newton's philosophical preoccupations. Among the many drafts and manuscripts that they translated, there was one extended treatment of Descartes's philosophy. This manuscript, which was left untitled and undated by Newton, is now known as *De Gravitatione*, after its first line: "De gravitatione et aequipondio fluidorum." Since the text had never been published before, Hall and Hall's edition made it widely available to scholars for the first time in its original Latin and to a wider audience, who read it in their English translation (see also Biarnais and De Gandt 1995, Steinle 1991). The text begins with a treatment of some questions in natural philosophy but then veers off into a very extended—roughly 30-page—treatment of Descartes's views in both natural philosophy and metaphysics. This discussion of Descartes greatly illuminates Newton's own metaphysical views, and the views of space, time, and motion he came to articulate in the Scholium to the *Principia* (most famously), and in other texts. We do not know why Newton never published *De Gravitatione*, but its importance is clear from the way that its discussions reflect many themes of Newton's published works.[9]

In *De Gravitatione*, Newton's criticism focuses on an essential tension between Descartes's first two laws of motion, on the one hand, and his proper concept of motion, on the other hand. Newton deftly demonstrates that this tension is essential in at least the sense that it cannot be eliminated through any reasonable reinterpretation of either the laws or the concept. This means, in turn, that Newton generates a dilemma for the Cartesian: either choose the laws and jettison your proper concept of motion—the horn of the dilemma that Newton embraces—or retain the concept and jettison the laws.

The conceptual tension between the laws and the concept can be seen as follows. The laws of motion indicate, as we have briefly seen, that any body moving rectilinearly will continue to move in that fashion unless caused to do otherwise; any body moving curvilinearly, however, will tend to move away from the center of its curvilinear trajectory. Any motion that deviates from a rectilinear path, in other words, must be due to some causal factor that influences the moving body. Finally, a body at rest will remain at rest until caused to do otherwise. As we have also seen, these laws do not *define* motion or rest; hence, even if I know the laws, I may not ipso facto know which bodies are moving and which are at rest. For that, I may require some concept of what motion (or rest) consists in, which may enable me, in turn, to discover which bodies are moving.[10] Newton focuses on the tension that these laws exhibit with the proper concept of motion. Fundamentally, Descartes's idea is that motion involves a change in relations between the moving body and one or more other bodies. Motion is relational in that precise sense. More specifically, Descartes contends that a body moves just in case it changes relations to its vicinity, namely, to those bodies that surround it. To move is to change one's relation to another body or bodies.[11] Newton then argues that the laws indicate that the motion of a body does not consist in a change in its relations to other bodies. According to the laws, that is, motion is not relational. That may not tell us what motion is, but it does indicate that the concept of motion found in the *Principles* is inconsistent with the laws.

To see Newton's point, suppose that some body, B, is moving rectilinearly—the laws tell me that B will continue moving rectilinearly until something causes B to change its state of motion. Suppose, too, that we understand B's rectilinear motion using the proper concept of motion: this would mean that B is moving in the sense that it continually changes relations with various vicinities which are regarded as at rest. Its motion at $time_1$ (say) consists in its transference from V_1 to V_2; its motion at $time_2$ consists in its transference from V_2 to V_3; and so on. But notice that we can *stop* B's motion by causally interacting with V_3, ensuring that it continues to surround B at $time_3$ and $time_4$. If B does not change its relation to V_3, then it is no longer truly moving. This violates our law, for we have not causally interacted with B in any way. Thus, we find that the laws regard motion as nonrelational, and this conflicts with Descartes's relational concept of motion in the proper sense (see Newton 2014, 30–32).

Newton's criticism poses a basic dilemma for the Cartesian: either we should jettison the laws and retain the proper concept of motion, or we should retain the latter and jettison the former. But we cannot endorse both. Newton's choice was to endorse the laws—although he clearly rewrote them by the time of the *De Motu* drafts of 1684–1685 that led to the writing of the *Principia* a year later, using the concept of an impressed force (see Chapter 5)—and to jettison the Cartesian proper concept of motion. Newton realized, moreover, that the tension in question did not derive from the specific Cartesian view that a moving body's vicinity is the key to understanding its motion; he saw beyond that view, recognizing that the laws indicate that true motion is not relational. That is, if the principle of inertia is correct, a body's true motion does not consist in a change in relations between it and *any other body*. It may *involve* such a change in relations, but it does not *consist* in it. The reason is simply that Newton's arguments, which focus on a body's vicinity, hold also for any view that regards true motion as relational. As long as we think that a body's true motion is relational, we must admit that the body's motion can be altered by causally interacting with some other body or bodies (those to which the moving body has some specified relation). We could alter a body's state of motion—whether it is at rest or moving rectilinearly—by leaving it alone and interacting with something else. And that basic idea involves a violation of

Descartes's first two laws. In this way, Newton developed a deep insight into ideas about space, time, and motion that reflect what he regarded as the laws of nature.

Newton's criticism highlights what we might regard as a fundamental tension between our ordinary idea of motion and the principle of inertia. This does not involve the common idea that the principle of inertia is itself counterintuitive, at least when compared with the perceptual evidence available to ordinary observers of material bodies. Instead, it involves a deeper—one might say metaphysical—point. Fundamentally, we might ordinarily think that motion is a relational concept, that is, a concept that concerns a body's relation to other things. In fact, we might ordinarily think that a body's motion is concerned especially, although perhaps not exclusively, with its distance from certain other things. And distance of course is a relation. Typically, if we think of a car as moving along the highway, as (say) heading toward Chicago, we think of it as changing its relation to Chicago, as getting progressively closer to it. Similarly, to walk across the proverbial college quad is to begin from some place that is close to one building and to end up closer to another one. It is to change one's relations to other things. This is a perfectly reasonable way to think about motion. However, as we have seen, the principle of inertia indicates otherwise: to move is not ipso facto to change one's relations to other things. One basic reason is this: our ordinary idea of motion is relational in part because it is not dynamical, that is, it ignores the *causes* of motion (or more precisely, of changes in states of motion). As far as the ordinary idea is concerned, as long as a person gets closer to her destination, and eventually reaches it, it makes little difference whether she has been caused to move closer to her destination or whether her destination has been caused to move closer to her. But of course, these are two different dynamical situations, and the principle of inertia is focused on the dynamics: a body's state of motion can be altered only if something causally interacts with that body. (We have not yet said what that causal interaction *involves*, which is a further and very significant topic (see Chapter 5).) If there is a causal interaction not involving that moving body, regardless of what it involves, then that causal interaction may change that body's *relations*, but it will not change its *state of motion*. This is a negative result, but one which is sufficient to recognize a tension between the principle of inertia and our ordinary conception of motion. This does not tell us what true motion consists in—it merely indicates that our *ordinary* idea of *what motion is* cannot be our guide to what *true* motion is.

If we endorse the laws of motion, even in their Cartesian formulation, we realize from reading Newton that true motion is not relational. But this does not tell us what it *is*. We should not conclude, moreover, that the idea that motion is not relational itself indicates that it is *absolute*, for we have not explained that notion yet, and there are both historical and conceptual points to be made about it. Conceptually speaking, the very idea of absolute space, and of absolute motion, requires work and cannot be generated merely by recognizing that true motion is not relational: a body's motion might be nonrelational in the sense of being an intrinsic feature of the body. That is, a relational feature of a body might be contrasted with an intrinsic feature of it. The laws certainly do not indicate that motion cannot be considered an intrinsic feature of moving bodies: they simply say that rectilinear motion will continue until something causally interacts with the moving body. And the causal interaction between the moving body and something else, in turn, could be thought of as altering an intrinsic feature of the body. To see this, we must recognize the distinction between intrinsic and essential properties: very roughly, a property is intrinsic just in case it is compatible with the loneliness of the bearer (hence, it cannot rely on the bearer's relations to anything else), and a property is essential just in case it constitutes, or helps to constitute, what the body is (see Langton and Lewis 1998). For instance, being 6 ft tall is an intrinsic feature of me: if the world disappeared, I would remain that height; hence, my height is not a relational feature of me. But my height is not *essential* to me: I used to be shorter, and when I age I may shrink a bit, but of course, I would not become a new person! It is possible to believe that all essential properties are intrinsic properties—although I doubt that—but it clearly is not true that all intrinsic properties are essential. Consider another example: having my legs crossed is an intrinsic feature of me, but it surely is not essential to me. (Again, the property of having crossed legs is compatible with loneliness.)[12] So at a minimum, the laws indicate only that true motion is not relational, and this is consistent with the idea that true motion is an intrinsic feature of a body, one that will remain intact unless that body interacts causally with something else. Obviously, the idea that motion is an intrinsic feature of something sounds bizarre from the ordinary point of view, but the latter is no guide in physics.[13]

We can therefore see that if we accept Newton's arguments in *De Gravitatione*, and if we endorse the principle of inertia, we have a reason to think that true motion is not relational. We therefore have a reason to uncover the right contrast between a relational conception of motion and some other conception. And that, finally, is precisely what Newton does when he develops his famous, and infamous, concept of absolute space in the Scholium to *Principia Mathematica*.

Now that we know that true motion is not relational, we must proceed by developing some contrast between relational and nonrelational motion that will enable us to capture what the laws tell us about motion. If you like, we need a concept of nonrelational motion that is consistent with the law of inertia (one that is dynamically tractable). This is a key context for understanding Newton's famous threefold distinction within the Scholium on space and time, which appears at the beginning of the *Principia*. Instead of contrasting a relational feature of a body with an intrinsic feature of it, Newton contrasts what he calls *relative* and *absolute* motion. Clearly, the idea of an absolute feature of something requires explanation. And in the most famous discussion of space and time in the modern history of what we now call science and philosophy, Newton provides one:

> Thus far it has seemed best to explain the sense in which less familiar words are to be taken in this treatise. Although time, space, place and motion are

very familiar to everyone, it must be noted that these quantities are popularly conceived solely with reference to the objects of sense perception. And this is the source of certain preconceptions; to eliminate them it is useful to distinguish these quantities into absolute and relative, true and apparent, mathematical and common. (*Principia* 408)

The first important thing to notice here, obviously, is that Newton does not merely settle for the idea that we can contrast a relative feature of a body with an absolute feature of it (whatever that turns out to mean), but that this contrast is somehow parallel to two other contrasts: common versus mathematical features, and true versus apparent features. To grasp each nuance of Newton's thinking, one must grasp this threefold contrast in its totality (see Huggett 2012). The tendency for commentators to focus exclusively on *absolute* space, time, and motion tends to obscure the crucial role played by the other aspects of Newton's threefold contrast.

It should be clear that none of Newton's contrasts is particularly self-evident. In Descartes, as we have seen, the common idea of motion is contrasted with the proper idea; in Newton, however, the common idea of motion is contrasted with the mathematical idea. But what is a mathematical idea of motion, or a mathematical motion? The idea of a true motion is contrasted not with the idea of a false one, but rather with the idea of an apparent one. What does that mean? And finally, we know that Newton thinks of true motion as nonrelational, and we may already understand what a relative motion is—it might be understood as the same kind of thing as a relational motion—but we have no idea yet what an absolute motion might be.

Let us begin with true motion. We know that true motion, consistent with the principle of inertia, is not a relational feature of bodies. There are two points to be made about it at the outset. First, we contrast true motions with *apparent* ones: there can of course be cases in which an object seems to be moving, when it really is not moving, just as there can be cases in which a body does not appear to be moving, but really is. For instance, we can look out a train's window when we are at the station, and for a moment, we may think that our train has started moving, only to realize that the train besides us is actually moving. (Cases like that fit nicely with the ordinary idea that motion is relational.) More importantly, it can certainly seem for all the world that the earth is not moving, but it might really be moving for all that. So the two come apart. There is nothing particularly sophisticated or technical about this idea. Second, we come to the complex move: Newton then says that since true motion is not relational, we should think of it as absolute motion. That is, true motion is absolute motion. What does that mean? In order to capture the idea from the laws of nature that true motion cannot properly be conceived of as relational, we need to regard true motion as something other than a change in object relations, and to do that, Newton proposes that we postulate an empty space whose parts (or places) can serve as the arena for true motion. In particular, a true motion is a change in absolute place. Hence, it is specifically not a change in object relations, so we cannot think of these absolute places as being defined by any objects that happen to inhabit them. For if they were so defined, a body's true motion would once again depend on its relation to some other object, and we have seen the problem with that basic concept. So the distinction between relative and absolute motion is introduced so that we can make the novel suggestion that true motion is absolute motion. The former distinction, in turn, requires us to distinguish between relative and absolute space. So we can see now that the following is true: we postulate absolute space in order to understand true motion in the right way.

Does the postulation of absolute space enable Newton to evade Descartes's problem? We can answer this question by employing a simple test: if a body is moving rectilinearly, and if we understand its true motion as absolute motion, does this give us the proper result, namely, that it will continue moving until something causally interacts with it? It does! A body's absolute motion is independent of its relations to other bodies, so we cannot alter its absolute motion by causally interacting with those bodies. Even if all of those bodies were to vanish, this would not disrupt the body's absolute motion, its true motion, at all; this is a conceptual point, and not an empirical claim. The same is true of a body at rest: a body at absolute rest cannot be disturbed by causally interacting with other bodies, for that will not alter its absolute position. So we now have a view of true motion that is consistent with our laws of nature.[14] Newton has successfully evaded what he regarded as a fundamental problem hampering the Cartesian program.

As important as this result is for Newton, however, we still lack a clear idea of what the other aspects of the threefold contrast are. We might think of it in this way: the contrast is a threefold one in that the items on either side of the contrast line up with one another in an intriguing way. For instance, we find that true motion is absolute motion, and this is also identified with a mathematical concept of motion. The reason might be this: since we think of true motion as absolute, and since we therefore require the idea of absolute space in order to conceive of true motion, and since absolute space, in turn, is clearly the space of Euclidean geometry, we find that this mathematical notion of space is required for us to conceive of true motion. Of course, this does not entail that we must understand anything especially specific or technical about Euclidean geometry in order to grasp what Newtonian true motion is, but we do require, at a bare conceptual minimum, the idea of Euclidean space. *Prima facie*, Descartes could never accept that claim: although he may endorse the idea that we can think of motion within geometry—for instance, the motion of a point can be thought of as generating a line, and the motion of a line as generating a plane, and perhaps the motion of a plane as generating a solid—he would certainly deny that motion in the real world can be thought of as occurring within absolute space, since space is identical to matter. This is an obvious point of difference with Newton, and it helps to illuminate some of the metaphysical views that he discusses already in *De Gravitatione* (as I note in the following). For Newton, it seems, the space of the real world just is the space of geometry.

Does Newton's view that true motion is absolute motion require us to postulate that space is independent of all bodies and their relations? (That is the canonical formulation of *absolutism* about space.) Does it require us, for example, to take a stand on the thorny question of whether space itself would continue to exist if all objects and their relations disappeared? Perhaps. But for our purposes here, there is a more important point: we are required to think that the places that constitute absolute space are not themselves *defined* by the objects filling those places. Of course, we could simply interpret Newton as stipulating that absolute places are not object dependent. But there is another point here. If we define two absolute places, P_1 and P_2, by the objects that filled them, and if we think that the true motion of body B is its absolute motion, and if, finally, we think that B's true motion consists in its transference from P_1 to P_2, then we realize that this would actually render true motion relational once again. For if the objects that defined P_1 and P_2 were to move, then those places would move—hence, the true motion of B would depend on those objects. So this is no mere stipulation: Newton has a reason to contend that the places constituting absolute space are object independent. In order to endorse Newtonian true motion, we have to postulate a Euclidean space whose constituent places are independent of objects.

In the Scholium, however, Newton does not merely suggest that we must think of true motion as absolute motion in order to capture what the laws tell us about motion. He also provides us with an ingenious *Gedankenexperiment*, one indicating that the Cartesian concept of true motion is inconsistent with ordinary experience (and not merely inconsistent with the laws). We discover this fact by thinking about the effects of true motion, which we have bracketed thus far. This is the famous bucket example. Imagine that we take a bucket, tie a long rope to its curved handle, turn the rope around so that it is quite twisted, fill the bucket with water, and then hold the end of the rope while letting it untwist. What would happen? At first, as the bucket spins around, the water would be at rest; then, as the bucket makes the water spin with it, the water would begin rotating with the bucket; and finally, as the bucket and water spin around together, the water would become concave at its surface. The genius behind Newton's example is that everything he says about this situation originates with ordinary experience: every farmer from Newton's hometown would know what would happen to this water. None of our knowledge here is technical, nor have we presupposed anything about true motion, absolute space, or anything else. We can tell that the water is actually moving, in this case, because of the concavity of its surface: if we were to rotate things around the water, without moving the water itself, then its surface would remain flat. So based on ordinary experience, we can say this much: changing the water's relations to other things would not render its surface concave; only spinning water has that feature. So we can tell that the water is truly moving.

The next step of the argument is to attempt to grasp this situation using the Cartesian view of true motion: the water's true motion consists in its transference from its vicinity, the bucket, to some other vicinity. But as ordinary experience would also indicate, the water and the bucket spin around at the same speed toward the end of our experiment, which means that the water is not being transferred away from its vicinity. Yet it is truly moving. Therefore, we have a reason to think that true motion is not relational in Descartes's specific sense. Does that *prove* that true motion is absolute motion? No. But it does indicate that the Cartesian view of true motion cannot account for this ordinary phenomenon. And, of course, it should be obvious that if we deny that true motion is relational, contending that it *just is* absolute motion, then we *can* account for this ordinary phenomenon. Otherwise put: even in ordinary cases, there are effects of true motion—the concavity of the water's surface—that indicate why true motion is not relative motion, for those effects are absent in cases of relative motion.

If that is the upshot of the bucket example, why does Newton give another example of circular motion on the very next page of the Scholium, namely, the case of the two rotating globes? Here is one reason: Newton recognizes that we can solve Descartes's problem if we say that true motion is absolute motion, but he also recognizes that the assertion of this identity generates another problem. If true motion is change of absolute place, then the imperceptibility of absolute place (or of absolute space) may entail that we cannot discover any true motions. It would be as if I had said that true motion is a change in relations with an invisible marker! How would anyone discover it? The case is not hopeless, Newton tells us. For once again, as with the bucket, we can sometimes discover the effects of true motion, and the key is that the identification of true motion with absolute motion does nothing to prevent us from perceiving those effects. Consider Newton's second example: suppose we take two wooden balls and connect them with a long cord (perhaps a rope). If we were to spin the balls over our heads—in a kind of Olympic event—we would notice that the tension in the cord between the balls would be affected by their rotation, increasing in proportion to an increase in the rotation. The tension would indicate to us that the balls are truly moving.[15] And the further idea that their true motion consists in a change in absolute place does nothing to undermine our capacity to perceive the tension in the cord. It is a brilliant example for that very reason. Finally, if we were to rotate anything else around the balls, or indeed, to rotate the entire universe around the balls, the tension in the cord would be unaffected. Hence, the effect indicates that the balls are truly moving.

Of course, Newton was well aware that although we can detect true (i.e., absolute) motion in certain cases, there are plenty of cases in which we cannot detect it. That might be true regardless of how we understand true motion, and one could certainly come to believe that if true motion is an intrinsic feature of a body, then there are cases in which we cannot detect it. But Newton's particular way of understanding true motion—namely, as change of absolute place—may raise special problems, since absolute place is inherently undetectable. Relative places can be detected under various circumstances, but absolute ones never can. So the question is, does Newton's view raise special detection problems? Here, we might use the laws of nature as our guide once again. First of all, the laws help us to understand when we can detect the effects of absolute motion. If we return to the bucket example, we see that the laws indicate why the water runs up the sides of the bucket: the truly moving water tends to move in a straight line, but when it is constrained by the bucket, it cannot do so; hence, it runs up the sides. As Newton puts this point, the truly moving water recedes from the axis of motion. The same is true of the globes: as they *try* to fly off along the tangent to their mutual orbit, they stretch out the cord between them, increasing its tension, which we can detect. Secondly, and more importantly, the laws tell us not only why we can detect the effects of true motion in some cases but also why we cannot detect the effects of true motion in other cases. More specifically, what the laws tell us, as Newton was the first to point out, is *that we cannot detect the unchanging velocity of a body, we can detect only its acceleration.* Since a rotation is an acceleration—any change in direction represents a change in velocity since the latter is a vector quantity, rather than a scalar quantity like speed—we can in principle detect it, or as Newton shows, we can detect its effects. What we cannot do, however, is to detect the true motion of a nonaccelerating body—more precisely, we cannot detect that a nonaccelerating body is truly moving! *Yet this is simply a consequence of the laws of nature (and their corollaries or implications)*[16]; *this is not a special consequence of Newton's view of space.* Hence, if you endorse the laws, then you must conclude that we cannot detect any motion that does not involve acceleration. This would also be true if we conceived of true motion as an intrinsic property, rather than as absolute motion: if a body were traveling rectilinearly, there would be no detectable effects of its motion—there would be nothing analogous to the water rushing up the sides of the bucket or to the tension in the cord between the rotating balls—so it would be undiscoverable.

Stepping back, we can see how Newton's Scholium serves at least two useful purposes: first, it helps to undermine Descartes's view that true motion is relational; and second, it enables Newton to move toward the positive view that true motion is absolute (nonrelational, in a particular way). This also indicates what Newton does *not* do in this text: he does not set out to "prove that space is absolute," a common refrain among his interpreters (see Rynasiewicz (1995a, b) for helpful details). It is not completely clear what such a proof might consist in, or why Newton would attempt it. Leaving that aside, Newton obviously thinks that relative spaces—spaces that are determined by relations among material bodies—exist as well, so he does not think that space is not relative in that specific sense. What he does think is that we must distinguish between different conceptions of space, time, and motion if those conceptions are to reflect what we learn from the laws of nature. And we can thereby avoid Descartes's unfortunate fate.

Newton may have avoided Descartes's problem, but that does not entail that he was above reproach in introducing the concept of absolute space in order to reflect his conclusion that true motion is not relational. Indeed, the claim that space is absolute, or that we can regard it as such, landed Newton in all sorts of hot water with numerous philosophers throughout the eighteenth century. Figures such as Leibniz, Berkeley, and Kant had little in common with one another, philosophically or even historically, but they were all agreed that the very idea of absolute space was problematic or worse. To see what bothered them, we have to wade into deep metaphysical waters.

4.4   Newton's New Metaphysics: *De Gravitatione* as Foundational Text

In *De Gravitatione*, which was most likely written before the first edition of the *Principia* in 1687, and probably before 1684 (Ruffner 2012), Newton indicates that he was committed to rejecting not only Cartesian physics, especially its conception of true motion, but also its foundation, Cartesian metaphysics. In fact, he rejected nearly every single principle or conclusion within the *Meditations* and part one of the *Principles*, including the view that space (or extension) and matter are numerically identical, the idea that the mind is a nonextended substance, the claim that God does not exist within space, and, most fundamentally, the presupposition that any item within our ontology must fit within a basic substance/property metaphysical framework. In rejecting Cartesian metaphysical doctrines and presuppositions, Newton was heavily influenced by his older colleague at Cambridge, Henry More, a leading figure of *Cambridge Platonism* in the mid-seventeenth century, a personal friend of Newton's, and the person who coined the term *Cartesianism* (Gabbey 1982). More's infatuation with Cartesian ideas early in his career gave way to a strong rejection of Descartes's views by the time his most influential philosophical works were published in the 1650s and 1660s (Henry 2013, 129–131). Newton read nearly all of More's mature works, citing them approvingly, for example, in his 1664 undergraduate notebook at Trinity College (McGuire and Tamny 1983). More's break with Descartes can be traced back to his celebrated correspondence with the aging philosopher in 1648–1649, where we find him pressing Descartes again and again to clarify his insistence that we must always distinguish extended from nonextended substances. This exchange of views, therefore, is the perfect entrée into a discussion of Newton's own break with Descartes's metaphysics a generation later.

Much as Princess Elisabeth forced Descartes to confront some of the thorny problems concerning mind–body causal interactions generated by his dualism in their 1643 correspondence (Shapiro 2007), More pressed Descartes to recognize some thorny problems involving God's causal interaction with the material world generated by the view that God is a nonextended being. In his first letter to Descartes, written in December 1648, More argues that if one endorses the view that God causally interacts with material bodies—remember that

Descartes had argued 4 years earlier in the *Principles* that God is the "primary cause of motion"—then one must admit that God is extended in some way. He writes (AT V: 238–239):

> And, indeed, I judge that the fact that God is extended in his own way follows from the fact that he is omnipresent and intimately occupies the universal machine of the world and each of its parts. For could he have impressed motion on matter, which he did once and which you think he does even now, unless he, as it were, immediately touches the matter of the universe, or at least did so once? This never could have happened unless he were everywhere and occupied every single place. Therefore, God is extended in his own way and spread out; and so God is an extended thing [*res extensa*].

More attempts to harness the common view (endorsed by Descartes) that God acts on material bodies, which latter of course are located somewhere in space, to show that God must in some sense be located where those bodies are located. And the idea that God is located, in turn, is said to entail the idea that God is extended, for surely a nonextended being must lack location.[17]

One might expect Descartes simply to reject everything that More says in his letter. But Descartes leaves More with an opening that he exploits later. In February 1649, Descartes replies to More, quoting from his earlier letter (AT V: 269–270):

> "But," you say, "God, or an angel, or any other self-subsistent thing is extended, and so your definition is too broad." It is not my custom to argue about words, and so if someone wants to say that God is in a sense extended, since he is everywhere, I have no objection. But I deny that true extension as commonly conceived is to be found in God or in angels or in our mind or in any substance which is not a body. Commonly when people talk of an extended being, they mean something imaginable. In this being—I leave on one side the question whether it is conceptual or real—they can distinguish by the imagination various parts of determinate size and shape, each nonidentical with the others. Some of these parts can be imagined as transferred to the place of others, but no two can be imagined simultaneously in one and the same place. Nothing of this kind can be said about God or about our mind; they cannot be apprehended by the imagination, but only by the intellect; nor can they be distinguished into parts, and certainly not into parts which have determinate sizes and shapes... Some people do indeed confuse the notion of substance with that of extended thing. This is because of the false preconceived opinion which makes them believe that nothing can exist or be intelligible without being also imaginable, and because it is indeed true that nothing falls within the scope of the imagination without being in some way extended.

Descartes insists on a series of points here which, as it turns out, More fully endorses: in saying that God is extended, we should not be understood as saying that God has parts, that we can represent God clearly and distinctly by imaging some substance, or more generally that every being or substance must be understood through the imagination. But given this insistence, why does Descartes leave an opening here? Why does he say that although it may delve into semantics, he does not object to the idea that God is extended *in a sense*, just not in the common meaning of that phrase? Why not reject the claim that God is extended per se?

The reason for Descartes's reluctance to reject More's view outright emerges later in the correspondence. Seeing his opening, More pounces again: we agree that God can act on material objects, and we obviously agree that material objects have locations, *so surely we must admit that God's action or power has a location.* If God decides to create a miracle, engulfing a bush in flames without it being consumed by the fire, then God's power or action is located where that bush is located. And since God's power or action can be located *anywhere*, we must conclude that God is *everywhere*. So says More. In April 1649, Descartes replies as follows:

> I do not agree with this "everywhere." You seem here to make God's infinity consist in his existing everywhere, which is an opinion I cannot agree with. I think that God is everywhere in virtue of his power; yet in virtue of his essence he has no relation to place at all. But since in God there is no distinction between essence and power, I think it is better to argue in such cases about our own mind or about angels, which are more on the scale of our own perception, rather than to argue about God.

Thus, More presses Descartes to admit that God's power is located everywhere. Now that view is obviously connected with what is often called Descartes's occasionalism, which is roughly the thesis that all causal powers within the world, or perhaps all causal interactions within the world, are ultimately due to God's power and not to the self-subsistent causal powers of the bodies in the world. Yet we can leave that aside here. For even if Descartes is not an occasionalist, he *does* think that God could act anywhere in the world, and so he does have a reason to say that God's action or power could be anywhere. If God were to act everywhere in the world, then God's action or power would be everywhere. But as Descartes also must admit, there is no distinction within God between his power and his essence, so he has now seemingly admitted that God's essence is located everywhere. He continues to insist that God is not extended in the usual sense—God has no parts, we cannot represent God through images, etc.—but he now endorses the idea that God is extended in some special, philosophically significant sense. This is a remarkable admission. From it and from it alone, one can see not only the key maneuver that leads to certain aspects of Henry More's early metaphysics, but also the fundamental origins of Newton's own rejection of Cartesianism in favor of a Morean-influenced position.

The correspondence between Descartes and More, which Newton read, illuminates his fundamental rejection of Cartesian metaphysics in *De Gravitatione*.[18] That rejection transcends the rejection of those aspects of

Cartesian metaphysics that are presupposed by Cartesian natural philosophy, for Newton does not merely challenge Descartes's conception of the metaphysics of body, but also his understanding of the mind and of God (and he rejects the latter in ways that do not involve the derivation of the first two laws of nature from divine immutability). Newton forcefully rejects Cartesian dualism, and he strongly endorses More's view that all beings or substances are extended in some way. But he begins at the beginning, noting that for Descartes, extension and body are identical (a view found in the *Meditations* and repeated in part Two of the *Principles*, which Newton cites). About that identification, he writes:

> And as this has been taken by many as proved, and is in my view the only reason for having confidence in this opinion, and lest any doubt should remain about the nature of motion, I shall reply to this argument by saying what extension and body are, and how they differ from each other. For since the distinction of substances into thinking and extended, or rather into thoughts and extensions, is the principal foundation of Cartesian philosophy, which he contends to be known more exactly than mathematical demonstrations: I consider it most important to overthrow [that philosophy] as regards extension, in order to lay truer foundations of the mechanical sciences. (Newton 2014, 35)

Newton does not merely reject the Cartesian view that extension and body are identical—he also rejects the notion that extension or space must be considered either a property of some substance or a substance in its own right. In doing so, he discusses classic metaphysical topics, challenging not only the Cartesian presupposition that all items within our ontology must fall somewhere into the substance/property matrix but, even more fundamentally, arguing that we require a new concept of substance.

From Descartes's point of view, any item that can be said to exist—the Taj Mahal, my mind, God, my height, the idea of a triangle—must either be a substance or a property of one. More technically speaking, any item must be a substance, a basic property of one, or an alterable property that involves various potential *modes*. What does that mean? Consider the Taj Mahal: it is an extended substance, which means that extension is its essence, or essential property (or attribute). In virtue of having that essential property, there are lots of features that it might also have: it might be 100 m tall, it might be white, it might be made of stone, and so on. These features are modes of the Taj, which means that *they are ways that it is extended*. Not all extended things are white, not all are made of stone, but some are. What modes must it lack? It cannot have an idea of triangle. For that, it would have to be a thinking substance, like my mind, rather than an extended one. So the Taj is an extended substance, my mind is a finite thinking substance, God is an actually infinite thinking substance (see the following text), height is a mode of extended substances, and the idea of a triangle is a mode of thinking substances.

But what exactly is a *substance*? Famously, Descartes entertains two distinct conceptions of substance.[19] First and foremost, he thinks of substances as entities that have independent existence—they do not depend on any other entity (technically: on any other *finite* entity) to exist. Hence, if we take my laptop and use philosophical magic to make the rest of the world disappear, we find that my laptop remains. This is a metaphysical claim: it may in fact be empirically true that a laptop could only cohere into a single object under certain physical conditions (gravity? interparticulate forces? etc.), but that is beside the point. To see why, consider this: the *weight* of my laptop, 2 pounds, cannot exist independently—if we make the rest of the world disappear, including my laptop, then its weight disappears. It is merely a way that my laptop is extended; it is a mode of an extended substance rather than a substance in its own right. But secondly, the qualification in parentheses earlier is crucial: technically speaking, Descartes endorses the traditional view that all finite things, including my laptop, depend for their existence on God, and so if we take a substance to be an independently existing thing per se, then my laptop is not a substance. In fact, *only God* is a substance according to this second criterion. (This of course leads to Spinoza's monism, his view that there is in fact only a single substance.) Regardless of which criterion one chooses, however, Descartes does seem committed to the notion that items within our ontology must fit into the substance/property scheme.

Following an important mid-seventeenth-century tradition involving figures such as Isaac Barrow, Walter Charleton, and Gassendi, Newton rejects the substance/property scheme.[20] He begins by saying that space is certainly something that we should admit into our ontology, but then denies that it is either a substance or a property (or a mode). Why so? Shouldn't Newton say that space is a substance? After all, absolute space, "without relation to anything external," has certain features—it is *homogenous* and *immovable*—and so it would seem to have properties (or modes), which means that it looks like it is a substance. Moreover, it would seem to exist independently of all the matter in the world, which would seem to indicate that it meets the independence criterion (even if it would not meet the second criterion because it somehow depends on God). It would be historically accurate, but philosophically boring, to note here that *De Gravitatione* was almost certainly written before the *Principia* presented the mature conception of absolute space for the first time. Luckily, Newton is many things, but never boring. There are also important philosophical echoes of the treatment of space within *De Gravitatione* in the General Scholium to the *Principia*, added in its second edition of 1713, so it is certainly reasonable to infer that Newton retained his denial that space is a substance even in his later years.

According to Newton in *De Gravitatione*, space is not a substance if we recognize the proper criterion of substance-hood: action. A substance, says Newton, must be an active thing, a causally efficacious entity:

> For although philosophers do not define substance as an entity that can act upon things, yet everyone tacitly understands this of substances, as follows

from the fact that they would readily allow extension to be substance in the manner of body if only it were capable of motion and of sharing in the actions of body. And on the contrary, they would hardly allow that body is substance if it could not move, nor excite any sensation or perception in any mind whatsoever. (Newton 2014, 36)

So philosophers assume that substances are causally interactive things, an assumption that Newton proposes to use as his official criterion of substance-hood. He seems to think that *independence* is a red herring (as we have seen, it is also ambiguous). Here is the idea: if we were to take something Descartes *et al.* would regard as a substance, like my coffee cup, and to remove all of its causal interactions, then it seems that we would no longer consider it to be a substance, but rather just a part of space. After all, what is the difference between my coffee cup and its exact location, namely, the coffee-cup-shaped place that it currently occupies? They are both extended; indeed, ex hypothesi, they have precisely the same shape. But the coffee cup can move around, it can bump into things, it can reflect light rays of a certain wavelength (hence, it is blue), and so on. If we remove all of its causal powers, it would be rendered imperceptible and immovable. And what is an imperceptible, immovable, coffee-cup-shaped extended thing? It's a place! Surely a mere place is not a substance. And what is space but an infinite collection of places? Hence, for Newton, space is not a substance because it is causally inert. (Naturally, he had never heard of the general theory of relativity.) So we have abandoned the independence criterion and replaced it with what I will call the activity criterion.[21]

What if we reverse this process? What if we begin with space, then consider some place within it (arbitrarily chosen, if you like), and then analyze this issue: how would that place have to change in order for philosophers to consider it a substance in its own right? This is exactly the question that Newton ingeniously asks a few pages later in *De Gravitatione*; he does so in order to specify further what he takes the nature of body to be, since he has already rejected the Cartesian identification of body and space. So let us consider the coffee-cup-shaped three-dimensional place we encountered before: what would it take for this to *become*, or at least to be *considered*, a substance (an extended one)? Suppose the coffee-cup-shaped place were to be endowed with the property of impenetrability. The place would now have a surface in the sense that light rays and sound waves would bounce off it—hence, it would be perceptible, at least in principle—and it would prevent other things, like my hand, from occupying its place. My hand would feel the place and be able to grasp it. But wait: remember that in this *Gedankenexperiment*, we have endowed the place with impenetrability, but not yet with mobility, so I could grasp the cup but I couldn't lift it! It could not move. So let us now add mobility to its features: now, I can see the coffee-cup-shaped place, lift it up, set it down, and so on. But wait: we have not yet stipulated that this mobile, impenetrable thing would follow the laws of nature. That is a crucial further stipulation, because without it, we might have a thing that behaves arbitrarily when it causally interacts with other things. For instance, it is compatible with the thing's mobility and impenetrability that it accelerate arbitrarily when I throw it. Or even that it suddenly starts floating in the air—after all, uncaused floating is compatible with impenetrability and mobility. So Newton is clever to add that the thing in question must behave in accordance with the laws of nature, just like any other ordinary object (see Biener and Smeenk 2012, Brading 2012). Newton concludes that this coffee-cup-shaped place would be indistinguishable from an ordinary coffee cup, and so we would conclude that it was an extended substance. We have said nothing about the cup's *independence* from anything else; we have focused solely on its action, its ability to interact with other things in the world, including perceivers. But that is not all. Intriguingly, Newton also characterizes this little *Gedankenexperiment* as a story about how God could have created matter. He does not claim to *know* how God created the material world, but he does think that we might be able to render that idea intelligible to ourselves by following his lead, distinguishing between space and body, and then imagining that God endowed various regions of space with impenetrability and mobility (cf. Bennett and Remnant 1978). Because this creation story was known to Locke and to French *philosophes* through his French translator, Pierre Coste, the fact that *De Gravitatione* was unpublished during Newton's lifetime did not prevent it from becoming part of the early modern philosophical conversation.[22]

What implications does this new criterion of substance-hood have for the rest of Newton's metaphysics? All substances are active: bodies move and bump into things, minds think and will things to happen, and God thinks and also acts in various ways. This is what all substances have in common. Moreover, we should consider all substances—bodies, minds, and God—to be extended. (That is, different kinds of substance cannot be distinguished from one another based on the Cartesian idea that only some of them have extension as their essential attribute.) Hence, all substances are active, extended entities. What, then, distinguishes them? Newton thinks that whereas ordinary bodies are impenetrable, the mind (and God) is not. Thus, the mind is not perceptible—it does not reflect sound waves, light rays, etc.—and it cannot be touched by anything. But the mind is active: its action consists in cognition and willing. Anything that is inactive, like space, is not a substance.[23]

More's debate with Descartes highlights the benefit of Newton's view that all substances are extended. Under pressure from More, Descartes admits that God's action or power—and therefore God's essence—is located everywhere. A parallel story might be told about the mind. With a finite thinking substance like my mind, we can distinguish between its power and its essence (for technical reasons that need not detain us here), so we are not required to infer that the mind's essence is present at some point in space. It is not: the mind is essentially nonextended; it is essentially a thinking substance. But it remains the case that if we think of the mind as active, as Descartes does, and if we think that the mind can interact with the body in particular, as Descartes does, then we have a fundamental question to answer: if my mind has no location, why is its power located only at my body? Why can I snap my fingers but not yours? Of course, Descartes might simply say that God creates a mind–body union for each person, which means that each mind is somehow connected to each body. But this is unsatisfying, as appeals to divine fiat often are. Newton can answer the fundamental question more satisfyingly: my mind is located where my body is located. My mind can interact with my body, but not with yours, because it is located at my body, and not at yours. So for Newton, my mind's power is located where my body is located because that, too, is where you will find my mind. The claim that all substances are extended, then, removes one dimension of metaphysical difference between the mind and the body. But Newton does not reduce the mind–body distinction into nothing. He still maintains that the mind is not impenetrable, unlike the body, which is an ordinary physical substance. So he still has trouble indicating how the mind can interact causally with anything: how can a substance that cannot touch anything, that cannot come into direct contact with anything, causally interact with anything? This remains a mystery. But what philosopher has completely solved the mind–body problem (cf. Gorham 2011)?

For those who are accustomed to thinking of Newton as a mathematician or a physicist, it may seem odd that he would devote so much attention to metaphysical topics. Why did he bother? Otherwise put, why did Newton simply not provide his internal critique of Cartesian physics, choose to endorse the principle of inertia, and then argue that true motion is not relational? This would set up his conclusion in the *Principia* that true motion is absolute, and he would then be prepared to develop the amazing details of what we now call his mathematical physics. Newton himself answers this question directly: since Cartesian natural philosophy is founded upon Descartes's conception of the metaphysics of extended substances and of the mind, Newton must present a new conception of these metaphysical topics if he is to *overthrow* the Cartesian program. That is, the internal critique of the Cartesian concept of motion is not sufficient to demolish the whole structure of Cartesian philosophy, since it rests explicitly on a metaphysical foundation. Hence, Newton says that the proper conception of extension will serve as part of the "truer foundations of the mechanical sciences." Much as we find in More, and later in Leibniz, Newton proposes to overthrow Descartes, propounding a new philosophy, and not merely a new physics with a new concept of true motion. This is evidence for the conclusion that Newton was a natural philosopher.

notes

1 In this, Newton was not alone: as Heilbron puts it, as of the mid-seventeenth century, "Descartes then replaced Aristotle as the foil against which British physics tested its metal" (1982, 30); cf. Henry (2013). For various perspectives on Newton's relation to Descartes and Cartesian ideas, see, inter alia, Koyré (1968), Cohen (1990), the groundbreaking approach of Stein (1970, 2002), and Janiak

(2010). Newton's relation to Cartesianism was mediated through the Cambridge Platonist Henry More's well-known criticisms of Descartes's views in natural philosophy and metaphysics. More was originally a strong supporter of Cartesian natural philosophy, calling its competitors in the 1640s mere *shrimps* (Heilbron 1982, 30); he later changed his mind. Newton had 11 of More's works in his personal library (see Harrison 1978), including More (1655, 1659, 1662), and was substantially influenced both by his eventual criticisms of Cartesian metaphysics and by his own positive views in that field.

2   That fact gives some evidence concerning its dating—but that topic remains controversial and I will not deal with it in any depth here.

3   In the preface to the French edition of the text (1647), he writes (AT IX-2: 14): "Ainsi toute la Philosophie est comme un arbre, dont les racines sont la Metaphysiques, le tronc est la Physique, & les branches qui fortent de ce tronc sont toutes les autres sciences, qui se reduisent à trois principales, à scauoir la Medecine, la Mechanique & la Morale, j'entens la plus haute & la plus parfait Morale, qui, presupposant une entière connoissance des autres sciences, est le dernier degree de la Sagesse."

4   Indeed, it is perfectly reasonable to interpret Descartes as an occasionalist, as holding the view that all causal activity in nature must in fact be directly attributed to God's activity. This view is defended in Garber (1992). Even if Descartes is not an occasionalist, however, he certainly held that God is the primary cause of motion in nature (the laws are called the secondary causes of motion), and so it is uncontroversial to hold that God's causal activity plays an ineliminable role in our understanding of physical interactions.

5   That is: "nihil aliud est quàm *actio, quâ corpus aliquod ex uno loco in alium migrat.*" The italics are in the original Latin and in the original French.

6   This is an element of Descartes's metaphysics that need not detain us here—for an illuminating discussion, see Garber (1992, 159–162). It may also conflict with section 26 of part two, which indicates that despite appearances to the contrary, the motion of a body does not require more action than rest.

7   Obviously, there are deep questions about how this derivation from the immutability of God's *concursus* might work. I bracket them here because these questions apparently did not exercise Newton: he was willing to grant Descartes the derivation, focusing instead on what he may have regarded as a more fundamental problem. The problem is roughly this: even if one can derive the laws of nature (at least the first two) from one's knowledge of God, it remains the case that the conception of motion expressed by those laws is in tension with the concept of proper motion that one also finds in part two of the *Principles*. As we will see, Newton made that tension the highlight of his criticism.

8   Descartes's understanding of the laws of nature is complex. For instance, although he takes God to be the *primary* cause of motion (section 36), he considers the laws to be *secondary* causes of it. For an illuminating treatment of this possibly confusing notion, see Schmaltz (2008, 105–116).

9   Moreover, despite the fact that the text was not published until the middle of the twentieth century, it may have been known to Locke, and through him (and the French translator of his *Essay*, Pierre Coste), to others as well, including French Newtonians in the eighteenth century. For discussion, see Bennett and Remnant (1978), Tamny (1979), and Stein (2002, 272–274), and see the discussion in Chatelet's work (1742, §73).

10 Of course, Newton points out in depth that a clear concept of motion may be insufficient to discover what bodies are actually moving in nature. Indeed, depending on the details of that concept, it may in fact be very difficult to discover what bodies are truly moving. I tackle those issues in the following.

11 As noted earlier, Descartes adds the thought that we must regard the vicinity as being at rest in order to conceive of a body's changing relationship to its vicinity as a true motion. Newton criticizes this aspect of Descartes's view in depth in *De Gravitatione*, on the grounds that it introduces a subjective element into the very concept of true motion (since distinct observers may disagree on whether a vicinity is at rest). See Newton (2014, 29–30). I bracket this issue here because it is not central to understanding the tension in the Cartesian program that Newton highlights.

12 One might object that the property of having one's legs crossed involves relations after all: for without legs, I could not have that property. But this may be misleading. After all, my legs are parts of me, and we presumably do not want to say that only simple bodies, that is, bodies without parts, can have intrinsic features. One might reply: bodies with parts can have intrinsic features, but those features cannot be borne by the bodies in virtue of the relations among their parts. But now take my shape: I have a certain complex shape, one which we could model with clay, and this feature of me presumably supervenes on, or depends on, the relations among my parts. After all, my shape depends on the relation between my head and my feet, for if we alter that relation, we alter my shape. But presumably we do not want to deny that my shape is intrinsic to me (leaving aside very technical questions about the potential curvature of space in connection with the distribution of matter–energy). Shape is a paradigm case of an intrinsic property because it is obviously compatible with loneliness. Cf. Langton and Lewis (1998). Thanks to Sally Halanger for discussion of these issues.

13 We might go further and say that the principle of inertia actually suggests that the motion of a body is intrinsic to it. After all, it tells us, perhaps counterintuitively, that a body moving rectilinearly will continue to do so indefinitely if nothing impedes it, so that may suggest that the body would continue moving even if it were a lonely body. Why so? Well, if it were lonely, then there would be nothing to impede its progress! So it would continue moving. And a property that is compatible with loneliness just is an intrinsic property. Of course, there is more to be said about all of this. But the basic point remains that Descartes's laws of motion (at least the first two) are perfectly consistent with the idea, and may even suggest the idea, that true motion is an intrinsic property.

14 Newton saw some of these points in *De Gravitatione*, where he notes (after his detailed criticism of Cartesian proper motion): "So it is necessary that the definition of places, and hence of local motion, be referred to some motionless being such as extension alone or space in so far as it is seen to be truly distinct from bodies" (Newton 2014, 35).

15 The second example also indicates how we might go about measuring the rotation by noticing how an increase in rotation tends to increase or decrease tension in the cord.

16 Newton discusses aspects of these issues in the fifth and sixth corollaries to the laws of motion (*Principia* 423).

17 More's argument here presupposes that a substance or being, even God, must be located wherever it acts; that presupposition requires an extended discussion of its own—see Janiak (2010) and Reid (2008).

18 Among Newton's papers in the archive at University Library, Cambridge, I discovered a notebook apparently belonging to one Thomas Clarke that contains a complete transcription of More's correspondence with Descartes. This transcription is remarkable because it is dated 1654, which was 1 year before Descartes's full correspondence was sent to Clerselier for later publication. Hence Mr. Clarke, whoever he was, must have seen Henry More's own copy of the correspondence; Clarke and More were obviously in Cambridge at the same time. At that time, however, Newton was a child—he did not enroll in Trinity College until 1660. How Clarke's notebook ended up with Newton's papers remains unclear. Newton read Descartes's correspondence in the Clerselier edition, citing it on occasion, and that edition included the More letters. See Newton (2014, 50), where he cites Descartes's "epistle 96 to Mersenne," which turns out to be a letter from January 9, 1639 (AT 2: 479–492). I owe this last reference to Alan Gabbey.

19 He explains his view in section 51, part one, of the *Principles* (AT VIIIA: 24).

20 Barrow, Gassendi, and Charleton (following Gassendi) all doubt that space and time must fit into the substance/property framework developed by Descartes and others. See Barrow (1734, 164), Charleton (1654), and, for discussion of Gassendi, LoLordo (2007, 106–124).

21 Remarkably, another very influential post-Cartesian thinker, one who would end his career in the midst of a wide-ranging philosophical debate with the Newtonians, would independently endorse a very similar view of substance in his own metaphysics. That would be Leibniz.

22 In addition to Bennett and Remnant (1978), see Stein (2002, 272–274).

23 This idea leaves open another question that Newton actually addresses: why should we think that space is also not a property of any substance? To answer this question, however, Newton tackles a series of very complex neo-Platonic (or Platonic) metaphysical concepts, relying in part on his fascinating conception of God. I discuss these concepts, and that conception, in Chapter 7.

making philosophy mathematical

'Tis great pity *Aristotle* had not understood Mathematicks as well as Mr. *Newton*, and made use of it in Natural Philosophy, with as good success.

John Locke

In the preceding books I have delivered principles of philosophy that are not, however, philosophical but strictly mathematical—that is, those on which the study of philosophy may be based. These principles are the laws and conditions of motions and of forces, which most pertain to philosophy. But in order to prevent these principles from becoming sterile, I have illustrated them with some philosophical scholia, treating topics that are general and that seem to be the most fundamental for philosophy, such as the density and resistance of bodies, spaces void of bodies, and the motion of light and sounds. It still remains for us to show the system of the world from these principles.

Isaac Newton

5.1   Applying Mathematics to Nature

Today's scientists take it for granted that one cannot study nature without employing mathematics. Whether one is engaged in experimental physics, molecular biology, or organic chemistry, mathematical techniques—from solving differential equations to running statistical analyses on large datasets—are part and parcel of the scientific enterprise. We might wonder: how else can we understand the features of light in an experiment, the movements of nutrients through a cell, or the structure of some molecule? Our historical understanding is hampered by the fact that we regard the employment of mathematical techniques as an obvious and essential aspect of the sciences. Why did any figure in history oppose the use of some mathematical technique in a particular science? And why would some figures have gone so far as to oppose mathematics more generally? Is there any way for us to render their concerns rational?

Newton, First Edition. Andrew Janiak.
© 2015 Andrew Janiak. Published 2015 by John Wiley & Sons, Ltd.

As the seventeenth century began, many thinkers—such as Galileo in the Italian-speaking world and Descartes, a bit later, in the French- and Dutch-speaking regions of Europe—came to maturity at a time when Scholastic, or *neo-Aristotelian*, thinking dominated natural philosophy.[1] It is impossible to do justice to this rich and varied tradition in a short space, for it spans many centuries, many texts, and many debates (French and Cunningham 1996). But one thing seems clear: according to the Scholastic natural philosophy that was predominant at the beginning of the seventeenth century, the study of nature was typically separated from mathematics. Natural philosophy was understood as a distinct discipline, one separate from the mathematical disciplines, such as geometry and arithmetic, on the one hand, and from the so-called mixed mathematical disciplines, such as music or optics, on the other (Kuhn 1977, Murdoch 1982). Thus, a figure like Galileo or Descartes certainly could not take it for granted, for example, that geometry might be employed to understand natural phenomena. One reason hailing from antiquity is this: the world of nature is the world of becoming, constant change, and messy structures; but the world of geometry is the world of being, changeless objects, and perfect figures. Mathematics more generally concerns abstract objects such as numbers, triangles, and circles rather than concrete objects such as tables, chairs, and carrots. The methods of the one seemed unsuited to the entities of the other. Indeed, Isaac Beeckman, who met Descartes in 1618 and who had a crucial formative influence on his work, wrote an entry in his diary after their meeting, writing of Descartes that he "says he has never met anyone other than me who pursues his studies in the way I do, combining physics and mathematics in an exact way. And for my part, I have never spoken with anyone apart from him who studies in this way."[2] It is in this context that we ought to interpret Galileo's famous pronouncement in 1623 concerning the book of nature: "philosophy is written in this most grand book ... (I am speaking of the universe) ... [which] is written in the language of mathematics, and its characters are triangles, circles, and other geometrical figures..."[3] This slogan was not expressing a widely shared view among natural philosophers—it was an expression of a particular side of a debate that would continue throughout much of the rest of the century.

One might imagine that the self-proclaimed *moderns*, the proponents of the new science who had joined together in their opposition to Scholastic natural philosophy, would have also happily endorsed the employment of mathematical techniques for studying nature. After all, the seventeenth century saw an amazing plethora of mathematical discoveries: Descartes's invention of what we now call analytic geometry, his use of coordinates to find equations expressing curves[4]; Wallis's attempt to solve long-standing geometric problems, such as the quadrature of the circle, using new techniques involving the summation of arithmetic sequences; and, of course, Newton's discovery of the generalization of the binomial theorem and his codiscovery, with Leibniz, of the integral and differential calculus. There were obviously very powerful techniques in analysis available to philosophers in 1700 that were simply unknown in 1600, and as the list above indicates, many of the leading philosophers studying nature during this time were *also* leading mathematicians. So one would expect to find a consensus about the use of mathematics, including well-established geometric techniques and the use of the new analysis, among the proponents of the new science, with their colleagues in the schools serving as the ideological opposition. But like many narratives, however tempting it is to view seventeenth-century natural philosophy in these terms, it is not historically accurate.

Some of the most vociferous mathematical debates between, say, 1650 and 1670, occurred between major proponents of the new philosophy. We saw in Chapter 3 that Hobbes plays an important role in helping us to understand the fact that opposition to Boyle's experimental philosophy was not irrational within its own historical context, even if it appears to be so from our present point of view. Rendering philosophy experimental would appear to be an obvious aspect of the emergence of the modern physical sciences in the seventeenth century. Similarly, rendering philosophy mathematical would be appear to be equally obvious, and equally important. Hence, we are in danger again of thinking that any opposition to the employment of algebra, arithmetic, or geometry within the study of nature must have been ideological or irrational, perhaps the product of outmoded conceptions of studying the world. Once again, I propose that Hobbes can come to our rescue: he helps us to grasp some of the details of the opposition to certain uses of mathematical techniques within natural philosophy, and is especially helpful in showing the modern reader that many important philosophers of the early modern period—Newton may have been among them, as we will see—were concerned that new methods in algebra and arithmetic may have lacked the kinds of mathematical beauty and the types of certainty associated with geometric methods since the time of Aristotle (Guicciardini 2009). Hobbes's debate with Wallis during the 1650s to the 1670s was perhaps even more notorious than that with Boyle (Jesseph 1999). But as we will briefly see, Hobbes's opposition to Wallis's methods is useful historically for its portrayal of the complexity of the situation facing philosophers concerned about mathematics.

In *Arithmetica Infinitorum*, which Newton read and commented on as a young student at Trinity College,[5] Wallis sought to create a new *arithmetic of indivisibles* to parallel Cavalieri's famous *geometry of indivisibles*.[6] The goal was to make progress on an old problem tackled by Cavalieri, among many others, namely, the problem of the *quadrature* of curvilinear figures, which included both the calculation of the area under some curve and the calculation of a volume enclosed by some curvilinear surface. Wallis argued in particular that any plane surface can be conceived of as comprising an infinite number of parallelograms—this obviously required him to think of the parallelograms as infinitesimals or as indivisibles, since they must somehow sum to a finite quantity expressing a feature of the plane surface. Wallis proposed to use this general method as a means of *squaring the circle*, which involved finding a

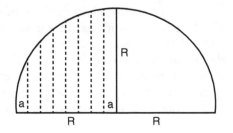

Figure 5.1 John Wallis, quadrant of the circle.

rectilinear figure with the same area as a given circle. He tackled the quadrant of the circle in part as follows (Figure 5.1):

The parallelograms comprising the circle would have equal bases a, such that

$$a = \frac{R}{\infty}.^{7}$$

Wallis argued that we could use a summation of an infinite number of indivisible or infinitesimal quantities in order to make the analysis of some finite quantity—such as the area under a curve—tractable. The key to Wallis's summation techniques, which help to transform geometric problems through the use of arithmetic sequences, is to remember that his infinite number of constituents of any finite quantity, such as a plane surface, retain a definite ratio to that original quantity, such that they sum to the original quantity.

This technique obviously raises many questions. One of them is this: how precisely are we to think about Wallis's infinitesimals or indivisibles? The question of how to think about infinitesimals would confront many of the leading mathematicians between Wallis in the seventeenth century and Euler in the eighteenth (Guicciardini 1999, 159–163). For instance, is an infinitesimal parallelogram, which we are meant to conceive of as a constituent of some finite quantity, distinct from a line? That is, does it have any width? Wallis apparently thought that the infinitesimal parallelogram differed from a line because the former's width is not zero; instead, its width is smaller than any assignable finite width. One question, of course, is whether such a notion can be made rigorous and clear. For his part, Wallis did not seem especially concerned with this issue (Stedall 2010, xxix). He dealt very freely with infinite products and infinitesimals (Guicciardini 2009, 146), even as others, most prominently Hobbes, raised objections against his practice.

Like the debate between Leibniz and Newton in the early eighteenth century, the debate between Hobbes and Wallis became protracted, repetitive, and personal. Unlike the calculus priority dispute, however, there is no doubt that Hobbes was no match for Wallis mathematically: his own attempts to *square the circle* were deeply flawed, as Wallis enjoyed indicating whenever he could (Jesseph 1999). But if we sift through their debate and focus instead on the question of the nature of indivisibles, or infinitesimals, we can recover a rational argument within Hobbes's work. He wisely noted that Wallis had not made his notion of the infinitesimal particularly clear and precise. Wallis's perspective is especially evident in the first proposition of his *De sectionibus conicis* (quoted in Jesseph 1999, 180):

> I suppose, as a starting point (according to Bonventura Cavalieri's geometry of indivisibles) that any plane is constituted, as it were, from an infinite number of parallel lines. Or rather (which I prefer) from an infinite number of parallelograms of equal altitude, the altitude of each of which indeed may be $1/\infty$ of the whole altitude, or an infinitely small part (for let ∞ denote an infinite number), and therefore the altitude of all taken together is equal to the altitude of the figure.

This short sentence, which opens Wallis's tract, encapsulates the problems that Hobbes would find in his work. In his 1656 criticism of Wallis, he quotes Wallis's notion that a geometric figure such as a triangle can be thought of as containing an infinite number of constituents, writing:

> Well, the Lemma is true. Let us see the theorems you draw from it. The first is (pag. 3), *that a triangle to a parallelogram of equal base and altitude is as one to two*. The conclusion is true, but how know you that? Because, say you, *the triangle consists as it were (as it were* is no phrase of a geometrician) *of an infinite number of straight parallel lines*. Does it so? Then by your own doctrine, which is, *that lines have no breadth*, the altitude of your triangle consists of an infinite number of *no altitudes*, that is, of an infinite number of nothings, and consequently the *area* of your triangle has no quantity. If you say that by the parallels you mean infinitely little parallelograms, you are never the better; for if infinitely little, either they are nothing, or if somewhat, yet seeing that no two sides of a triangle are parallel, those parallels cannot be parallelograms. (Hobbes 1656, 46; italics in the original)

Hobbes was on to something: Wallis had noted, in the quotation above, that he *preferred* to employ infinitesimal parallelograms rather than lines in his reasoning, but he did not seem clearly to distinguish the two. If the infinitesimals are actually like lines, as Hobbes notes, then they will lack width, in which case they will be unable to sum to some finite quantity. But if they are distinct from lines in the sense that they bear some width, however small, then presumably an infinite number of them will sum to an infinite quantity. Either way, Wallis's view is not fully clear.

Despite Hobbes's criticism, Wallis's technique of solving geometric problems by using the summation of arithmetic sequences and his way of thinking about finite geometric figures and quantities as consisting of infinite numbers of infinitesimals proved to be extremely influential. He certainly had a very important impact on a young Isaac Newton in 1664–1665, who understood immediately from Wallis that one infinite extension can be greater than another. In that sense, the fact that Wallis's idea of the infinitesimal could not be rendered clearer, or defended against Hobbes's criticism, was perhaps ultimately irrelevant. Other mathematicians, such as Newton, simply adopted many of his ideas and techniques, and then proceeded from there: for instance, Newton discovered the generalization of the binomial theorem soon after reading Wallis, and there is no doubt that Wallis's ideas helped lead to the discovery of the integral calculus. But none of these facts about the development of mathematics in this period show that Hobbes's criticism was simply irrational or misguided. He was perfectly right in claiming that Wallis's ideas lacked the precision that one might expect from a mathematician.

Hobbes's skepticism about Wallis's new arithmetical techniques reflected a broader conception of the status of different mathematical domains. It was quite common in the seventeenth century for a philosopher or a mathematician to believe that the gold standard for certainty within mathematics is Euclidean geometry. Indeed, some would limit geometry itself to the classic straight line and compass constructions carried out in Euclid's *Elements*, excluding any other techniques. When Descartes considered various classes of curves in his *Géometrie* of 1637, introducing some of the ideas that we now associate with analytical geometry, many of his readers were skeptical that what we might call his extension of the classical ideas and methods was sufficiently rigorous. Indeed, none other than a young Isaac Newton wrote "non est geom!" in the margins of his own copy of the *Géometrie* (in the significantly expanded, Latin edition by van Schooten). Although figures such as Descartes and Wallis, not to mention Newton and Leibniz, made tremendous strides using new algebraic and arithmetic methods, these techniques remained highly controversial throughout the century. Newton himself often seemed to suggest that classical geometry exhibited a level of certainty that the new methods could not match (Guicciardini 1999, 31–32, 101–104). In this context, then, one can understand the rationality of Hobbes's criticism of Wallis's use of infinitesimals, despite the fact that Wallis was in fact successful in ways that Hobbes never was. One way to encapsulate many of these facts is to think of the seventeenth century as the end of the Renaissance, rather than as the beginning of the modern period: many mathematicians and philosophers, including Newton, were highly enamored of the idea of the *prisca scientia*. They believed that the ancients, especially the Greeks, had achieved a high level of mathematical and philosophical insight and understanding, one that could not be easily matched by the new techniques and ideas of their own century. Many leading *moderns* attempted to form a community of practitioners who would eventually be comfortable using new mathematical techniques for thinking about nature.

And yet this reluctance to embrace fully the new analytical techniques, even among leading mathematicians such as Newton, was coupled with a strong endorsement of the idea that the new methods would enable philosophers to think about certain classic problems in refreshing ways. This was true, for instance, with problems concerning infinity, a philosophical and mathematical domain rife with potential paradoxes and contradictions, as had already been clear in antiquity. For his part, Newton clearly believed that

Wallis's broad point of view in *Arithmetica Infinitorum* would assist philosophers and theologians in escaping some of the paradoxes of infinity that plagued earlier work. Although he read Wallis as a young man in 1664, he cited his principal work nearly 30 years later when discussing some difficulties that Richard Bentley had encountered in attempting to articulate how Newton's views in *Principia Mathematica* could be employed to undermine atheist conceptions of the world. In particular, Bentley was pondering how to understand the case in which the world consists of an infinite space containing infinite matter within it. Newton writes:

But you argue in the next paragraph of your letter that every particle of matter in an infinite space has an infinite quantity of matter on all sides & by consequence an infinite attraction every way & therefore must be *in equilibrio* because all infinites are equal. Yet you suspect a paralogism in this argument, & I conceive the parallogism lies in the position that all infinites are equal. The generality of mankind consider infinites no other ways than definitely, & in this sense they say all infinites are equal, though they would speak more truly if they should say they are neither equal nor unequal nor have any certain difference or proportion one to another. In this sense therefore no conclusions can be drawn from them about the equality, proportions or differences of things, & they that attempt to do it, usually fall into paralogism. So when men argue against the infinite divisibility of magnitude, by saying that if an inch may be divided into an infinite number of parts, the sum of those parts will be an inch, & if a foot may be divided into an infinite number of parts, the sum of those parts must be a foot, & therefore since all infinites are equal those sums must be equal, that is, an inch equal to a foot. The falseness of the conclusion shows an error in the premises, & the error lies in the position that all infinites are equal. There is therefore another way of considering infinites used by mathematicians, & that is under certain definite restrictions & limitations whereby infinites are determined to have certain differences or proportions to one another. Thus Dr Wallis considers them in his *Arithmetica Infinitorum*, where by the various proportions of infinite sums he gathers the various proportions of infinite magnitudes: which way of arguing is generally allowed by mathematicians & yet would not be good were all infinites equal. According to the same way of considering infinites, a mathematician would tell you that though there be an infinite number of infinitely little parts in an inch, yet there is twelve times that number of such parts in a foot; that is, the infinite number of those parts in a foot is not equal to, but twelve times bigger than, the infinite number of them in an inch. And so a mathematician will tell you that if a body stood *in equilibrio* between any two equal and contract attracting infinite forces, & if to either of those forces you add any new finite attracting force: that new force how little so ever will destroy the equilibrium & put the body into the same motion into which it would put it were those two contrary equal forces but finite or even none at all: so that in this case two equal infinites by the addition of a finite to either of them become unequal in our ways of reckoning. And after these ways we must reckon if from the consideration of infinites we would always draw true conclusions. (*Correspondence* 3: 239)

We might read Newton here as explaining to Bentley that mathematicians such as Wallis and, presumably, Newton himself have ways of thinking about infinite quantities or infinite processes—such as infinite divisibility—that avoid the false assumption guiding philosophical discussions, namely, that all infinites are equal. In particular, mathematicians following Wallis understand that the proportion between two finite quantities is preserved when one considers each of those quantities to be infinitely divisible. Hence, an infinitely divisible foot remains 12 times the size of an infinitely divisible inch. Since there can be preserved proportions between items that are infinite, or that have an infinite feature, such as being infinitely divisible, it follows, says Newton, that there can be different-sized infinities. Newton had already grasped this exact point in 1664–1665 as a student at Trinity College reading Wallis (*Mathematical Papers*, vol. 1: 89)! So we have a specific mathematical view that enables us to reject the faulty philosophical presumption guiding reasoning about the infinite. As we will see in Chapter 7, the concept of infinity was important for Newton not only for mathematical reasons, and not only so that he could understand natural phenomena such as motion in a sophisticated way, but also, and perhaps even more significantly, it was central to his ideas about space and the divine. Newton embraced the concept of actual infinity in a way that few of his predecessors did (see Janiak 2014).

5.2 Applying Mathematics to Nature: The Cartesian Legacy

Despite Galileo's immense importance, the question of whether natural philosophy could legitimately—or perhaps fruitfully—employ mathematical principles and methods was brought to center stage by the subsequent work of Descartes. It is probably safe to say that by the middle of the century, Descartes had set the agenda of natural philosophy for philosophers throughout Europe, certainly for those working in England (Heilbron 1982, 30). As Beeckman already recognized in the early part of the century, Descartes would become a great champion of employing mathematical methods in order to understand nature and its parts. His *Géometrie* (1637) was translated into Latin and widely read as the most advanced text in that field. If we conceive of the seventeenth century as involving a grand struggle between the traditional conception of natural philosophy espoused in the schools—the so-called Scholastic conception—and the great *moderns* of the day, Descartes was firmly, and self-consciously, on the side of the new movement.

But as with many narratives involving grand struggles, the historical facts are more complicated. As it turned out, Descartes actually pursued a program in natural philosophy that exhibited a much more vexed relationship with the modern mathematics that he himself had invented and promulgated. During his early years, from the time he worked with Beeckman in 1618 through the 1620s, Descartes's plan may have been to follow through on his promise to establish a fully mathematical approach to understanding problems in natural philosophy, especially the motions of material bodies. Part of his conception may have been to follow Aristotle in one crucial respect: working out the details of an (admittedly anti-Aristotelian) physics first, worrying about various metaphysical questions later. And as the decade of the 1620s came to a close, Descartes wrote and prepared to publish a grand text in natural philosophy entitled *Le Monde*. However, he stopped the presses in 1633 after he learned of Galileo's house arrest by the Vatican for his advocacy of a Copernican orientation toward the question of the earth's place within the universe, for he had endorsed a similar view in *Le Monde* (see Chapter 7 for details).[8] The withdrawal of *Le Monde* from the press had a dramatic impact on Descartes's life, serving to invert his Aristotelian plan by leading him to write a text in metaphysics, the *Meditations* (1641), first and then to follow it with his work in natural philosophy, the *Principles* (1644). This decision had two profound effects. First and foremost, Descartes would forever after be known for developing a strong conception of the metaphysical foundations of physics—indeed, he has been described as propounding a *metaphysical physics* (Garber 1992). Secondly, Descartes would also become known for failing to live up to his original promise of articulating a mathematical natural philosophy in detail.

Why did Descartes's promulgation of a metaphysical foundation for physics prevent him from articulating a mathematical orientation toward natural philosophy? First and foremost, as we have seen, Descartes's metaphysics takes there to be two substances in the world: extended substances, like tables and chairs, and thinking substances, like the human mind (and perhaps God). Descartes thought in particular that the essence of extended substances is exhausted by their extension, by their three-dimensionality. Hence, tables might be blue or green, they might be wooden or plastic, and they might be expensive or cheap, but these are all accidental features of them: their only essential feature lies in being extended. (And in fact, Descartes would say that the other features of a table are merely modes of its principal attribute, namely, its extension.) Hence, as Daniel Garber has put it, for Descartes, material bodies like tables are "the objects of geometry made real" (Garber 2012, 34). In that sense, one might think that Cartesian metaphysics paves the way for the employment of mathematical methods, especially geometric methods, within natural philosophy: if an object like a rock is essentially an extended thing, we can treat it like an object in geometry and then understand its motion using geometrical techniques. As Lisa Shabel indicates, the classic early modern problem of the applicability of mathematics to nature and its quantities is, in a sense, easily solved by Descartes, for he contends that the essence of material bodies is the very extension of which we have a clear and distinct idea when we consider our representations of geometric objects. We know that geometry, and the rest of pure mathematics perhaps, applies to natural objects because the essence of those objects is just extension (Shabel 2005, 38).

But this is not the end of the story. For Descartes, it is indeed possible to think of ordinary material bodies as geometric objects, and if we consider them in abstraction from the rest of nature, then we can understand their changes mathematically. However, natural philosophy does not consider objects in abstraction from the rest of nature: it considers them as participants in the great system of objects that constitutes the natural world. So to conduct investigations in natural philosophy, we have to embed our little rock in the world in which it actually exists. When we do so, however, we encounter a further problem generated by Descartes's metaphysics. As it turns out, Cartesianism is not exhausted by the view that the essence of material bodies is extension—it also includes the related claim that extension itself is indistinct from matter or substance. For Descartes, as we have seen, it is a conceptual confusion to adopt the idea of empty space: extension for Descartes is a property, and as such, it must be regarded as a property of *some substance*. Hence, an empty space—an empty extension—is incoherent because it presents a property without anything serving the function of bearing that property. (It is sort of like saying that I walked down the street yesterday and saw *red*—not a red car, a red bike, or anything red, but just red itself.) So for Descartes, the whole of nature consists of an indefinite multitude of extended substances. When we look across a lawn or stare into space, it may *appear* to us as if space can be empty, but in fact, all of space is full of objects big and small. Hence, Descartes believes that nature is a plenum.

If nature is a plenum, the motion of our little rock, which seemed so straightforward in the abstract, becomes incredibly complex (Nelson 1995). Suppose, for instance, that I am standing on the main quad at my college and I throw a rock across the lawn. When the rock leaves my hand, it immediately becomes ensnared in a vast network of other objects on its trajectory toward the grass. To get a basic grasp on the Cartesian view, we might think of the rock as entering a kind of conveyor belt of tiny particles as it sails through the air: it pushes the numerous particles in front of it and is also perhaps pushed along by the particles behind and surrounding it. But the complexity of the situation exceeds even this picture, for we must also conceive of the rock as bearing some weight toward the earth—hence, there are also numerous particles flowing downward toward the ground that impede the rectilinear motion of the rock, giving it a classic parabolic trajectory and eventually bringing it to rest on the lawn. The complexity is overwhelming. We are obviously very far from thinking of a point generating a curved line by its motion through space.

In part three of his *Principles*, Descartes famously extended this picture of nature into the heavens, arguing that the motions of the heavenly bodies, including the planets and their satellites, can be understood by a vortex theory of motion. This theory presented celestial motions as involving the motion of giant, imperceptible, swirling fluids permeating the solar system. He presented the following diagram of his vortices (Figure 5.2).

Just as our rock is surrounded by imperceptible particles of air throughout its parabolic journey across the quad, the planets are surrounded by imperceptible vortical particles as they make their orbital journeys across the solar system. Geometers like Descartes were prepared to think about the motions of objects through geometric space in sophisticated ways, but they of course

Figure 5.2 Descartes, vortex theory of planetary motion.

tended to think of that space as otherwise empty. Descartes's heavenly plenum involves the causal interactions of innumerable particles for every orbital path. Its immense complexity may lie beyond the grasp of any geometer.

Thus, Descartes's legacy is twofold and characterized by a certain tension. On the one hand, he followed in Galileo's (and Beeckman's) footsteps by strongly opposing Aristotelian natural philosophy, advocating the use of mathematical methods to understand motion and natural change, presenting an austere metaphysics that would be welcome to geometers, and declaring at the end of part two of the *Principles* that he would employ mathematical demonstrations within the rest of his text.[9] On the other hand, his plenist view of nature presented a picture in which the motion of ordinary objects like rocks and balls is fantastically complex, exceeding the capacity of even the greatest mathematicians[10]; and in parts three and four of his *Principles*, Descartes presented a largely qualitative—rather than a quantitative or mathematical—science of nature, preferring to present a text that was filled with numerous images of, for example, the earth and the sun but largely unencumbered by the myriad of complex geometrical diagrams that fill his *Géométrie* and that would later fill Newton's own text. It is probably fair to say that Descartes never resolved this tension within his work in natural philosophy.

As with so many other central aspects of Newton's program in natural philosophy (see Chapter 4), this tension within the Cartesian system helped to set the stage for Newton's approach. He struggled to avoid this tension by presenting what he regarded as a set of truly mathematical principles for natural philosophy to apply to objects within nature, including everything from our flying rock to the orbital paths of the planets. As we will see, however, the history of this Newtonian maneuver contains an intriguing and surprising element: one of the most significant and controversial aspects of Newton's newly mathematical program in natural philosophy did not involve the employment of a particular analytical technique, or a newfound use for an old geometric one. Instead, it involved Newton's attempt to present what he called a *mathematical* treatment of force in *Principia Mathematica*, something quite foreign to his Cartesian predecessors.

5.3   Newton's Program in Natural Philosophy

A young Isaac Newton picked up the *Meditations*, the *Géometrie*, and Wallis's works, including the *Arithmetic of Infinites*, in the early 1660s in Cambridge. He read Descartes's *Principles* in depth, and it is safe to say that he considered Descartes the greatest natural philosopher, if not the greatest mathematician, in the previous generation. (A young Leibniz, working far away on the Continent, may have felt similarly.) When Newton gave some lectures in the early 1670s as part of his charge as Lucasian Professor of Mathematics, he lamented the state of natural philosophy, noting in particular that the profound developments in mathematical techniques had thus far exhibited little impact on the discipline. His inaugural Lucasian Professor lectures in 1670 included the following comment:

> the generation of colors includes so much geometry, and the understanding of colors is supported by so much evidence, that for their sake I can thus attempt to extend the bounds of mathematics somewhat, just as astronomy, geography, navigation, optics, and mechanics are truly considered mathematical sciences even if they deal with physical things: the heavens, earth, seas, light, and local motion. Thus although colors may belong to physics [ad Physicam pertineant], the science of them must nevertheless be considered mathematical, insofar as they are treated by mathematical reasoning. Indeed, since an exact science [accurata scientia] of them seems to be one of the most difficult that philosophy is in need of, I hope to show—as it were, by my example—how valuable mathematics is in natural philosophy. I therefore urge geometers to investigate nature more rigorously, and those devoted to natural science [scientiae naturalis] to learn geometry first.[11]

From Newton's point of view, then, the Cartesian program in natural philosophy had not lived up to its rhetoric. As we have seen, Newton also wrote an extensive critique of Cartesian metaphysics and its plenist view of nature (as discussed in Chapter 4). Whether he did so because he recognized that Descartes's views in metaphysics, especially his advocacy of a plenum, ultimately undermined the employment of mathematics by natural philosophers, remains an intriguing open question.

These developments set the stage for Newton's own magnum opus, whose title emphasized his use of *mathematical principles*. In a famous exchange with Edmond Halley—the discoverer of the comet by the same name and the person often credited with encouraging Newton to write and publish his work—Newton explains that for his *Principia Mathematica* to be considered a work in *natural philosophy*, he must include what would become its third book, with its focus on the motions of falling bodies on earth and on the motions of the heavenly bodies. Without the application of Newton's mathematical methods and conclusions from the first two books of *Principia Mathematica* to the natural objects in our solar system, we would have instead a book more aptly titled *De Motu corporum*, or *On the motion of bodies*. Hence, the natural philosopher, from Newton's point of view, is not concerned with the motion of any arbitrary body in any medium, under any physical conditions we might conceive; he is concerned with the motions of bodies within nature. It is no surprise, then, that for Newton, as for many natural philosophers in this period, one of the great outstanding questions is how to understand the earth–sun system, including the question of whether the earth is at the center of the system and is moving or at rest.

For a committed Cartesian reader, one might say that this move from the first two books of *Principia Mathematica*, in which we consider the motions of bodies in abstraction from various factors involving nature as we find it, to the third book, in which those factors are explicitly invoked, would be problematic. As we have seen, a Cartesian would regard the actual motions of material bodies as occurring within a plenum with a huge multitude of moving parts; this would render those motions intractable from a geometrical point of view. And it seems plausible that a Cartesian reader would understand Newton's books II and III as committing him, explicitly or implicitly, to the falsity of the plenist conception of nature found in Descartes. Indeed, Newton explicitly attempted to vanquish the Cartesian plenist, vortex-based, view of motion in Book II of *Principia Mathematica* by considering numerous cases in which bodies move through resisting media.

There are two distinct aspects of Newton's attempt to render natural philosophy a mathematically rich investigation into nature. The first aspect is relatively obvious: Newton ingeniously employed a number of complex geometrical techniques throughout *Principia Mathematica*. Although his text was not primarily written in the language of the new analysis—what we would now call the calculus—he also showed from the very opening of the text that he was perfectly comfortable using new methods to think about limits (Cohen 1999, 115). This aspect of the text was profoundly influential, and from the very beginning, it was clear to Newton's readers that he would

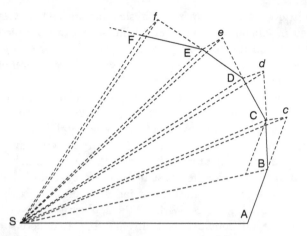

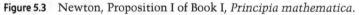

Figure 5.3 Newton, Proposition I of Book I, *Principia mathematica.*

be thinking about motion in a different way from his Cartesian predecessors. But this aspect of *Principia Mathematica* does not exhaust its mathematical character, and as we will see in the next section, it was Newton's *mathematical* treatment of force that generated tremendous controversy among his readers.

One aspect of Newton's mathematical approach to motion is evident right from the start, in Book I, proposition I (cf. Dunlop 2012). The proposition and its accompanying figure are as follows (Figure 5.3):

Proposition 1   The areas which bodies made to move in orbits describe
                 by radii drawn to an unmoving center of forces lie in unmoving
Theorem 1   planes and are proportional to the times.

Newton informs us that we should think of a body as moving rectilinearly (inertially) from points A to B, such that this body is moving in a straight line from A to B.[12] It is then to be thought of as struck by an instantaneous force at B directed toward S, which knocks the body into a new trajectory from B to C, where that trajectory is also to be thought of as occurring along a straight line. So the force in question here is understood as what Newton calls a *centripetal force*, which he has just introduced in the definitions that precede the beginning of Book I. Newton makes it clear that by his first law, the body would have traveled in the same temporal interval from B to c (so that AB = Bc) if it had not been struck by a force at B. Similarly, the body travels from B to C, and is then struck by an instantaneous force that propels it along the new trajectory from C to D, and so on. He notes that the body will remain in *the same plane* throughout its trajectory along the polygon with center S. Hence, each force that strikes the body changes its direction with respect to the polygon but nothing else. Finally, we are to think of these forces as impacting on the body in equal intervals of time, such that the time elapsed from A to B is equal to the time elapsed from B to C. He then notes that triangle SAB will have an area equal to triangle SBc (because they have equal bases AB = BC and the vertex S in common) and also with triangle SBC (noting that SB and Cc are parallel), and indeed, the other triangles—SBC, SCD, SDE, etc.—will also be equal.

Newton then makes two intriguing points before concluding his discussion of the figure. First, he draws a conclusion from the points mentioned previously: "Therefore, in equal times equal areas are described in an unmoving plane," a claim that shows that he has his eye already at the very beginning of the text on Kepler's so-called area law, which states that planets orbit the sun so that the radius vector joining the sun to the planet sweeps out equal areas in equal times. Second, and perhaps even more strikingly, Newton boldly shows that he is not merely thinking here about some arbitrary polygon, but rather wishes his analysis to be one step toward thinking about properly curvilinear motions. He writes:

> Now let the number of triangles be increased and their width decreased indefinitely, and their ultimate perimeter ADF will (by lemma 3, corollary 4) be a curved line; and thus the centripetal force by which the body is continually drawn back from the tangent of this curve will act uninterruptedly, while any areas described, SADS and SAFS, which are always proportional to the times of description, will be proportional to those times in this case. (*Principia* 445)

Echoes of Wallis's *Arithmetica Infinitorum* can be heard at the very beginning of Newton's text. Just as we are taught to think of a plane as consisting of an infinite number of infinitesimal parallelograms, here Newton teaches us to think of a curved figure as consisting of an infinite number of triangles. Just as Wallis's parallelograms must have some width that is smaller than any finite width, Newton's triangles here must have their width *decreased indefinitely* until they compose the curved figure.

In the very first proposition of Book I of *Principia Mathematica*, then, we encounter two aspects of Newton's mathematical approach to questions in natural philosophy, especially his understanding of motion and its causes. Clearly, Newton proposes that we think of motion as being described not merely by standard geometrical techniques, but as involving the new and complex ideas about infinitesimals and limits that figures like Wallis had employed to great effect in the previous generation. And even in this opening book, which considers the motions of bodies under all sorts of conditions, without any focus on the actual motions of terrestrial or celestial bodies in nature, which occurs in Book III of *Principia Mathematica*, we already find that Newton is clearly interested in thinking about Kepler's laws. They will turn out to be fundamental to his understanding of the planetary orbits. What is perhaps just as remarkable, however, is that in this proposition and its discussion, Newton also makes important use of his new notion of a centripetal force. He had just introduced this notion in the definitions as a way to think about the causes of motion (or, rather, of changes in states of motion), for centripetal forces are a kind of impressed force for Newton. What he may not have expected is the following: although many authors would follow in his footsteps by using new techniques for thinking about infinitesimals, limits, and many related ideas, his notion of a centripetal force would become a matter of philosophical controversy. Hence, that notion would require a considerable amount of defense on Newton's part. Intriguingly, moreover, this very notion was also a crucial component of what Newton called his *mathematical* treatment of force.

In one way of thinking, Newton's use of what he calls the *mathematical* treatment of force was one of the most revolutionary aspects of *Principia Mathematica*. It was certainly one of the most controversial. This is not to say that Newton's use of various geometrical, algebraic, and analytical techniques in *Principia Mathematica* generated no controversy; it did (Guicciardini 1999). But it was Newton's unique approach to thinking about forces *mathematically* rather than *physically* that generated some of the most vociferous philosophical debates. Unlike Descartes, Newton placed the concept of a force at the very center of his thinking about motion and its causes within nature. In that regard, his reactions to the shortcomings of Cartesian natural philosophy parallel Leibniz's, who coined the term *dynamics*. But Newton's attitude toward understanding the forces of nature involved an especially intricate method that generated intense scrutiny and debate among many philosophers and mathematicians, including Leibniz (Garber 2012). The reason is that he had found a way of thinking about causation that would enable him to use his mathematical techniques to determine the motions of bodies under all sorts of conditions. He could so do, moreover, without committing himself to, or endorsing, any particular mechanical idea of how the causation in question would actually operate. As has often been noted, Newton's mathematical treatment of forces exhibits an uncanny parallel to his work in optics in the early 1670s (see especially Harper and Smith 1995). In each case, Newton found a way to make what he considered to be important progress in thinking about certain kinds of natural phenomena without endorsing any particular mechanical model of the phenomena and their causes. History looked upon this tactic favorably: generations of students would learn about the forces of nature because of Newton's way of thinking. But as we have come to expect, his contemporaries did not see things that way. As always, we have to try to understand why.

5.4 Newton's Mathematical Treatment of Force

Newton's canonical notion of a force, which he calls a *vis impressa* or *impressed force*, is given in definition four of *Principia Mathematica*, which appears before Book I begins:

> Impressed force is the action exerted on a body to change its state of either of resting or of moving uniformly straight forward. This force consists solely in

making philosophy mathematical

the action and does not remain in a body after the action has ceased. Moreover, there are various sources of impressed force, such as percussion, pressure, or centripetal force. (*Principia* 405)

Suppose a ball is resting on a flat surface like a table: when I strike it with my hand, I change its state of motion, so this means that I have impressed a force on the ball. This would be a case of what Newton here calls *percussion*. We have a decent idea of how the physical interaction between my hand and the ball works, at least in broad outline, because we are dealing with two ordinary material bodies, each of which is impenetrable and therefore able to engage in percussive interactions. But what exactly is this *force* that I impressed on it? The ball and my hand are ordinary physical things, but is the force also physical in some way? Is it not physical? It does not seem likely that a force is itself a physical thing or a substance (as we saw in Chapter 3). Importantly, Newton says that the force "consists solely in the action and does not remain in a body after the action has ceased." So when I push the ball, the force I impressed on it was the action of pushing the ball, or an action associated with pushing the ball, and not a property of me or of the ball after the action ceased. This basic idea confused many of Newton's readers. By the mid-eighteenth century, the time of Hume's analysis of causation in the *Treatise* and the *Enquiry*, many philosophers started to think that actions and other kinds of event are important items to have in one's ontology, and they often contended that causal relations hold between events, rather than between substances or objects. But in Newton's day, philosophers typically regarded objects or substances as the causal relata in nature and in metaphysics more generally—for instance, God is the primary cause of motion for Descartes, and of course God is a substance (perhaps the only one). So actions were difficult to analyze or often left out of analyses.

Happily, Newton's readers did not merely have definition four to guide them in understanding him; they also had the laws of motion, which also appear before Book I begins. Every high school student learns Newton's three laws of motion. However, it is important to look at how Newton wrote down his own laws. As was customary in his time, he often expressed his ideas in terms of ratios and proportions, a method of thinking about both geometric topics and topics within natural philosophy that has its roots in antiquity (of which Newton approved). He did not write down, "$f = ma$"! Instead, he spoke of a certain type of proportionality. In particular, his second law is as follows: "A change in motion is proportional to the motive force impressed and takes place along the straight line in which that force is impressed." But how should we understand this reference to motion? In definition three, he had written: "Quantity of motion is a measure of motion that arises from the velocity and the quantity of matter jointly." But what is a body's quantity of matter? For that, we must turn back to definition one, which states: "Quantity of matter is a measure of matter that arises from its density and volume." More helpfully,

Newton indicates that he means *mass*—a neologism that he coined in 1687 in this very text—whenever he speaks of the quantity of matter. (Of course, he means what we would now call inertial mass.) So in order to understand what a force is, we look to the second law of motion. But in order to understand that law, we must return to definition three, which brings us back to definition one. When we put all of this together, we find that an impressed force is proportional to mass and to velocity or to what Newton calls *change in motion*—ultimately, for reasons that we can ignore here, it is proportional to acceleration. So in sum, the action that changes a body's state of rest or of uniform rectilinear motion is proportional to mass and to acceleration.[13]

This idea leads to the heart of Newton's *mathematical* treatment of force. Newton did not really clarify the idea that a force is an action exerted on a body. Instead, he clarified his notion of force by showing us that an impressed force can be thought of as a *quantity*. The reason that we can think of Newtonian forces as quantities is that, at least in principle, we can *measure* them by measuring those quantities to which they are proportional (viz., mass and acceleration). There is a sense in which Newton is implying here that his readers need not worry about what kind of action a force really is; instead, they should concentrate on the role that the notion of force plays in the laws, and then they will come to recognize that Newton is providing his readers with a method for measuring forces. He is telling us to treat them as quantities. And of course, mathematicians deal with quantities in numerous ways. That is certainly one reason that Newton's treatment of forces is *mathematical*.[14]

But Newton decided that his method of thinking about causation via the notion of an impressed force was sufficiently novel that he had to add a lengthy caveat for his readers at the end of the definitions before beginning Book I of *Principia Mathematica*. It remains one of the most famous of all of Newton's methodological statements:

> Further, it is in this same sense that I call attractions and impulses accelerative and motive. Moreover, I use interchangeably and indiscriminately words signifying attraction, impulse, or any sort of propensity toward a center, considering these forces not from a physical but only from a mathematical point of view. Therefore, let the reader beware of thinking that by words of this kind I am anywhere defining a species or mode of action or a physical cause or reason, or that I am attributing forces in a true and physical sense to centers (which are mathematical points) if I happen to say that centers attract or that centers have forces. (*Principia* 408)[15]

This struck Newton's readers as confusing. He has already told us that an impressed force is an action (in some sense), but he is now telling us a few pages later that he is not defining a "mode of action or a physical cause or reason." And he is not doing the latter, apparently, *because* he is treating forces from a mathematical point of view (hence the use of "therefore" here). What does this mean?

Newton seems to think that he can treat forces as actions in an abstract sense. That is, he can tell us two things: first, when we think about causation within nature, we can think about forces as quantities that are proportional to other things, in particular, to mass (the quantity of matter) and to acceleration; and second, we need not think of forces as involving *any particular physical interaction or model of such an interaction*. If we limit ourselves to the kinds of percussive cases mentioned previously—for example, a hand pushing a ball—then we might fail to grasp the import of Newton's method. After all, there is really no reason to abstract away from the physical aspects of a hand pushing a ball: that kind of physical interaction is perfectly intelligible and therefore in no need of philosophical explication. So we must remember that for Newton, as he tells us right at the beginning, impressed forces involve cases of percussion, but they *also* involve pressure and centripetal cases. The latter, in turn, involve such things as magnetism and gravity. Forces of nature in Newton's sense, therefore, encompass many causal interactions that may not be mechanical in any clear way (Stein 1993, 195–97). The true benefit of this abstract method is that it enabled Newton to consider a wide range of causal interactions, including some types that were not physically understood.

For Newton, then, the earth impresses a force on the moon that makes it continue in its orbit (it causes it not to rest or to move uniformly straight forward). So now the plot thickens. What this makes us realize is that we were using our ordinary sense of how impact (or percussive) cases might actually work *physically* to enable us to grasp what Newton means when he speaks of an impressed force. But if he says that the earth impresses a force on the moon that is proportional to mass and acceleration, then we see that we actually must treat this force in the abstract sense that Newton suggests. We must think of it as a quantity that is proportional to these other quantities. The key here is to recognize two points: first, we think of the centripetal force as a quantity because that idea is helpful to us; but second, we think of it as a quantity because we have no other way to think of it! For what does it mean to say that the earth acts on the moon? How could it do so? Remember the caveat that if Newton says that the earth acts on the moon, he is not specifying any physical cause; that is, he is not saying that the earth shoots particles at the moon or pushes a giant swirling fluid that pushes the moon or anything of the kind. He is abstracting away from all such possible physical ideas about the earth's action and instead treating that action *abstractly*. This is a mathematical treatment because we regard the force as a quantity and ignore its physical characteristics or the physical characteristics of the system of which it is a part (Cohen 1980). That is an aspect of the mathematical perspective of his book.

The parallel with Newton's experiments in optics from the 1670s is compelling (Harper and Smith 1995). Just as Newton insisted to Hooke and Huygens that he was in a position to claim that ordinary sunlight consists of a number of blue and red rays without specifying the physical nature of those colored rays, he thought he could claim that the earth impresses a force on the moon without specifying what the earth's action on the moon consists in physically.

Newton was perfectly well aware that some philosophers regarded colors such as blue and red as nothing but sensations caused by the physical impact that material particles have on the human visual apparatus, and he certainly understood that rays of light were argued to be either particulate or wavelike. Yet he professed a desire to remain neutral on such questions; or at least, he claimed that he could remain neutral on them even while making his claim about light's heterogeneity (along with some claims about *refrangibility*). Newton was also perfectly well aware that some philosophers regarded the earth and the moon as surrounded by giant swirling fluids called vortices. Yet he professed a desire to remain neutral on whether vortices, or anything else, existed when he made his claim that the earth acts on the moon. His idea in the latter case was bolstered, he believed, through his extensive mathematical methodology: one could remain neutral on the *physical* question of what kind of action was involved in the earth–moon causal relationship by focusing instead on the *mathematical* question of how to measure that action by understanding its proportionality to other quantities.

As important as the mathematical treatment of force was for the reception of Newton's methodology, it was his application of that method to the case of gravity that led to the greatest debate. Newton did not develop the abstract characterization of a cause merely in order to pave the way for future treatments of the forces of nature, although as he indicated in other texts, such as the queries to the *Opticks*, that was certainly part of his overall goal.[16] He also employed his method in Book III of *Principia Mathematica* when arguing, in its first seven propositions, that there is a force of gravity acting on all bodies in proportion to their quantity of matter. That is, he argued for the radical and transformative concept of *universal gravity*. He contended, in particular, that this force, which is not only proportional to the quantity of matter of the bodies that experience it, but also inversely proportional to the square of their spatial separation, can be postulated and understood through these proportionalities despite the fact that he was not able to give it a physical characterization. This is where the abstract description of a force played its more important role in Newton's theory, since it enabled him to characterize gravity as both a centripetal force, which is one kind of impressed force, as we have seen, and also as a quantity that is proportional to other quantities, even while remaining silent on the physical aspects of the force. More precisely, he remained silent on the question of gravity's *cause* or its *physical seat*, which is to say he did not—and presumably could not—provide any description of gravity in physical terms.

What would a physical description of gravity look like? The most influential competitor to Newton's theory, both in 1687 and even at the end of his life, of course, was some kind of vortex theory (Aiton 1972). Indeed, despite Newton's tremendous efforts, in Book II of *Principia Mathematica*, to undermine vortex theories of planetary motion, they remained prominent among leading philosophers such as Leibniz and later Euler until years after Newton's death (Euler questioned them around 1750). A vortex theory gives a physical description of gravity along the following lines: the action of gravity between, say, the earth and the sun involves one or more giant swirling fluids that (say) carry the earth around the sun. The fluid might consist of minute particles that are imperceptible under normal perceptual conditions. Newton attempted to remain neutral on this kind of question in his description of the force of gravity. That is, although he argued against vortex theories, he never provided an *alternative* physical characterization of gravity of any kind. This became the most controversial aspect of Newton's work in *Principia Mathematica*, for it involved his attempt to evade answering exactly the question that most philosophers regarded as the key question for any theory of planetary motion to answer. In this sense, Newton's mathematical point of view in *Principia Mathematica* generated controversy because of what it *failed* to do. It failed at the task that philosophers set themselves when trying to explain planetary motion. Perhaps more than any mathematical method or technique that Newton employed, this failure to provide a physical model of gravity prevented many of Newton's contemporaries from endorsing his theory.

Not every leading philosopher demanded that Newton provide a physical characterization, or mechanical model, of gravity. Perhaps most famously, Locke's previously stalwart defense and acceptance of the mechanical philosophy underwent an intriguing transformation after he read the first edition of *Principia Mathematica*.[17] The clearest expression of this transformation is evident in one of his letters to Bishop Edward Stillingfleet, in which he discussed his presentation of a thoroughly mechanist understanding of causation in the first edition of his *Essay*.[18] He writes:

It is true, I say, that 'bodies operate by impulse and nothing else'. And so I thought when I writ it, and can yet conceive no other way of their operation. But I am since convinced by the judicious Mr. Newton's incomparable book, that it is too bold a presumption to limit God's power, in this point, by my narrow conceptions. The gravitation of matter toward matter by ways inconceivable to me, is not only a demonstration that God can, if he pleases, put into bodies, powers and ways of operations, above what can be derived from our idea of body, or can be explained by what we know of matter, but also an unquestionable and every where visible instance, that he has done so. And therefore in the next edition of my book, I shall take care to have that passage rectified. (Locke 1699, 408; see also Locke 1823, vol. 4: 467–468)

What Locke's sentiment indicates is that even Newton's strongest supporters could not articulate an alternative to the mechanist requirement that a theory provide a physical characterization or explanation of gravity. Locke lacked any alternative physical view: he simply endorsed Newton's theory of universal gravity, expressing defeat regarding the mechanist intelligibility criterion by attributing this feature of nature to God's intervention, explicitly admitting that we cannot understand this fact any further. From his own point of view, Newton's theory does not provide Locke with a novel method of conceiving of causation: he still can conceive of it only via the concept of impulse (or contact). And so the mathematical treatment of force has failed to give him an alternative to mechanist ideas about causation; he simply thinks that the former gives him an exception to the latter involving God's intervention in nature. Divine exceptions were not foreign to seventeenth-century natural philosophy.

For his part, Leibniz understood Locke's defeat all too well: after quoting this very same passage from Locke's letter to Stillingfleet, he then argued in the preface to the *New Essays* (written in 1705 but published only 60 years later):

> I cannot but praise our renowned author's modest piety here, when he acknowledges that God can do what is beyond our understanding and hence that there may be inconceivable mysteries within the articles of faith, but I would not like to be obliged to resort to miracles in the ordinary course of nature and to admit absolutely inexplicable powers and operations. Otherwise put, under the guise of what God can do, we may give too much license to bad philosophy; and we may admit these *centripetal powers* and *immediate attractions* at a distance without the possibility of making them intelligible. I do not see what is to prevent our Scholastics from saying that everything simply comes about through faculties and from promoting their intentional species that travel from objects to us and enter our souls. (Leibniz 1921, 22)

Leibniz highlights what he regards as the key shortcoming of Locke's approach: to admit that universal gravity is, as it were, a brute fact due to God's miraculous intervention in the course of nature is to relinquish the intelligibility criterion of the mechanist approach. And once we do that, we have nothing to distinguish our view from the widely derided Scholastic approach to understanding and explicating natural phenomena.

It is clear that many of Newton's contemporaries, including especially Leibniz and Huygens, believed that he had endorsed action at a distance among the planetary bodies with the theory of celestial motion propounded in Book III of his text. Even Newton's supporters, such as Locke, did not appear to deny this fact. And this aspect of Newton's theory proved to be especially prominent in later reactions to his work—for instance, the issue remained centrally important for Kant in 1781–1786 (Friedman 2012).[19] But this aspect of the reaction to Newton's theory can be overemphasized: it was central to the reaction to Newton's theory, but did not exhaust it. Even if his philosophical critics were to ignore the question of action at a distance, they would retain what is perhaps a more fundamental objection. Newton had failed altogether at the key task of the natural philosopher: he had simply failed to provide any physical model of gravity. If he wanted to reject a vortex theory, then that would perhaps be acceptable, so long as he provided some *other* physical model for the action of gravity among the planetary bodies. This could involve flowing particles, the action of the aether, or something else entirely. After all, none of the major proponents of vortex theories between 1644, when Descartes proposed his view in the *Principles*, and 1750, when Euler began questioning the wisdom of that approach, had any strong empirical evidence in its favor. Vortices and their cousins were postulated on theoretical, not empirical, grounds. Hence, Newton's critics could not have fundamentally objected if he had postulated some other physical—by which they would mean *mechanical*—model for understanding gravity. Rather, it was the reluctance to provide *any* physical model, involving *any* mechanism, which amounted in their minds to a broad failure at developing the kind of theory that philosophers sought.[20]

As with Newton's optical work in the 1670s, his *mathematical* point of view for thinking about the causes of motion within nature was fundamentally contested by many of the leading philosophers who read *Principia Mathematica*, including most prominently Leibniz (see Chapter 6). Many of Newton's contemporaries were prepared to make a distinction that was, quite ironically, precisely the kind of idea that Newton had sought to transcend in *Principia Mathematica*. They distinguished between the first and the second aspects of the mathematical nature of Newton's text described previously. That is, they distinguished the mathematics within Newton's text from its role as a work in natural philosophy. They were ready in broad strokes to endorse many of the new mathematical techniques that Newton had employed in his text in order to understand problems about motion. But they were not prepared to endorse his ideas about force and its characterization. Huygens's response to Newton's work 1 year after its publication is illustrative in this specific respect: he accepted the fact that Newton had provided an accurate mathematical derivation of an inverse square force acting on the planetary bodies, and yet he continued to reject Newton's theory overall because it failed to provide a physical account of gravity in the way that vortex theories did.[21]

Huygens was not alone. The first edition of Newton's *Principia Mathematica* was met with four reviews in England and on the Continent. One of these reacted to Newton's mathematical approach by contending that in fact Newton had failed to provide a work in natural philosophy at all! According to the reviewer, he had merely provided a mathematical treatise that does not characterize the motions of bodies in nature (Cohen 1971, 145–158). This conception of Newton's work continued into the next century, even among leading philosophers. For instance, in a letter from 1707, Malebranche writes: "Although M. Newton is not a physicist, his book is very curious and very useful to those who have good principles of physics; he is, moreover, an excellent geometer."[22] Newton's contemporaries were often eager to endorse his text as mathematically profound, even while denying that he had contributed to natural philosophy. They resisted his attempt to link the two by discussing forces from a *mathematical point of view*. In that sense, Newton's book can be viewed as unsuccessful, as Kuhn indicates:

> It does not, I think, misrepresent Newton's intentions as a scientist to maintain that he wished to write a *Principles of Philosophy*, like Descartes, but

that his inability to explain gravity forced him to restrict his subject to the *Mathematical Principles of Natural Philosophy*. Both the similarity and the difference of titles are significant. Newton seems to have considered his magnum opus, the *Principia*, incomplete. It contained only a mathematical description of gravity. Unlike Descartes's *Principles* it did not even pretend to explain why the universe runs as it does. It did not, that is, explain gravity, or so Newton thought. (Kuhn 1957, 259)

The view that Newton had not *explained* gravity was not his alone—indeed, it was probably the dominant view among his contemporaries.

But these facts lead us to a historical irony. Although Newton's contemporaries strongly resisted the abstract characterization of forces from a mathematical perspective and although they did so in part because they regarded this method as deviating from the mechanist consensus among philosophers studying nature, Newton's method would (broadly speaking) eventually become the standard way of thinking about forces within physics. Norwood Russell Hanson is especially clear on this point (1958, 91):

> As the *Principia* won over the physicists' thinking, however, it became a model for every other field of inquiry. Soon it ceased being a merely mathematical aid to the prediction of how bodies behave, and became a system, indeed *the* system of mechanics. The word "mechanistic" was used to mark processes which permitted explanation in terms of the *Principia*. Newton gave new meaning to causal explanation. Mechanics became the paradigm of a causal theory. Thus its central concepts—force, mass, momentum—were sometimes regarded as the ultimate causal powers.

The success of Newton's theory and the model for understanding nature that his articulation of the law of universal gravity would provide for future philosophers, despite his failure to characterize gravity through some mechanical model, would eventually become so profound that it would alter the meaning of the word *mechanical* and its cognates. Eventually, to provide a mechanistic or mechanical understanding of some phenomenon would simply mean to provide an explanation of it that employs Newton's three laws or similar generalizations. Eventually, physicists would relinquish the demand that their theories must provide mechanical models of the causes of natural phenomena, opting instead to think of forces in Newton's sense as the basic causal powers of the world. Alas, Newton never saw these developments.

notes

1 See Blair (2006) and the editors' introduction to *The Dynamics of Aristotelian Natural Philosophy from Antiquity to the Seventeenth Century*.
2 Quoted by Gaukroger (2008); see also Garber (2000).

3   Quoted by Mahoney (1998, 703).

4   Although Descartes did not use *Cartesian* axes in the modern sense, he did use coordinates to express plane curves in some circumstances (see Descartes (1954, 94–95)). Thanks to Niccolo Guicciardini for discussion of this point.

5   In his Trinity notebook, whose title McGuire and Tamny translate as *Certain Philosophical Questions*, Newton may have made use of some of Wallis's techniques from *Arithmetica Infinitorum* (Newton 1983, 106–107, footnote 168), and he made two pages of annotations from Wallis in that text (*Mathematical Papers*, vol. 1: 89–90). (In another pocket book from 1664 to 1665, he made detailed entries concerning Wallis's text, as Whiteside indicates (*Mathematical Papers*, vol. 1: 91–141.)) In the *Que[a]estiones quedam Philosoph[i]cae*, Newton noted that "one infinite extension may be greater than another," a key point from Wallis that Newton would describe to the theologian Richard Bentley some 30 years later. See *Mathematical Papers*, vol. 1: 89. Whiteside notes, intriguingly, that Newton may have read Hobbes's attack on Wallis first and then proceeded to read Wallis for himself (*Mathematical Papers*, vol. 1: 89, note 1). Newton also retained a copy of Wallis's *Opera Mathematica* in his personal library (Harrison 1978). David Rabouin points out that by roughly 1680, Newton had decided that he no longer needed the techniques of Wallis. This is an important point, but it is compatible with the fact that Newton still regarded Wallis as indicating how we can avoid various kinds of paradoxes when thinking about infinitesimals, infinite divisibility, and infinity more generally, as his later correspondence with Bentley indicates.

6   For discussions of Wallis's work, see Guicciardini (2009, 140–147), which places it in the context of understanding Newton's work in mathematics; Stedall (2010), which places it within the history of mathematics more broadly; and Jesseph (1999, 22–28), which places it within the context of Wallis's protracted debate with Hobbes.

7   Wallis is credited with having introduced the "∞" symbol to represent an infinite quantity or infinite number of items or features. He appears to have employed the symbol with considerable relish.

8   *Le Monde* was published only posthumously in Paris in 1664. This description of the historical record is actually somewhat simplified, although it is the description one will often find, and it may be the best characterization of Descartes's own understanding of the events in question. However, many scholars would now argue that Galileo was not placed under house arrest in 1633 for advocating a Copernican view, but rather for abrogating to himself the authority to pronounce opinions on various issues with theological import, issues that many theologians and officials in the Vatican took to fall under their own purview. As for the use of mathematics in *Le Monde*, Friedman has argued that Descartes may have been prepared to use mathematics in that text because it was an essay in optics, at least in part, and that is traditionally considered *mixed mathematics* (Friedman 2008).

9   The last section of part two of the *Principles* (section 64; AT VIII-1: 78) reads: "The only principles that I admit or require in physics [in physica] are those of geometry or of pure mathematics—these principles explain all natural phenomena, allowing us to provide quite certain demonstrations of them."

10 The other great post-Cartesian natural philosopher, Leibniz, had his own metaphysical commitments that led him to intriguing views of the application of mathematics. One intriguing aspect of Leibniz's conception of the relation between mathematics and metaphysics bears mentioning here, as it distinguishes his view from those of his most important predecessor, Descartes, and his most important interlocutor, Newton. From Leibniz's point of view, reality consists of an infinite series of nonspatial, noninteracting, simple substances called monads. The objects of our experience—tables, chairs, and the like—are merely the *appearances* of these monads when viewed from the human perceptual point of view. Given this metaphysical distinction between the appearances and the reality that underlies them, the question of how mathematics applies to the world takes on a new meaning: we might ask this of the natural world, the realm of our scientific or physical investigations, but we might also ask this of the reality discovered and described by fundamental metaphysics. It seems clear that for Leibniz, the monadic realm is not describable mathematically: he insists that monads lack spatial properties, thereby limiting any geometric characterization of them, and he denies that monads are mathematical points, thereby preventing any arithmetic characterization of them. So in a special Leibnizian sense, mathematics does not apply to reality (see Shabel 2005, 42–43). It does, however, apply to the natural world.

11 See *Optical Papers*, vol. I: 86–87, Shapiro translation. Isaac Barrow preceded Newton as the Lucasian Professor at Cambridge; for a helpful discussion of his influence on Newton's conception of the role of mathematics within natural philosophy, see Shapiro (1993, 30–40).

12 Newton says that the body is moving by "its inherent force," by which I take him to mean its quantity of matter or mass, since he has already indicated that we should think of inherent force or "vis insita" in that way (see definition three in *Principia* 404–405).

13 On the complications involved in these moves and related issues, including the question of whether Newton shifts between thinking of forces as acting like an impact and as acting continuously, see Westfall (1971, 470–476), Panza (2003, 162–163), and Stein (2002, 283–287).

14 If one thinks of forces as measurable quantities, moreover, then one can attempt to identify two seemingly disparate forces as in fact the same force through thinking about measuring them. Newton does this in Book III of the *Principia*, when he argues in proposition five and its Scholium that the centripetal force maintaining the planetary orbits is in fact gravity, namely, the force that causes the free fall of objects on earth. This culminates in the claim in proposition seven that all bodies gravitate toward one another in proportion to their quantity of matter. This helped to unify what were once called superlunary and sublunary phenomena, a unification that was obviously crucial for later research.

15 In the Scholium to proposition 69 in section 11 of Book I, Newton adds a similar caveat, one that ends with a reference to the earlier caveat following the definitions (*Principia* 588): "I use the word 'attraction' here in a general sense for any endeavor whatever of bodies to approach one another, whether that endeavor occurs as a result of the action of the bodies either drawn toward one another or acting on one another by means of spirits emitted or whether it arises from the action of aether or of air or of any medium

whatsoever—whether corporeal or incorporeal—in any way impelling toward one another the bodies floating therein. I use the word 'impulse' in the same general sense, considering in this treatise not the species of forces and their physical qualities but their quantities and mathematical proportions, as I have explained in the definitions."

16 For instance, the famous opening of Query 31, which first appeared in the 1706 Latin edition of the *Opticks* and was renumbered in later English editions, indicates the broad scope of Newton's thinking about the forces of nature (1952, 375–376): "Have not the small particles of bodies certain powers, virtues, or forces, by which they act at a distance, not only upon the rays of light for reflecting, refracting, and inflecting them, but also upon one another for producing a great part of the phenomena of nature? For it's well known, that bodies act one upon another by the attractions of gravity, magnetism, and electricity; and these instances show the tenor and course of nature, and make it not improbable but that there may be more attractive powers than these. For nature is very consonant and comfortable to herself. How these attractions may be performed, I do not here consider. What I call attraction may be performed by impulse, or by some other means unknown to me. I use that word here to signify only in general any force by which bodies tend towards one another, whatsoever be the cause. For we must learn from the phenomena of nature what bodies attract one another, and what are the laws and properties of the attraction, before we enquire the cause by which the attraction is performed. The attractions of gravity, magnetism, and electricity, reach to very sensible distances, and so have been observed by vulgar eyes, and there may be others which reach to so small distances as hitherto escape observation; and perhaps electrical attraction may reach to such small distances, even without being excited by friction."

17 Locke wrote a celebratory, but anonymous, review of *Principia Mathematica* for the journal *Bibliothèque Universelle* in its March 1688 issue (Cohen 1971, 145–148). That journal also published excerpts of Locke's *Essay Concerning Human Understanding* in 1687; the first edition of the complete text was published in 1690. For his part, Newton had the first edition of the *Essay*, along with all three editions of Locke's correspondence with Stillingfleet and eight other works by Locke, in his personal library (Harrison 1978).

18 Stillingfleet was certainly open to hearing Locke's endorsement of Newtonian ideas: he himself was known for having compared Descartes's views unfavorably with Newton's (Gascoigne 1985, 65). For more on Stillingfleet's philosophical views and the influences on them, see Beiser (1996, 134–138), and see Reedy (1985, 112–113, 136–139) for a discussion of his theological beliefs, including Stillingfleet's opinion that Locke's views of substance might undermine the Trinity, at least in its Anglican interpretation.

19 For a history of the issue, see Hesse (1961). I present an extended argument concerning Newton's own surprising rejection of action at a distance in Janiak (2008)—the view presented therein has been challenged in detail by Ducheyne (2011), Henry (2011), and Schliesser (2011); defended in Janiak (2013); and challenged again in Henry (2014).

20 Hence, one might say that Newton disrupted the previously established mechanist consensus concerning the aims and aspirations of physical theories by refusing to restrict his theorizing to physical models of causal interactions. In

Janiak (2008), I contend that Newton upended that consensus, a view endorsed by Chomsky (2013, 667–668, 681); but this idea remains controversial—for a different interpretation of Newton's relation to the mechanical philosophy, see Machamer *et al.* (2012).

21 Huygens's reaction occurred in 1688: see *Oeuvres* 21: 143 and 21: 446. For an illuminating discussion, see Guicciardini (1999, 122–123). My only difference with Guicciardini is one of emphasis, perhaps even of semantics: he notes that Huygens accepted Newton's mathematical derivation of the inverse square force that is central to Newton's theory in Book III of *Principia Mathematica*, but adds that Huygens "could not accept the physical theory of universal gravitation." I concur, but simply add that, in a way, Huygens rejected the theory of universal gravitation in part because it was not really a physical theory in the proper sense, since it lacked a physical model for gravity.

22 See *Oeuvres completes de Malebranche*, 19: 771–772; I owe this reference to Tad Schmaltz.

newton's struggle with leibniz

When historians and philosophers mention Leibniz and Newton in the same breath, they typically have the protracted debate over the discovery of the calculus in mind. One finds dramatic titles such as *Philosophers at War* (Hall 1980) because the calculus priority dispute was one of the most famous philosophical debates of the early eighteenth century, consuming the attention of numerous important mathematicians and philosophers (Bertoloni Meli 1993). The drama of this debate, and the way in which it poisoned numerous relationships between thinkers in England and their colleagues on the Continent, tends to suggest to contemporary readers that Leibniz and Newton were destined for disagreement. But if we reconsider some basic historical facts that precede the calculus debate, which gained steam roughly in 1708 with a remark of the Newtonian John Keill's and continued unabated until Leibniz's death 8 years later, we find that it is not at all obvious that Leibniz and Newton should have ended up bitter enemies. Indeed, from a certain point of view, it is rather surprising. First and foremost, Leibniz and Newton grew up in the same philosophical environment: each came of age during the heyday of Cartesianism, and each argued in particular that Cartesian views in natural philosophy failed to include a sufficiently robust conception of the forces of bodies in nature (Garber 2012). Force would lie at the center of Newton's mature physics (Westfall 1971), as we have seen in Chapter 5, and would become even more central to Leibniz's thinking, playing an essential role in his metaphysics as well. Indeed, it was Leibniz who coined the term *dynamics* (*le dynamique*). In that specific sense, their philosophical orientations would appear to be quite *sympatico*.

Secondly, unlike their great predecessor Descartes, who, as we have seen, did not provide a robustly mathematical philosophy of nature, both Leibniz and Newton were committed to developing precisely such a program. This is obvious from even the briefest glance at *Principia Mathematica* and from Leibniz's *Essay on the Causes of Celestial Motions* (*Tentamen*), published just 2 years later in the February 1689 issue of the *Acta Eruditorum*. Each is a

Newton, First Edition. Andrew Janiak.
© 2015 Andrew Janiak. Published 2015 by John Wiley & Sons, Ltd.

fundamentally different text than Descartes's *Principia*. The two knew one another as mathematicians already in 1676 and developed considerable respect for one another on that basis (this respect is still evident in their only other direct correspondence, from 1693—see the following text). Indeed, they communicated some of their thoughts about what we would call the calculus through third parties in 1676, and for his part, Leibniz told others that "Newton's discoveries are worthy of his genius" already in that year (*Correspondence* 2: 65–71, Westfall 1980, 262–267). Thirteen years later, Leibniz called him "the renowned Newton" in his *Tentamen* (Bertoloni Meli 1993, 138). Thirdly, since each developed a version of the calculus, it is also clear that each was committed specifically to employing new analytical techniques for understanding problems concerning motion and related natural phenomena.[1] Fourthly, both Leibniz and Newton regarded Kepler's laws as essential to any understanding of the planetary orbits and therefore as crucial for any more general theory of planetary motion (Bertoloni Meli 1993, 127–128). Finally, Leibniz's famous attempt to prevent certain neo-Aristotelian ideas from being thrown into the dustbin of history by modern mechanistic thinkers is actually mirrored in Newton's equally strong commitment to *prisca scientia*, to various kinds of ancient wisdom both in mathematics (Chapter 5) and in theology (Chapter 7).

Why, then, did Leibniz and Newton become so deeply opposed to one another's philosophical methodologies and ideas? By the time of the calculus priority dispute in the early eighteenth century, Leibniz had already decided that Newtonian natural philosophy was deeply mistaken. He spent considerable energy in his final years attempting to convince his contemporaries of that point. Why?

6.1   Newton versus Leibniz, 1693–1712

The opposition between Leibniz and Newton was fundamentally philosophical in character, centering on Newton's failure to endorse the mechanical philosophy as the guiding methodology for studying nature. This fact is especially evident after the publication of the *Principia* in 1687, when Leibniz began to develop a substantial critique of Newton's approach. Although Leibniz told some of his contemporaries that he had learned of Newton's views in natural philosophy only by reading the review of *Principia Mathematica* in the *Acta Eruditorum* of June 1688—the anonymous review in that journal was written by Christoph Pfautz—we now know that Leibniz actually read the text and took substantial notes on it.[2] As Bertoloni Meli writes, "Leibniz realized immediately the philosophical implications of the *Principia*" (1993, 99). Just 2 years after the *Principia* appeared, Leibniz published his *Tentamen*. In Chapter 5, we have encountered some aspects of Newton's methodology in *Principia Mathematica*, especially his mathematical treatment of force. Part of that treatment is evident in the Definitions, when Newton discusses his ideas of impressed force and of centripetal force. Intriguingly, in his notes on *Principia Mathematica*, Leibniz pays special attention to the Definitions (Bertoloni Meli 1993, 97). How does Newton's approach in *Principia Mathematica* compare with Leibniz's approach in his *Tentamen*?[3] Unlike Newton's text, Leibniz's essay makes it perfectly evident from the very beginning that it is a thoroughly mechanistic text. More specifically, it is evident that despite Newton's challenge to Cartesian natural philosophy in *Principia Mathematica*, including its specific challenge in Book II to vortex theories of planetary motion, Leibniz's *Tentamen* is associated with the Cartesian tradition.[4] After *Principia Mathematica*, however, Leibniz and others developed more sophisticated mathematical vortex theories than the more qualitative theory found in Descartes's *Principles*.

After discussing the approach to astronomy in antiquity and indicating the key importance of Kepler's laws, which of course was also understood by Newton, Leibniz's first two propositions, which characterize not only the laws of nature and the nature of motion but also the cause of the planetary orbits, are as follows:

(1) To tackle the matter itself, then, it can first of all be demonstrated that according to the laws of nature *all bodies which describe a curved line in a fluid are driven by the motion of the fluid.* For all bodies describing a curve endeavor to recede from it along the tangent (because of the nature of motion), it is therefore necessary that something should constrain them. There is, however, nothing contiguous except for the fluid (by hypothesis), and no conatus is constrained except by something contiguous in motion (because of the nature of the body), therefore it is necessary that the fluid itself be in motion.

(2) Hence it follows that *planets are moved by their aether,* namely they have fluid orbs which are deferent or moving. In fact by universal agreement they describe curved lines, and it is not possible to explain phenomena by supposing rectilinear motions alone. Therefore (by the preceding paragraph) they are moved by an ambient fluid. The same can otherwise be demonstrated from the fact that the motion of a planet is not uniform, or describing equal spaces in equal times. Whence, also, it is necessary that a planet be driven by the motion of the ambient fluid. (Bertoloni Meli 1993, 128–129).

The difference between Newton's mathematical treatment of force and Leibniz's approach in these first 2 propositions of the *Tentamen* could not be sharper. Instead of insisting that the deviation of the planetary bodies from the tangents to their solar orbits is due to something called a centripetal force, which can be abstractly characterized through its proportionality to various quantities in the system, Leibniz argues right at the beginning of his text that this deviation is due to *something* that must constrain the planets, adding that this thing must be contiguous to them. The abstract characterization of a centripetal force is not compatible with this notion, since the *something* that Leibniz has in mind must be a physical element of the system, one that interacts directly with the planets. As we saw in Chapter 5, Newton insists that we need not settle the question of what physical items are interacting directly with the planets in such a way as to maintain them in their orbits; Leibniz insists, on the contrary, that we must have a mechanical model of such physical items if we are to understand why it is that the planets maintain their orbits.

A few pages later in the *Tentamen*, by the time we reach the eighth and ninth propositions, Leibniz makes it perfectly clear that the Newtonian idea of the sun's *attraction* of the earth is nothing more than a *façon de parler*. This can be harmless, as long as it is always understood within an overarching mechanist framework:

(8) Thus we suppose that *a planet moves with a double motion composed of the harmonic circulation of its fluid deferent orb, and the paracentric motion*, as if it had a certain gravity or attraction, namely an impulsion *towards the Sun or—if it is a satellite—the planet* ...

(9) Having explained the harmonic circulation, we must come to the *paracentric motion of the planets, born of the outward impression of the circulation and solar attraction* combined. Moreover, it may be permitted to call it an attraction, although in reality it is an impulse, inasmuch as the Sun in a certain sense can be conceived to be a magnet; the magnetic actions themselves, however, are derived doubtless from the impulsions of fluids. (Bertoloni Meli 1993, 132)

We are free to speak of the sun's attraction of the earth, as long as we recognize that as a matter of fact—as Leibniz writes, *in reality*—the earth's orbit around the sun is due to *impulse*, a direct physical interaction between the earth and the circulating imperceptible fluids that fill the solar system. We can conceive of the sun as like a giant magnet, pulling the earth toward it, thereby preventing the earth from following the tangent to its orbit, as the laws indicate it would do if not constrained by something, but this is merely a heuristic device, since the fact remains that the earth is pushed or carried along by imperceptible fluids.

From Newton's point of view, we ought to assess the first two propositions of Leibniz's *Tentamen* in roughly the following manner: Leibniz introduces the idea that the solar system contains a circulating fluid by hypothesis (ex hypothesi), and so the question is, does he have any empirical evidence to support this claim? There is no such evidence, but from Leibniz's point of view, the lack of any such empirical evidence is irrelevant. For Leibniz would reject the idea that we can ignore *physical questions* about the planetary orbits and simply attribute them to the action of the force of gravity itself; he requires from the start that we postulate *something*, by which he means *something mechanical*, to constrain the planets in their orbits. This kind of disagreement runs deep, and it already signals the fact that Leibniz and Newton would spend the rest of their careers disagreeing about the most fundamental aspects of methodology in natural philosophy. Leibniz's commitment to the mechanical philosophy guides his work in natural philosophy in a direct and lasting way; for his part, as we have seen in Chapter 5, Newton simply lacks that commitment.

What is perhaps more remarkable is that many years after the *Tentamen* was published, Newton wrote out a few notes on Leibniz's text during the height of the calculus priority dispute (between 1713 and 1715). In these notes, Newton makes a number of criticisms of Leibniz's arguments in favor of a vortex theory (Bertoloni Meli 1993, 186–190), but one of them stands out as potentially unique among Newton's many reactions to that theory. He writes (*Correspondence* 6: 116):

Hypothesis 1. All bodies describing a curved line in a fluid are impelled by the motion of that fluid. For the endeavor to recede from the center is overcome only by a contiguous and moving [body].

Absurdity 1. Therefore a body is moved only by a corporeal agent, not by the human mind (unless it is corporeal), nor by God (unless corporeal).

Absurdity 2. God does not rule the world, and thus is not the Lord God.

Here, we see, perhaps for the first and only time in Newton's long dispute with Leibniz, that he wishes to object to Leibniz's introduction of a premise ex hypothesi not only methodologically, and not merely because there may be agents in nature that are not mechanical in Leibniz's sense, but also because Leibniz has limited his physical analysis of planetary motion in a way that would restrict the possibility that the human mind and also God are causal agents. This move is remarkable because it changes what we might call the scope of the conversation: instead of limiting his debate with Leibniz to the question of whether forces (as causes of changes in states of motion) must somehow be reduced to, or conceived in terms of, mechanical models, Newton broadens the discussion dramatically, contending that Leibniz's mechanist commitment is incompatible with the idea that the human mind and indeed God himself are causally efficacious.

What are we to make of Newton's fascinating comment on the *Tentamen*? One might construe Newton's move narrowly by contending that he is claiming specifically that planetary motion might be caused by God (presumably, not by the mind!). That is a perfectly plausible reading. Yet one might also construe it more broadly, contending that Newton intends here not to claim something specific about the causes of planetary motion, but rather to claim that the mechanical philosophy more generally cannot be used to support a hypothetical premise in the *Tentamen* because that philosophy conflicts with more fundamental commitments. That is, if one is committed to thinking that the mind moves the body and to thinking that God causes various events to happen (as More reminds Descartes in 1648), then one must ipso facto avoid the commitment that bodies are moved *only* by contiguous and moving bodies.[5] Thus, the mechanical philosophy cannot be a generally true account of natural change involving bodies. And if that is the case, it follows that one cannot introduce Leibniz's kind of premise ex hypothesi, since its support has collapsed, and it has collapsed on substantive rather than on methodological grounds.

Four years after Leibniz published his *Tentamen*, he sent Newton a short but pithy letter (Newton 2014, 140–142). When Leibniz initiated this discussion in March 1693, he proceeded by highlighting Newton's "astonishing discovery" that the elliptical planetary orbits found by Kepler can be the result of gravitational attraction within the solar system and then by contending that these motions must be caused by "the motion of a fluid medium" (Newton 2014, 141). He had described such a fluid medium, or vortex, in detail in his own *Tentamen*. The background to Leibniz's comment is his unwavering commitment—one shared by Huygens, whose theory of gravity's cause Leibniz mentions in the same letter—to the mechanical philosophy's requirement that all changes in motion must be the result of bits of matter impacting on one another. Thus, Leibniz reminded Newton in this short letter that even after the publication of the first edition of *Principia Mathematica*, Leibniz remained a firm believer in a vortex theory of planetary motion and was thereby following in the tradition of Descartes (Aiton 1972, 30–64, Gaukroger 2002, 150–153).

When he replied in October 1693, however, Newton did not accept Leibniz's philosophical olive branch by focusing on what would appear to be their agreement that Kepler's laws are fundamental to understanding planetary motion or Leibniz's more important claim that the vortex theory of planetary motion "would not at all detract from the value and truth of your discovery" that Kepler's ellipses result simply from the conception of attraction or gravitation (Newton 2014, 141). Instead, Newton focused on their *disagreement*, noting that vortices would disturb the motions of planets and comets through the solar system. Newton writes that some *very fine* matter fills the heavens, adding:

> For since celestial motions are more regular than if they arose from vortices and observe other laws, so much so that vortices contribute not to the regulation but the disturbance of the motions of planets and comets; and since all phenomena of the heavens and of the sea follow precisely, so far as I am aware, from nothing by gravity acting in accordance with the laws described by me; and since nature is very simple, I have myself concluded that all other causes are to be rejected and that the heavens are to be stripped as far as may be of all matter, lest the motions of planets and comets be hindered or rendered irregular. But if, meanwhile, someone explains gravity along with all its laws by the action of some subtle matter, and shows that the motion of planets and comets will not be disturbed by this matter, I shall be far from objecting. (Newton 2014, 143–144)

This passage is obviously rich with meaning. Leibniz clearly insisted that vortices, or some physical object or fluid, must be in contact with the planets if we are to explain why they deviate from the tangents along their orbital paths when circling the sun. Newton's reply is that swirling fluids in the heavens would actually disturb the regular orbital paths and the paths of comets through the solar system. That reply might be thought of as empirical in character, for it depends on observational data regarding the actual paths of the heavenly bodies. But Leibniz's perspective is obviously not merely empirical in character: he does not postulate vortices (or anything akin to them) on observational grounds; he infers their existence because he thinks we know (perhaps we can add, we know a priori) that in the ordinary course of nature, physical bodies such as comets or planets can deviate from a rectilinear path—they can accelerate—only if some other physical item impacts upon them. Newton has a reply to that type of view as well: he insists that the phenomena of the motion of the heavenly bodies *follow* solely from gravity itself—an impressed force, as we have seen, and therefore an *action*—in accordance with the laws of motion and the law of universal gravitation. Since gravity is an action—clearly, a causal notion—it seems clear that Newton's answer to Leibniz's idea that vortices cause the planetary orbits is that gravity itself causes them. And it is not much of a leap to conclude, in turn, that this reply commits Newton to the idea that bodies involved in gravitational interactions, such as the sun and the earth, act at a distance on one another through the force of gravity. It is not hard to divine why Leibniz (and Huygens) would have concluded that Newton had relinquished any commitment to the norms of the mechanical philosophy.

Leibniz's *Tentamen* and his 1693 correspondence with Newton were not idiosyncratic: indeed, the other leading mathematical philosopher of that time, Christiaan Huygens in Holland, had a similar reaction to the theory of universal gravity in *Principia Mathematica*.[6] In the very text of Huygens's that Leibniz mentions to Newton, the *Discours sur la cause de la pesanteur* of 1690, Huygens makes the following comment on the very first page: we must attempt to discover "an intelligible cause of gravity [*une cause intelligible de la pesanteur*]," not by supposing that bodies have some tendency or inclination to approach one another, but solely by considering their "different sizes, shapes and motions" (Huygens 1690, 129). This was a reasonably polite way of shirking Newton's procedure. Writing to Leibniz that same year (on November 18), Huygens was more pointed, explaining in private what he took himself to have already implied in his *Discourse*:

> Concerning the cause of the flux given by Mr. Newton, I am by no means satisfied, nor by all his other theories that he builds upon his principle of attraction, which to me seems absurd [*qui me paroit absurde*], as I have already mentioned in the addition to the *Discourse on Gravity*. And I have often wondered how he could have given himself all the trouble of making such a number of investigations and difficult calculations that have no other foundation than this same principle. (Huygens, *Oeuvres*, 21: 538)

Huygens clearly sides with Leibniz: he does not claim that Newton's theory of universal gravity—his *principle of attraction*—is merely mistaken in some regard or even false; he claims that one of its primary principles is *absurd*. Insightful readers of the *Discourse* may have understood this implication in Huygens's remark that Newton's theory fails to provide us with an *intelligible* cause for gravity. Thus, Huygens rejects Newton's universal gravity out of hand on grounds similar to those articulated by Leibniz.

What had been a reasonably polite exchange in public between 1689 and 1693, even if it happened in parallel with sharper exchanges in private, was eventually transformed into a highly polemical philosophical debate from roughly 1711 to Leibniz's death in 1716. This was no doubt spurred on in part by the calculus priority dispute, but it also reflected continuing fundamental differences between Newton and his major Continental critics. In February 1711, Leibniz wrote a letter to Nicholas Hartsoeker that was highly critical of the Newtonians; it was published the next year in English translation in the *Memoirs of Literature*, a journal to which Roger Cotes, the editor of the *Principia's* second edition, held a subscription (Newton 2014, 157). After Cotes brought Leibniz's criticisms to Newton's attention—especially the claim that the *Principia* renders gravitation a *perpetual miracle* because it does not specify the physical mechanism underlying it—Newton wrote an intriguing, but only posthumously published, rebuttal. Here is part of Newton's paraphrase of Leibniz's original letter: "But he [i.e. Leibniz] goes on and tells us that God could not create planets that should move round of themselves without any cause that should prevent their removing through the tangent. For a miracle at least must keep the planet in" (Newton 2014, 152). Newton's response to this Leibnizian charge is illuminating:

> But certainly God could create planets that should move round of themselves without any other cause than gravity that should prevent their removing through the tangent. For gravity without a miracle may keep the planets in. And to understand this without knowing the cause of gravity, is as good a progress in philosophy as to understand the frame of a clock and the dependence of the wheels upon one another without knowing the cause of the gravity of the weight which moves the machine is in the philosophy of clockwork; or the understanding of the frame of the bones and muscles and their connection in the body of an animal and how the bones are moved by the contracting or dilating of the muscles without knowing how the muscles are contracted or dilated by the power of the mind, is [in] the philosophy of animal motion. (Newton 2014, 152)

Thus, Newton repeats the view he mentions to Leibniz in 1693, namely, that the force of gravity itself causes the planets to follow their orbital paths rather than their inertial trajectories along the tangents to those orbits, independently of any fluid medium in the heavens. He attempts to defend this idea by presenting two analogies: one is the classic conception of a mechanical clock, the other is a more unusual conception of an animal's musculature and its role in its movement. Newton then argues as follows: just as the mechanical philosophers had been insisting throughout the seventeenth century, we can understand a clock's internal movements by understanding the way that its hands are moved by gears and levers behind the clock face; this understanding is not undermined by the fact that we do not grasp the cause of the gravity of the weight that moves one of the gears in the clock. Similarly, our understanding of the various muscles within a lion, along with their connections to sinew and bone in the lion's legs, is not undermined by our ignorance of how the lion's will causes the muscles that move the legs to move themselves. The fact that we lack a *complete* understanding does not entail that we have *no* understanding.

It is easy to miss the philosophical import of Newton's analogies—they are carefully chosen. Firstly, mechanical philosophers had often argued that understanding mechanical clocks—a wonderful new invention in the early modern period—is akin to understanding aspects of nature itself, adding that the world is like a great machine. It is especially ironic, then, for Newton to argue as follows: your (admittedly significant) explanation of how a mechanical clock works is predicated implicitly on the notion that we can take for granted the fact that there is a weight within the clock that plays a key role in causing the motions of its gears and levers. Despite the fact that many mechanists had various ideas about how gravity worked, there was certainly no consensus at all among them in understanding it. This means that a key aspect of the clock's internal motion *must* be taken for granted: the mechanists did not know why a weight within the clock behaves as it does. What makes it pull down on the lever connected to it? A stream of particles pushing it toward the earth's center, an imperceptible rotating fluid, or something else entirely?

Secondly, although it will not seem obvious to contemporary readers, there was actually a well-known and long-standing tradition of forging an analogy between gravity and thinking or willing, one explored in great depth by Newton's old friend John Locke in his celebrated correspondence with Bishop Edward Stillingfleet. In the letter quoted already in Chapter 5, we find this analogy expressed in precisely the same passage in which Locke famously commits to altering his *Essay* to accord with his understanding of Newton's theory of universal gravity:

> What I have above said, I take to be a full answer to all that your Lordship would infer from my idea of matter, of liberty, and of identity, and from the power of abstracting. You ask, how can my idea of liberty agree with the idea that bodies can operate only by motion and impulse? Answer: by the omnipotence of God, who can make all things agree, that involve not a contradiction. 'Tis true, I say, that bodies operate by impulse and nothing else. And so I thought when I writ it and yet can conceive no other way of their operation. But I am since convinced by the Judicious Mr. Newton's incomparable book, that 'tis too bold a presumption to limit God's power in this point, by my narrow conceptions. The gravitation of matter towards matter, by ways unconceivable to me, is not only a demonstration that God can, if he pleases, put into bodies, powers, and ways of operation, above what can be derived

from our idea of body, or can be explained by what we know of matter, but also an unquestionable and every where visible instance, that he has done so. And therefore in the next edition of my book, I shall take care to have that passage rectified. As to self-consciousness, your Lordship asks, what is there like self-consciousness in matter? Nothing at all in matter as matter. But that God cannot bestow on some parcels of matter a power of thinking, and with it self-consciousness will never be proved by asking, how is it possible to apprehend that mere body should perceive that it doth perceive? The weakness of our apprehension I grant in the case: I confess as much as you please, that we cannot conceive how a solid, no nor how an un-solid, created substance thinks; but this weakness of our apprehensions, reaches not the power of God, whose weakness is stronger than any thing in men. (Locke 1699, 408–409)

What is especially pertinent here is that Locke takes gravity and thinking (or self-consciousness) to pose similar problems for a mechanistic conception of the world: each would appear to require a kind of *superaddition* by God, since neither is consistent with the idea that objects in the world are *extended solid substances*. With this background in place, we can see that Newton takes the lion's mind or will to be analogous to the weight within the clock: our understanding of how all the muscles and sinew and bone within the lion's leg work together to produce a motion is predicated implicitly on the fact that we must take the original cause of all this motion—namely, something like the lion's decision to move its legs—for granted. Once again, the fact that we do not understand the latter should not undermine our confidence that we understand the former. Or so Newton argues.

And yet, however carefully Newton constructed these analogies, it seems that Leibniz would not accept them. For Leibniz would be in a position to argue that the case of the planetary orbits is actually not analogous to either the clock or the animal case. In the case of the planetary orbits, Newton's contention that gravity itself is the cause of their acceleration might be acceptable if *the rest of the explanation were mechanical*. That is, if Newton had claimed that gravity somehow caused some particles or some fluid or some other matter to push against the planet, thereby causing its acceleration around the sun, then that would be analogous to our two other cases. But Newton made no such claim: he thinks that gravity alone is the cause of the orbit, end of story. There is no *partial*, but mechanical, account of the planetary orbits in Newton's work. So Leibniz could argue as follows: a genuinely analogous case would be to argue that the weight in the clock moves the hands, without any intervening mechanical interactions among the gears and levers, or to argue that the lion simply moves his legs by willing it to be so, without any intervening mechanical interactions among his muscles and bones. And that would disrupt Newton's basic point.

Ironically, this last point might suggest that Locke's account of thought's superaddition to matter would actually be less objectionable to Leibniz than Newton's discussion of the lion. If God has superadded thought to the lion, thereby enabling a lion to will its legs to move, this is perfectly consistent with the idea that *the rest* of the internal workings within the lion are completely mechanical. That is, our ignorance concerning the lion's mind and its connection to the lion's body would extend only to our ignorance of how the lion wills its legs to move, where the latter is construed as some kind of causal interaction at the beginning of the *otherwise* mechanistic causal chain. Once the lion's will interacts, say, with some muscle, the rest of the causal chain can involve only mechanical links from muscle to sinew to bone, and so on. So our ignorance here would be limited in scope, and more importantly, it would enable us to endorse a fully mechanical account of the lion's motion, with only one nonmechanical feature. Leibniz could still object to that idea, of course, but his objection would be less profound than his dissatisfaction with the fact that Newton's account of gravity lacks any mechanical elements whatsoever.

The reasoning by analogy was not Newton's only attempt in this posthumously published letter to convince his reader that he could successfully reply to Leibniz's charges. He also included a wider discussion of mechanist norms within philosophy more generally. Again, he begins by quoting Leibniz:

But Mr. Leibniz goes on. "The ancients and the moderns, who own that gravity is an occult quality, are in the right, if they mean by it that there is a certain mechanism unknown to them whereby all bodies tend towards the center of the earth. But if they mean that the thing is performed without any mechanism by a simple primitive quality or by a law of God who produces that effect without using any intelligible means, it is an unreasonable and occult quality, and so very occult that it is impossible that it should ever be done though an angel or God himself should undertake to explain it." (Newton 2014, 151)

In this quoted passage, Leibniz returns to the kind of criticism that he would present against the *superaddition* view that Locke presented to Stillingfleet, arguing that philosophers must reject the idea that gravity could simply be a feature of bodies that God adds to them, despite the fact that we cannot possibly understand gravitational interactions based on our idea of body (our idea of extended solid substances or another similar idea). Indeed, Leibniz raises the stakes by contending that *God himself* could not explicate how such interactions are possible based on the idea of matter. Leibniz would argue, perhaps on metaphysical grounds, that any laws said to govern the interaction of bodies, and any qualities attributed to bodies, must be intelligible in the terms available to philosophers through the mechanist orientation. In particular, laws and qualities must be intelligible in terms of the shape, size, motion, and impenetrability (or solidity) of bodies. In this way, one might conclude that Locke and Leibniz do not necessarily disagree on whether gravity can be made intelligible in mechanist terms; they simply disagree on the propriety of the contention that God could *superadd* a feature to bodies that cannot be made intelligible in that way.

Newton's reply to Leibniz's argument is illuminating. Instead of presenting a narrow defense of his view, perhaps by denying that he has postulated any nonmechanical causation with his theory of gravity, he challenges the mechanical philosophy itself by contending that it should not be understood as holding for all natural phenomena:

> The same ought to be said of hardness. So then gravity and hardness must go for unreasonable occult qualities unless they can be explained mechanically. And why may not the same be said of the vis inertiae [force of inertia] and the extension, the duration and mobility of bodies, and yet no man ever attempted to explain these qualities mechanically, or took them for miracles or super-natural things or fictions or occult qualities. They are the natural, real, rea-sonable, manifest qualities of all bodies seated in them by the will of God from the beginning of the creation and perfectly incapable of being explained mechanically, and so may be the hardness of primitive particles of bodies. And therefore if any man should say that bodies attract one another by a power whose cause is unknown to us, or by a power seated in the frame of nature by the will of God, or by a power seated in a substance in which bodies move and float without resistance and which has therefore no vis inertiae but acts by other laws than those that are mechanical: I know not why he should be said to introduce miracles and occult qualities and fictions into the world. For Mr. Leibniz himself will scarce say that thinking is mechanical as it must be if to explain it otherwise be to make a miracle, an occult quality, and a fiction. (Newton 2014, 151–152)

The first aspect of Newton's argument, it seems, is to indicate that mechanical explanations are predicated on referencing certain kinds of qualities when investigating natural phenomena, and that these qualities themselves are therefore not subject to mechanical explanation. For instance, since mechanist explanations—say, of the way in which magnets attract iron filings across a table—must refer to qualities such as the extension of the bodies subject to the explanations, then we cannot give a mechanist explanation of extension itself. Of course, Leibniz might reply that we need not provide any explanation of the basic qualities of bodies that figure in mechanical explanations, for those prop-erties have been chosen by the *moderns* precisely because they are perfectly intelligible on their own, perhaps unlike various qualities attributed to *Scholastic* accounts of natural phenomena.

The second aspect of Newton's argument is more intriguing—it also harks back to Locke's discussion with Stillingfleet, for as we have seen, Locke had contended that God may have superadded not only gravity to material bodies, but also the power of thought, linking them because he believed that neither could be rendered intelligible using any philosophical means at his disposal. That is, from Locke's point of view, we know that human beings—which are, or at least contain, material bodies with size, shape, motion and solidity, along with parts characterized by those qualities—are capable of thought, but since we cannot discern how any material thing could possibly have that capacity, we conclude that God may have superadded that feature to us, or to our bodies. Thought and gravity are disanalogous in the sense that we did not require anything like Newton's theory to convince us that human beings can think, but they are otherwise analogous. Newton then attempts to make the following argument: since Leibniz would have to agree that thinking is not a mechanical process, and not mechanically explicable, he must agree that there is at least one aspect of the world that has the following two features—(1) it is not mechanical; and (2) it is clearly not to be rejected on that ground alone. He attempts to liken *gravity* (as he understands it) to *thinking* (as he believes Leibniz is required to understand it), arguing that despite the fact that it is not mechanical—it cannot be explained mechanically—it nonetheless should not be rejected. This argument may be predicated on the view that human beings, qua material things, or at least qua partially material things, do the thinking, rather than immaterial things, such as minds or souls, for if one attributes all thought to an immaterial mind or soul, then there is no pressure to say that anything in nature, or perhaps even any aspect of anything in nature, has a feature that cannot be mechanically explicated. If one accepts Locke and Newton's apparent view that we should in fact attribute thinking to material things, or to aspects of material things, then perhaps Newton has successfully followed Locke in likening gravity to thought, thereby making room for aspects of nature that are not mechanical after all. This vexing issue would continue to foment debates among Newton and Leibniz's various followers in England and on the Continent, respectively.

6.2 The Leibniz–Clarke Correspondence, 1715–1716

Leibniz's most extensive debate with the Newtonians would not occur until the very end of his life. His celebrated correspondence with Samuel Clarke, Newton's parish priest, friend, and supporter in London, is his most famous interaction with the Newtonians, occurring right before his death in 1716 (Clarke and Leibniz 1717). Leibniz fomented the correspondence in November 1715 by sending a short, pithy, provocative letter to Princess Caroline of Wales, one designed to provoke a response from Newton's circle in London (Bertoloni Meli 1999, 2002, Vailati 1997). Leibniz knew well that Princess Caroline was a leading intellectual and political figure in England at the time, one who would surely wish to see the views of her countrymen defended against Leibniz's rather shocking claims about the negative religious consequences of Newtonian thinking. He opens his initial letter by mentioning both Locke and Newton, along with the issues about materiality and thinking that arose in his near exchange with Newton in 1712:

> Natural religion itself seems to decay [in England] very much. Many will have human souls to be material; others make God himself a corporeal being. Mr. Locke and his followers are uncertain at least whether the soul is not material and naturally perishable. Sir Isaac Newton says that space is an organ which God makes use of to perceive things by. But if God stands

in need of any organ to perceive things by, it will follow that they do not depend altogether on him, nor were produced by him. (Clarke and Leibniz 1717, L 1: 1–3)

Thus, Leibniz charges both Lockeans and Newtonians with presenting philosophical views of the human and of the divine that lead to theologically unsavory consequences, such as the idea that the human soul might be material and the view that God must employ something akin to an organ in order to perceive happenings in the world. These were fighting words. Although Locke had died in 1704, he had various followers in England at the time (Gascoigne 1985, 172–173), and Newton himself was at the height of his influence: he had recently been knighted, as Leibniz acknowledges by calling him "Sir" in his letter, and was at that time President of the Royal Society. Moreover, Samuel Clarke had given the Boyle lectures in 1704 and again in 1705, so he was a public figure associated with the state of Christianity in England. Once Clarke took the bait, replying that same month to Leibniz's charges, Locke's views quickly dropped from view and the two focused specifically on Leibniz's numerous objections to Newtonian ideas and methods.

But why did Clarke respond on Newton's behalf, and what was Newton's actual role in the correspondence? These questions continue to puzzle scholars (see Bertoloni Meli 1999, 2002, Cohen and Koyré 1962). There is no documentary evidence, such as letters, between Clarke and Newton indicating the contours of his role; then again, at this time, since both men lived in London and Clarke was Newton's parish priest, the lack of letters or other papers is unsurprising. That fact alone is intriguing, for the theological differences between the two are salient: since Newton was a committed anti-Trinitarian—a fact known to figures like Locke and to others such as William Whiston, Newton's successor in the Lucasian Professorship at Cambridge (Force 1985)—he may have decided that Leibniz's contentions about *natural religion* in England would best be answered by Clarke, a rising star in the Church at that time and clearly a formidable theological thinker. On the other hand, Clarke himself was certainly not an orthodox Anglican thinker—his *Scripture-Doctrine of the Trinity* of 1712 was read by some as showing at least some sympathy for Unitarian ideas—so he was not an unproblematic figure in this regard. Perhaps just as importantly, Clarke was a serious metaphysician, a more systematic philosopher than Newton, as was evident from his *Demonstration of the being and attributes of God* (1704). He was therefore in a position to engage Leibniz on metaphysical territory, writing in depth about such issues as the principle of sufficient reason, which Newton apparently did not take seriously. In any event, there is no doubt that Clarke was taken by Leibniz and his followers to be speaking for Newton and his circle. Nonetheless, there are certainly aspects of Clarke's views that may deviate from Newton's own opinions, so it would be unwise to (as it were) remove Clarke from our conception of the correspondence by regarding it effectively as Newton's work.

Leibniz's letters to Clarke are methodologically characteristic: he leaves much of his own systematic and complex metaphysical theorizing—including the monadology—in the background, bringing to the fore only those elements that are both necessary for his criticisms of the Newtonians and also likely to garner support from Clarke. Thus, the key to many of Leibniz's criticisms is the principle of sufficient reason (PSR), which he knows Clarke will endorse, although with a distinct conception of its scope: Leibniz asserts, while Clarke denies, that the principle demands that each act of divine willing requires a reason; for Clarke, divine willing itself is reason enough for some physical state of affairs to obtain or for some event to occur. Leibniz argues in particular that several key aspects of the Newtonian worldview are incompatible with the PSR, including the idea of absolute space. If space were in fact completely independent of all physical objects and all relations among them, as the Newtonians seem to assert, then a problem arises:

> I have many demonstrations to confute the fancy of those who take space to be a substance or at least an absolute being. But I shall only use, at present, one demonstration, which the author here gives me occasion to insist upon. I say, then, that if space were an absolute being, something would happen for which it would be impossible that there should be a sufficient reason—which is against my axiom. And I prove it thus: space is something absolutely uniform, and without the things placed in it, one point of space absolutely does not differ in any respect whatsoever from another point of space. Now from this it follows (supposing space to be something in itself, besides the order of bodies among themselves) that it is impossible there should be a reason why God, preserving the same situations of bodies among themselves, should have placed them in space after one certain particular manner and not otherwise—why everything was not placed the quite contrary way, for instance, by changing east into west. But if space is nothing else but this order or relation, and is nothing at all without bodies but the possibility of placing them, then those two states, the one such as it is now, the other supposed to be the quite contrary way, would not at all differ from one another. Their difference therefore is only to be found in our chimerical supposition of the reality of space. (Clarke and Leibniz 1717, L 3: 5)

Leibniz's argument is clever at the outset: he bypasses the thorny problem of determining whether Newton's idea of absolute space commits him to thinking of space as a substance—a view, as we have seen in Chapter 4, which Newton explicitly considers and rejects in *De Gravitatione* (Newton 2014, 36)—by presupposing only that Newton thinks of space as existing independently of objects and their relations. If space is indeed independent in this way, then it would seem that God faces a choice: when creating the world, or matter, why place the earth in one particular part of space rather than any other? The parts of space, independently of all objects and all relations, obviously do not differ from one another in any salient respect, so it would seem that one could not even theoretically devise a reason for placing the earth anywhere in particular, as opposed to anywhere else in particular. (This argument, incidentally, does not depend on our having the capacity to refer to places within empty space.) But since space exists, with all its places, independently of the earth and everything else, then God must indeed have some reason to place the earth in one place rather than another—for Leibniz, even the divine will is inert independent of any reason for (as it were) inclining in one direction rather than another.

Finally, Leibniz argues that he himself avoids this problem by asserting that space is nothing above and beyond the objects in the world and all possible relations among them (hence, he holds a kind of modal relationalist view, in more modern terminology). God faces no problematic choice on this view, since space does not exist prior to the creation of the world or of material objects: to create objects with spatial relations just is ipso facto to create space itself, for it is nothing over and above objects and their relations. If you like, space for Leibniz just is a way of conceptually grasping all objects and all possible relations among them, all at once. Time, similarly, is a way of grasping the whole series of events that have characterized history. Clarke's reply is somewhat disappointing: he blocks Leibniz's inference by simply denying that the divine will must have a reason to place the earth in one place rather than another (Clarke and Leibniz 1717, C 3: 5). The PSR is not violated in this case, according to Clarke's interpretation of it, because it requires only this: if the earth appears in one place rather than another, there must be a reason that it appears there, and the reason in this case is simply the divine will; there is no further question about why the divine being made a particular choice rather than another.

In the quotation earlier, Leibniz speaks of the Newtonians as endorsing "the reality of space," which Leibniz regards as "chimerical." This remark highlights a second important aspect of Leibniz's conception of space and time, one that is often ignored in contemporary discussions, which tend to emphasize Leibnizian *relationalism* in opposition to Newtonian *absolutism*. Leibniz's view of space and time connects intimately with broader aspects of his metaphysical positions: unlike ordinary physical objects, which are constituted by their parts (they are discrete) and which exhibit features that involve internal distinctions among those parts, he thinks of space and time as continuous and homogeneous. Leaving aside the monadology, as he does in his correspondence with Clarke, this means that for Leibniz, it is physical objects that are real things; space and time are merely *ideal* or abstract entities whose continuity and homogeneity signal this special status. It is not merely that space and time are nothing over and above the events and relations of objects that exist in our world; it is also the case that they are ideal: they depend in some way on the human mind for their existence. Or so Leibniz seems to suggest. This aspect of his view would become of central importance to Kant's understanding of the Leibniz–Newton debate on the nature of space.

Leibniz also famously argued that the PSR, on his interpretation of it, entails a distinct and equally significant metaphysical principle, which he called the *identity of indiscernibles* (the PII for short). The PII states the following: qualitative identity entails numerical identity. Philosophers like to distinguish between different kinds of identity. If two snowflakes are qualitatively identical, then that means that they have all the same features: each is (say) 1 in. wide, 30 °F, an octagon, and so on. But there is another kind of identity: if we say that Superman is Clark Kent, or that Barack Obama is the President of the United States, we are not saying that these things have all the same features, we are saying that *they are the very same thing*. They are one and the same. Of course, I might not realize that Clark is Superman, so I can believe that they are two separate individuals, but my belief is false (the metaphysics tracks the truth, not my beliefs and the evidence I may have for them). It seems natural to think that there are at least these two kinds of identity. The PII then states: if two things were actually identical qualitatively, then they would have to be the same thing. That is, there cannot be two numerically distinct things that share all the same features. This may sound implausible. Remember that for Leibniz, this is a metaphysical, rather than an epistemological, principle, so the PII does not indicate that human beings are capable of finding the distinguishing features between any two items that exist. That is, it may appear for all the world that our two snowflakes are qualitatively identical. Perhaps they are qualitatively identical even at the molecular level, so that for all intents and purposes, any difference between them is simply imperceptible, maybe even unknowable. The PII simply demands that they are in fact distinct in some way, whether we can discover that way or not. Why is Leibniz entitled to such an idea? Because he thinks that God knows everything, and therefore God will be capable of distinguishing our two snowflakes from one another.

But why does Leibniz think that the PSR entails the PII? Roughly, he argues as follows: let us suppose that there could be two qualitatively identical snowflakes (*actually* qualitatively identical, not merely *apparently* qualitatively identical *for us*). Then suppose that God decided to place a snowflake on Aristotle's head during a snowstorm in ancient Athens. The problem is that although God could have a reason to place a snowflake on Aristotle's head, God could not have a reason to choose one of our two snowflakes instead of the other. Why not? Because all the facts about the one snowflake are also facts about the other, so any feature that God regarded as salient—weight, width, temperature, structure—would be shared by the two snowflakes. Thus, God could not have a reason to choose one snowflake rather than the other. But of course, God is omnipotent, so God can act on these snowflakes, which means, in turn, that there could be some divine-caused event involving them that had no reason. And that is a violation of the PSR.

So now the question is, does the Newtonian view of space and time also involve violations of the PII? Leibniz thought that it did, for the following reason. If one thinks that space and time exist independently of all objects and of all possible relations among objects—for Newton, before the creation, God was substantially omnipresent throughout all of actually infinite space (Chapter 7)—then one must think that space and time are like objects or substances in their own right. But if one thinks of them as objects or as substances, as independently existing items, then the PII will be violated, for the PII holds not only for objects and substances, but also their parts: just as no two snowflakes can be qualitatively identical, no two cells or molecules within snowflakes can be, either. So the PII demands that the parts of all objects or substances differ from one another. But the parts of space and time—the places within space, at any level, and the second or minutes or hours that constitute time—are in fact qualitatively identical with one another. One hour does not differ from any other, independently of what happens during that hour; and one place does not differ from any other, independently of whatever occupies that place. Leibniz thinks that his view of space and time avoids exactly this problem. If one thinks that space and time are just the order of relations among objects, and the order of events involving objects, respectively, then one does not think of them as objects or as substances in their own right. That is, space and time are merely ideal—they are not real things at all, in which case they do not have real parts. Hence, the PII does not apply to them. In this respect, space and time are akin to mathematical objects like triangles and planes and lines: these are not real things, so it is harmless if they are constituted by qualitatively identical features (e.g., the line might be composed of points). Indeed, for Leibniz, if something is composed of qualitatively identical items, such as points or lines, then that signals the fact that it is not a real thing, but rather ideal or merely mathematical. Space and time are like that.[7]

Obviously, Leibniz's arguments against the Newtonians highlighted a fundamental difference between his interpretation of the PSR and Clarke's: where Leibniz held what we might call the *rationalist* view that all willing, all choice, must occur for a reason—a requirement from which even the divine being is not exempt—Clarke held what we might call the *voluntarist* view that willing, or choice, need not occur for any reason, for it is itself a sufficient reason for some states of affairs to obtain or events to occur. From Leibniz's point of view, this renders the will, including the divine will, opaque or unintelligible: if an agent can act or make a choice without having any reason for it, then surely the agent is not rational, and if the PSR demands anything of the world, it is that the world must be rationally intelligible to us. This requirement must hold of agents and their wills as well. But from Clarke's point of view, this requirement is too stringent, especially in the divine case: if we hold that even God must have a reason for choosing to create one state of affairs rather than another—for choosing, say, to part the Red Sea rather than the Mississippi River—then we are ipso facto restricting God's freedom. Surely God has the freedom to choose to do anything at all or, at least, anything that does not contain or instantiate a contradiction, and for his part, Leibniz agrees that the principle of contradiction does not entail the PSR—the latter is a separate and independent principle which is necessary for metaphysics and natural philosophy to extend beyond mathematics, which requires only the principle of contradiction (Clarke and Leibniz 1717, L 2: 1). God does not need a reason to part the sea—God can simply do it! Leibniz replies: Clarke's view leaves us with a

God, and indeed with ordinary agents, who can act arbitrarily, with no reason at all, and that is not the kind of freedom that philosophy seeks; it wishes to see agents as engaged in rational action. In their differing interpretations of the PSR, and their correspondingly distinct conceptions of freedom and reason, the debate between Leibniz and Clarke hits rock bottom. Many philosophical debates do so, as one might expect from the issues I discuss in Chapter 2.

Leibniz's criticisms of the Newtonians were not restricted to questions about the nature of space and time; he also revived his old complaint—one shared with, and by, Huygens, as we have seen earlier—that Newton's physical theory commits him to the possibility, if not to the reality, of action at a distance among the planetary bodies. In one passage in his fourth letter, for instance, Leibniz writes (Clarke and Leibniz 1717, L 4: 45): "It is also a supernatural thing that bodies should attract one another at a distance without any intermediate means and that a body should move around without receding in the tangent, though nothing hinders it from so receding. For these effects cannot be explained by the nature of things." As a defender of the mechanical philosophy, Leibniz insists here, as he had before, that a material body like the earth would recede along the tangent to its orbit if it were not the case that it was impacted upon by some physical body or bodies, such as a vortex or another kind of fluid filling the solar system, as the Cartesians had discussed decades earlier. Clarke's reply to this charge is especially illuminating (Clarke and Leibniz 1717, vol. 4: §45): "That one body should attract another without any intermediate means, is indeed not a miracle, but a contradiction: for 'tis supposing something to act where it is not. But the means by which two bodies attract each other may be invisible and intangible, and of a different nature from mechanism, and yet, acting regularly and constantly, may well be called natural, being much less wonderful than animal motion, which yet is never called a miracle." This passage is bound to confuse readers. On the one hand, Clarke is clearly arguing that the Newtonians refuse to restrict their understanding of causal interactions in nature to mechanical cases; on the other hand, however, he does not accept what many at that time would have regarded as the obvious implication of this denial of mechanism, namely, that action at a distance is perfectly possible (a move embraced by some later in the eighteenth century, such as Kant). Instead, Clarke not only rejects action at a distance as Newton possibly had before him; he contends that it is not even *logically* possible! In his various pronouncements to Bentley and others, Newton never contended that action at a distance was simply a contradiction and therefore impossible. That kind of claim would presumably hold even for the divine being, for God is typically said to be capable of creating any situation that does not instantiate a contradiction (although Descartes's views on the eternal truths are more complicated). Clarke's view raises a serious problem for Newtonians: if action at a distance is simply a contradiction and therefore not a possible physical situation, even with divine intervention, then how ought one to interpret the theory of universal gravity, which certainly *appears* to indicate that distant action is perfectly possible and perhaps even actual? If we interpret the theory as postulating actual distant action, say between the moon and the earth, then it clearly must be mistaken; but even if we interpret it less strongly, as merely postulating that distant action between the moon and the earth is *possible*, that would presumably disqualify the theory as well. Perhaps one can save Clarke's view by contending that since distant action is logically impossible, Newton's theory must therefore be interpreted as neutral on that issue. This is one issue where Clarke's views may differ substantially from Newton's own. Regardless of whether Clarke represented Newton's own views faithfully, there is no doubt that his correspondence with Leibniz helped to shape the agenda of philosophy in the eighteenth century.

Leibniz's long debate with Newton and his followers, which began in earnest in 1693 and continued until Leibniz's death in 1716, indicates that he regarded the Newtonians as fundamentally mistaken both on the level of natural philosophy, where the explanation of natural phenomena like the planetary orbits occurs, and at the deeper level of metaphysics, where the explanation of the methodology of natural philosophy and indeed of the world as a whole occurs. The methodology of the mathematical treatment of force enables Newton to discuss gravity *abstractly*, without considering its physical aspects, but it is precisely this methodology that Leibniz must reject: if we treat gravity abstractly, we are allowing ourselves to think about a kind of force that is inexplicable from the basic properties of material bodies. The fact that gravity is said to be proportional to quantities that *are* mechanically intelligible, such as spatial separation, cannot obscure the fact that gravity itself is mechanically unintelligible. For Leibniz, it is as if Newton's methodology licensed him to say: there is a miraculous causal interaction between bodies, but that is perfectly acceptable because the miracle is proportional to mass and inversely proportional to distance!

Leibniz also argued that the Newtonians were mistaken at the more basic level of fundamental metaphysics. In fact, Newton was wrong both methodologically and substantively at the metaphysical level: first, he was wrong methodologically because he did not accept the overriding idea that natural philosophy requires a metaphysical foundation in the first place, as the Cartesians had always believed; and second, he was wrong substantively because his own views in natural philosophy conflict with the true metaphysical principles that Leibniz endorses when providing just such a foundation to his own work. At the deepest level, Leibniz and Newton thought about natural philosophy differently. As for the first point, although each was a great critic of Descartes, Leibniz worked within the Cartesian tradition in one important sense in which Newton did not: he accepted the fundamental idea that the study of nature requires a metaphysical foundation. He did not endorse the notion that there could be brute facts in nature. From his point of view, the philosopher studying nature could not discover just *any* laws of motion: the laws must reflect some fundamental features of the world expressed in metaphysical principles such as the PSR and its entailment, the PII. For instance, it might certainly *seem* that atomism is correct, and the empirical evidence might in fact suggest that it is correct, but we can know a priori that it must be false, since it would violate the PII. Newton never accepted this approach. He seemed comfortable with the idea that there can be brute facts about nature, or at least, facts with no deeper explanation than the inscrutable divine will. We have already seen the details of the second point. Leibniz argues that Newton's conception of space, time, and motion violates the PSR and the PII. So once one presupposes Leibniz's methodology, endorsing the idea that natural philosophy requires a metaphysical foundation, one finds that Newton's substantive views about space, time, and motion within natural philosophy cannot be accurate, since they conflict directly with the very metaphysical principles that serve as the centerpiece of that foundation. In the history of philosophy, there have been many protracted disputes, debates, and discussions among numerous figures. But it is hard to think of any conflict between any two philosophers in the modern period that was more thoroughgoing and complete than the conflict between these two. Because of their joint discovery of the calculus, Leibniz and Newton will always be mentioned on the same page of the history books. But philosophically speaking, they inhabited different worlds.

notes

1 Of course, they had distinct understandings of what we now call the calculus, in addition to differing on its discovery. Some of their later discussions were, to some extent, infected with the acrimony of the debates about the calculus—see, for example, Newton's letter to Conti of February 26, 1716 (*Correspondence* 6: 285–290), and Leibniz's letter to Conti, written in reply, of March 29, 1716 (*Correspondence* 6: 304–314).

2 Leibniz told Mencke this story in a letter written sometime in 1688—*Correspondence* 3: 3–5. For details of Leibniz's encounter of Newton's text, see Bertoloni Meli (1993, 96–104, 306).

3 As Guicciardini shows (1999, 145–156), Newton's extensive employment of geometric methods in *Principia Mathematica* differs substantially from Leibniz's use of the calculus when thinking about planetary motion in the *Tentamen*.

4 The *Tentamen* is a Cartesian text in both substantive and methodological respects. Substantively speaking, its postulation of vortices was understood at that time, and indeed well into the eighteenth century, as broadly following Descartes's explanation of planetary motion in the *Principles*. Methodologically speaking, Leibniz assumes a vortex—he introduces it ex hypothesi—just as Descartes does in part III, section 30 of the *Principles*. Newton himself endorsed a kind of vortex theory in his youth (Ruffner 2000), rejecting it only when working on the *De Motu corporum* drafts (1684–1685) in favor of Keplerian orbits that result from a central force. In the first edition of *Principia Mathematica*, Newton objects extensively to vortex theories in Book II (Smith 2001), and in the second edition, he emphasizes in sections like the General Scholium that he rejects the use of the *hypothesis* of vortices.

5 There is manuscript evidence from roughly this same time period that Newton regarded the study of the mind as a proper part of philosophy (in the relevant sense), which would have been a perfectly standard idea about natural philosophy (Hatfield 1996). In a draft of a new preface for a possible reissuing of *Principia Mathematica*, Newton writes: "What is taught in metaphysics, if it derived from divine revelation, is religion; if it is derived from phenomena through the five senses, it pertains to physics [*ad Physicam pertinent*]; if it is derived from knowledge of the internal actions of our mind through the sense of reflection, it is only philosophy about the human mind and its ideas as internal phenomena likewise pertain to physics" (Cohen 1999, 54; *Mathematical Papers*, vol. 8: 459).

6 On various significant aspects of Huygens's reactions to *Principia Mathematica*—since Huygens died in 1695, he saw only the first edition—see Guicciardini (1999, 121–125) and Koyré (1968, 115–138); for a more general discussion of Huygens and natural philosophy, see Westfall (1971, 146–193). The most systematic treatment of Huygens remains Yoder (1988).

7 This obviously raises the question of how Leibniz thinks in more depth about the relation between ideal entities and mathematical ones. I cannot delve into that topic here.

newton's god

One principle in philosophy is the being of a God or spirit infinite eternal omniscient omnipotent, and the best argument for such a being is the frame of nature and chiefly the contrivance of the bodies of living creatures.... These and such like considerations are the most convincing arguments for such a being and have convinced mankind in all ages that the world and all the species of things therein were originally framed by his power and wisdom. And to lay aside this argument is unphilosophical.[1]

Newton

...the late seventeenth century in England was an age obsessed with the formation of correct principles for interpreting the Bible.

Gerard Reedy

From a contemporary point of view, seventeenth-century natural philosophy is an odd mélange, an approach to studying the world that defies contemporary categorization (Lüthy 2000). A glance at Descartes's *Principles of Philosophy* indicates why this is so: in this text, we encounter everything from the nature of the human mind and the existence of God to the vortices causing the planetary orbits and the reason why glass is fragile. The philosophers who studied nature in this period expressed views in areas that we regard as fundamentally separate. Perhaps nothing is as confusing for a contemporary reader as the discussion of God in treatments of nature—this renders the relation between theology and natural philosophy especially important for contemporary historical understanding. The first step toward clarity involves the recognition that seventeenth-century theology encompassed three distinct fields or endeavors. Very roughly speaking, *natural* theology attempts to understand the divine by studying its creator, in a way that reflects one's faith; *revealed* theology attempts to understand the divine by studying scripture; and *systematic* theology attempts to understand the divine by using reason, often focusing on divine attributes such as infinity, omnipotence, and omniscience. Whereas infinity is a key attribute of God according to many systematic theologians, it is often said that it is not a scriptural concept. So there is not only a distinction between

Newton, First Edition. Andrew Janiak.

various branches of theology based on their focus and methods but also a distinction reflecting the concepts they employ. In contrast, the natural philosopher's discussion of the divine is centered on the book of nature—hence, he will interpret nature as the work of a creator, employing it as his guide, leaving aside scripture and emphasizing reason over faith. Just as importantly, the boundaries between natural theology and natural philosophy were not precise during the seventeenth century and they remained contested throughout it. Nonetheless, many authors, including Newton himself, insisted that discussing God by studying the phenomena was a proper part of natural philosophy, and not merely of natural theology.[2] What is perhaps most important, however, is that God was a philosophical concept *par excellence* in the seventeenth century (Funkenstein 1986), and Newton himself employed that concept in a number of key contexts, including most prominently the General Scholium to *Principia Mathematica* in the 1713 edition. Newton would have denied that this fact entails that natural philosophy encompasses religious ideas. As he wrote near the end of his life, "religion and philosophy are to be preserved distinct. We are not to introduce divine revelations into philosophy, nor philosophical opinions into religion."[3] Hence, Newton distinguishes between a discussion of God based on revelation and one based on natural phenomena. This does not mean that Newton's discussions of God within philosophy were banal or uncontested. Indeed, as we will see, a single characterization of the divine could be both theologically unproblematic and philosophically disputed.

The relationship between natural philosophy and other aspects of philosophy in this period was also contested and depended in part upon one's conception of philosophy more generally. For instance, as is the case now, metaphysics in the seventeenth century was understood in disparate ways: following the Aristotelian tradition of the thirteenth through the sixteenth centuries, it might be an analysis of *being qua being*; following Descartes's example in the *Meditations* of 1641, it might be thought of as "first philosophy," a philosophical inquiry that is prior to any other; or following the example of Leibniz, it might be thought to involve an analysis of the most basic principles of our reasoning and of their roles in guiding our thoughts about God and the creation (as we have seen in Chapter 6). But it was typically distinguished from natural philosophy, with its focus on nature and *natural* beings, like rocks, planets, and human beings, which would have included ideas about the human mind, the soul, or the will.[4] That is why Descartes was taking a substantive position in his *Principles* when he suggested that natural philosophy must rest on a logically independent metaphysical foundation. The key to avoiding anachronistic pitfalls is to remember that some philosophers, including Newton, regarded the study of nature as providing us with knowledge of its creator.

When one thinks about Galileo's house arrest in 1633 and about Descartes's subsequent decision to suppress *Le Monde* because of its Copernican perspective, it is easy to conclude that theology and religion hampered natural philosophy in this period. It is also easy, when thinking about Descartes or

Newton's discussions of God within natural philosophy, to conclude that they are parroting well-worn theological points.[5] But the actual historical relationship between theology and natural philosophy is more complicated than that (Harrison 2005). Indeed, the discussion of how to understand the basic distinction between theology and natural philosophy was one of the most fundamental disputes of the century. For if natural philosophy studies nature without considering what the Hebrew or Greek Bibles, or some Catholic or Protestant doctrine, teach us about nature, how can anyone guarantee that their conclusions will be mutually consistent? If one reads in Genesis that the Earth was created in 6 days or in Joshua that there was once a day when the Sun stopped moving, how can these characterizations be made to cohere with the view of nature that philosophers develop? This kind of question captured the attention of numerous philosophers and theologians working in numerous institutional and political contexts throughout the century. In what follows, I consider three famous attempts to deal with these issues, centered on the work of Galileo, Descartes, and Boyle, before turning to the unique approach developed by Newton.

Perhaps the most famous attempt at accommodating religion and natural philosophy was Galileo's 1615 letter to the Grand Duchess Christina, written just 1 year before the Church officially censured Copernican astronomical doctrine. Galileo wrote to Christina because in an earlier conversation with Castelli, she had objected to Castelli's Copernicanism on the grounds that it is incompatible with scriptural passages such as the one in Joshua, which indicates that the sun once stopped moving in the sky (Joshua 10: 12–14). Galileo's extremely long letter to Christina belongs to a tradition of theological interpretation that follows in the footsteps of Saint Augustine's *literal* biblical commentary, the *De Genesi ad Litteram*, which was written in the early fifth century in an attempt, among other things, to find a means of squaring natural knowledge with scriptural interpretation. Following Augustine's example, which he frequently cited, Galileo sought to defuse the tension between the latest thinking in natural philosophy—in Galileo's case, this included a Copernican-influenced conception of the world—and various scriptural passages.

The passage from Joshua, which received considerable attention from Galileo and his various adversaries (Blackwell 1991, 68–70), reads as follows:

Then spake Joshua to the Lord in the day when the Lord delivered up the Amorites before the children of Israel, and he said in the sight of Israel, Sun, stand thou still upon Gibeon; and thou, Moon, in the valley of Ajalon. And the sun stood still, and the moon stayed, until the people had avenged themselves upon their enemies. Is not this written in the book of Jasher? So the sun stood still in the midst of heaven, and hasted not to go down about a whole day. And there was no day like that before it or after it, that the Lord hearkened unto the voice of a man: for the Lord fought for Israel. And Joshua returned, all Israel with him, unto the camp to Gilgal. (*Joshua* 10: 12–14, Marks 2012, vol. 1: 418–419)

This passage does not explicitly mention the motion or rest of the earth, but it clearly indicates that the sun is in motion, since its motion was *stopped* on one important—and apparently unique—day in history to allow fighting to continue for a longer period.[6] If the Copernican view includes the contention that the sun is at rest at the center of the solar system, then presumably it would not be possible to cease its motion, as the passage indicates. For his part, Galileo makes his understanding of the astronomical facts perfectly clear near the very beginning of his lengthy letter to Christina: "I hold the sun to be situated motionless in the center of the revolution of the celestial orbs while the earth rotates on its axis and revolves about the sun" (Galileo 1959, 177). What can be done to resolve the conflict between that view and the Joshua passage?

Galileo was nothing if not clever. As is well known, he attempted to show that despite appearances to the contrary, the Joshua passage is actually easier to square with the Copernican view than with the Ptolemaic one. But of course, that solution to the problem may simply be an artifact of the particularities of the Joshua passage. Galileo understood this, so he did not put all his eggs in this basket. That is, he understood that there could in fact be other scriptural passages that are simply incompatible with some claim about nature made by a philosopher studying motion. So he grasped the need for a more general conception of how philosophers studying nature, especially those *moderns* employing mathematical techniques to understand the motions of terrestrial and celestial objects (Palmerino 2006), can approach the topic of scriptural interpretation, given the potential for conflict. He understood that the philosopher cannot simply contend that nature and the motions of its objects fall under his purview and leave scriptural interpretation entirely to the theologians. Instead, he had to articulate some conception of how scriptural interpretation ought to be approached in order to lessen its tendency to conflict with the new philosophy. One of his prominent tactics is to rely on a particular construal of the old saying that scripture is written in the language of the common person. Referring to a passage from Aquinas that he has just quoted, he writes:

Now from this I think one can obviously argue that analogously the Holy Scripture had a much greater reason to call the sun moving and the earth motionless. For if we test the understanding of common people, we shall find them much more incapable of becoming convinced of the sun's rest and earth's motion than of the fact that the space surrounding us is full of air; therefore, if the sacred authors refrained from attempting to persuade the people about this point, which was not that difficult for their understanding, it seems very reasonable to think that they followed the same style in regard to other propositions which are much more recondite.

Indeed, Copernicus himself knew how much our imagination is dominated by an old habit and by a way of conceiving things which is already familiar to us since infancy, and so he did not want to increase the confusion and difficulty of his abstraction. Thus, after first demonstrating that the motions which appear to us as belonging to the sun or the firmament really belong to the earth, then, in the process of compiling their tables and applying them in practice, he speaks of them as belonging to the sun and to the part of heaven above the planets; for example, he speaks of the rising and setting of the sun and of the stars, of changes in the obliquity of the zodiac and in the equinoctial points, of the mean motion and the anomaly and the posthaphaeresis of the sun, and other similar things, which really belong to the earth. We call facts these things which appear to us as facts because, being attached to the earth, we are part of all its motions, and consequently we cannot directly detect these things in it but find it useful to consider it in relation to the heavenly bodies in which they appear to us. Therefore, note how appropriate it is to accommodate our usual manner of thinking. (Galileo 2010, 132–133)

Galileo attempts here to articulate the basis for a distinction between the characterizations of space, time, and motion within natural philosophy and those found in scripture. Whereas the goal of the former is to describe the true system of the world, the goal of the latter is to describe the world in terms that are familiar to the common person, since the Bible was written with such readers in mind. The contention that the Holy Scripture is written in a *vulgare* language, the language of the *commoner*, is perfectly familiar: its well-known slogan, "Scriptura humane loquitur," hails from the thirteenth century and is itself a translation of a much older Hebrew interpretive guide (Funkenstein 1986, 213–218). The related idea that this interpretive guide should be understood specifically to mean that scripture describes space, time, and motion as they appear to ordinary people was not unique to Galileo or even to philosophers at this time: for instance, the theologian Foscarini had made a similar claim (McMullin 1998, 281 and appendix VI to Blackwell 1991). No less an authority than Augustine had prefigured this approach in his literal Genesis commentary. For instance, he wrote (see McMullin 1998, 297) that we must hold to "the pronouncement of St. Paul …that 'star differs from star in glory (brightness).' But, of course, one may reply, without attacking St. Paul, 'they differ in glory to the eyes of men on earth.'" Since it appears to us as if the earth is at rest and the sun revolves around it, with its emergence in the morning causing day and its disappearance below the horizon in the evening causing night, the Bible describes the world in precisely this way. Since the Bible is not an astronomical text, it does not attempt to provide a complete description of the heavenly bodies and of their motions; that is the task of the philosopher studying nature. This general conception, in turn, enables the philosopher to avoid problems involving texts that seem incompatible with some astronomical conception like Copernicus's. As we will see, this approach toward accommodation is mirrored in Newton's views.

Alas, Galileo's arguments in his letter to Christina did not prevent the wheels of history from turning (McMullin 1998, 319). Neither did the fact that Galileo was in the good graces of the future Pope (as we will see, that fact is reflected in Descartes's astonishment at what happened next). Pope Paul V had Cardinal Robert Bellarmine, probably the leading Catholic theologian of that time, meet with Galileo personally in 1616 to discuss Copernican astronomical ideas, but this did not save Galileo from future troubles.[7] When Gregory died in 1623, Barberini became Pope Urban the VIII, and in May 1630, Pope Urban met privately with Galileo, another sign of his stature in Italy in that era (Drake 2001, 86–87). In February 1632, the *Dialogo* was published in Firenze. The *Dialogue* includes a detailed analysis of the tides—the sloshing of water on the surface of the earth—along with the clear implication that the earth must be rotating. Despite his previous and by then well-known attempts in the letter to Christina to show that scriptural passages concerning the earth's various motions are not actually incompatible with astronomical pronouncements to the contrary, given the distinct role that scripture and astronomy are intended to play in Galileo's view of human knowledge, he was well aware of the problems with explicitly advocating a Copernican view as the true astronomical system of the world. The meeting with Bellarmine in 1616 would have ensured that much. So to guard against criticism, Galileo included in the *Dialogue* Simplicio's statement that God could create the tides without making the earth move at all, suggesting that no astronomical analysis could decisively prove how the divine agent chose to form the solar system (Galileo 1953, 464). After Salviati briefly concurs with this sentiment, Sagredo declares that the 4 days of argument are over, and the book ends. In his recent biography, Heilbron judges this move at the book's conclusion to be Galileo's principal mistake: by placing this comment in the mouth of Simplicio, rather than Sagredo or Salviati, Galileo had given Pope Urban and others ample reason to think that he did not really believe that this was a possible physical situation and, therefore, that he had not really succeeded in dealing with the two world systems *equally*, *mathematically*, and *hypothetically*, as required (Heilbron 2010, 302–303). His insistence in the preface to the reader that he had taken "the Copernican side" but considered it "a pure mathematical hypothesis" that could be defended successfully against Aristotelian objections was apparently also unpersuasive (Galileo 1953, 5). So in August 1632, the Pope convened a special panel to review Galileo's case, and in June of the next year, Galileo was placed under house arrest. Obviously, this momentous event overshadowed Galileo's attempt at reconciliation in the letter to Christina. It also had a huge impact on the life and work of Descartes.

In November 1633, Descartes reacted to Galileo's predicament by deciding to withdraw his newly completed work in natural philosophy, *Le Monde*, from publication. In a famous letter to Mersenne, he wrote:

> In fact I had intended to send you my *World* [*Le Monde*] as a New Year gift, and only two weeks ago I was quite determined to send you at least a part of it, if the whole work could not be copied in time. But I have to say that in the mean time I took the trouble to inquire in Leiden and Amsterdam whether Galileo's

World System was available, for I thought I had heard that it was published in Italy last year. I was told that it had indeed been published but that all the copies had immediately been burnt at Rome, and that Galileo had been convicted and fined. I was so astonished at this that I almost decided to burn all my papers or at least to let no one see them. For I could not imagine that he—an Italian and, as I understand, in the good graces of the Pope—could have been made a criminal for any other reason than that he tried, as he no doubt did, to establish that the Earth moves. I know that some Cardinals had already censured this view, but I thought I had heard it said that all the same it was being taught publicly even in Rome. I must admit that if the view is false, so too are the entire foundations of my philosophy, for it can be demonstrated from them quite clearly. And it is so closely interwoven in every part of my treatise that I could not remove it without rendering the whole work defective. But for all the world I did not want to publish a discourse in which a single word could be found that the Church would have disapproved of; so I preferred to suppress it rather than to publish it in a mutilated form. (AT 1: 270–271)

It has often been noted that Descartes was in Holland at the time and therefore far beyond the reaches of the Vatican; moreover, Mersenne's circle in Paris included philosophers who did not take Galileo's predicament to constrain their theorizing about the earth's motion. So what explains Descartes's suppression of his major work? The most common interpretation is that Descartes overreacted to Galileo's arrest and that he took the Vatican's pronouncements to provide what I will call a nonrational constraint on his theorizing. That is, he had reached the conclusion that the earth moves on the basis of independent philosophical reasoning, but refrained from endorsing this conclusion on (his own perhaps inflated sense of relevant) political grounds. On this reading, theological constraints have a political cast—they do not give the philosopher a reason to doubt the earth's motion. In this respect, Descartes would fall into Galileo's philosophical camp in a significant respect: he would regard theology as imposing a nonrational constraint on theories of motion and would differ from Galileo only in his method of avoiding political entanglements, perhaps learning from Galileo that suppression is wiser than caveat-laced publication.

Yet there is another interpretation of Descartes, one bolstered by his subsequent correspondence with Mersenne. For instance, in a lost letter of February 1634, Descartes tells Mersenne that he has abandoned his work of the past 4 years "in order to give my obedience to the Church, since it has proscribed the view that the earth moves." Two months later, in a letter that did reach Mersenne, Descartes explains his position further: he is under the impression—which Heilbron says was inaccurate (2010, 320–323)—that Galileo's views on the earth's motion were condemned "comme heretique," adding that he would not "wish, for anything in the world, to maintain" his views "against the authority of the Church." Finally, in August 1634, in a further letter to Mersenne (AT 1, 303–306), Descartes quotes from a document printed at Liège concerning the Church's judgment of Galileo: it indicates not that Galileo expressed a heretical opinion, as Descartes had said earlier, but only that he was under "strong suspicion of heresy"—"vehementer suspectum videri de hoeresi"—for following a doctrine that is "falsam & contrariam sacris ac divinas scripturis" (AT 1: 306). Descartes may have been unclear on the exact status of the judgment. But he does make strong statements of obedience to Church doctrine. These facts may suggest that Descartes did not misread the political situation within Holland, but rather that he suppressed *Le Monde* because as a believing Catholic, he took Church doctrine to give him a reason to doubt his view of the earth's motion.

Each of these two interpretations is consistent with Descartes's next maneuver: instead of finding a way to maintain his conception of the earth's motion à la Galileo—say, by adding the caveat that he is treating that motion merely hypothetically or mathematically, without describing the true motions of planetary bodies in the solar system—he alters his theory in the *Principles* of 1644, and he does so in part by providing a substantive metaphysical foundation for the physics of motion, something essentially lacking in *Le Monde* (Gaukroger 2002, 28–29). He chose an intriguing route: he would find a way to argue that the earth's motion could no longer be *demonstrated* from his principles.

As we saw in Chapter 4, Descartes's *Principles* introduces a novel distinction between what he calls the *vulgar* and the *proper* conception of motion. In the ordinary or *vulgare* sense, motion is "nothing other than *the action by which a body passes from one place to another*" [nihil aliud est quàm *actio, quâ corpus aliquod ex uno loco in alium migrat*] (AT VIII-1, 53). Descartes views this ordinary understanding of motion as problematic because its employment of *place* may presuppose the possibility of empty space, which Descartes now regards as prohibited on metaphysical grounds, and because it treats motion as the *action* by which a body is transferred from place to place, which may conflict with the principle of inertia articulated in the first two laws of the *Principles*.

In the next section (AT VIII-1, 53–54), Descartes jettisons the problematic notions of *place* and *action*, defining motion in the *true sense* as follows:

> If, on the other hand, we consider what should be understood by *motion*, not in common usage but in accordance with the truth of the matter, and if our aim is to assign a determinate nature to it, we may say that *motion is the transfer of one piece of matter, or one body, from the vicinity of the others which immediately touch it, and which we consider to be at rest, to the vicinity of others* [ex vicinia eorum corporum, quoe illud immediate contingent & tanquam quiescentia spectantur, in viciniam aliorum].

This distinction, in turn, helps to enable Descartes's famous maneuver regarding the earth's motion, which he makes in section 28 of part three of the *Principles*:

> The earth does not move, properly speaking, any more than the planets, although they are all transported by the heaven [Terram, propriè loquendo,

non moveri, nec ullos Planetas, quamvis à coelo transferantur]. Here we must bear in mind what I said above about the nature of motion (part II, section 25), namely that if we speak properly and in accordance with the truth of things, then motion is simply the transfer of one body from the vicinity of the other bodies which are in immediate contact with it, and which are regarded as being at rest, to the vicinity of others. But in accord with ordinary usage, it often happens that any action whereby a body travels from one place to another is called motion; and in this sense it may be said that the same thing at the same time moves and does not move, depending on how we determine its location. It follows that there is no motion in the case of the earth or even the other planets properly speaking; for they are not transferred from the vicinity of those parts of the heaven with which they are in immediate contact, in so far as these parts are considered as being at rest. Such a transfer would require them to move away from all these parts at the same time, which does not occur; but since the celestial material is fluid, at any given time different groups of particles move away from the planet with which they are in contact, by a motion which should be attributed solely to the particles, not to the planet; similarly, the partial transfers of water and air which occur on the surface of the earth are not normally attributed to the earth itself, but to the parts of water and air which are transferred. (AT VIII-1: 90–91)

Hence, for Descartes, there is a change in spatial relations between the earth and the vortex that surrounds it, in particular between it and the vortical particles that constitute the vortex, but the motion that involves this change of relations must be attributed to the particles rather than to the earth. This reflects Descartes's insistence that the motion in question be attributed to one and only one (set of) objects.[8] Descartes's view is perfectly consistent with the idea that the earth bears continually changing spatial relations to the sun, since he thinks that the sun lies at the center of the vortices that *carry* the earth and the other planets around the sun (section 30). These spatial relations would include distance relations, since Descartes denies that the planetary orbits are perfectly circular: hence the earth's distance to the sun, or to the sun's center, will vary as it is carried along by the vortex.

Descartes's view of the planetary bodies and of the earth is confusing. Since he claims in section 30 that the earth is *carried* around the sun by its vortex, like the other planets, there must be some sense in which the earth is moving, and yet according to his *proper* definition of motion, as he continually reminds his readers, the earth is not in motion. Descartes hints at an awareness of this puzzle in section 29 when he writes that if he seems to attribute some motion to the earth, he is speaking loosely, much as one might loosely say that passengers sleeping on the deck of a ship "nevertheless go from Calais to Dover" because the ship sails along the English Channel. Part of Descartes's motivation here might be to say that since the passengers are not the cause of their traveling from Calais to Dover, the motion must be attributed strictly speaking solely to the ship, and not to them; he hints at just this point in section 26, when he notes that he wishes to deny that the earth has any "innate tendency to motion." Thus although the earth is carried through the heavens by the vortex, it itself does not cause this to happen, and so the motion in question must be attributed to the vortex (to its particles) rather than to the earth.

There are two obvious objections to Descartes's view, the first of which can be found in Newton's Scholium in *Principia Mathematica*.[9] First, his view seems to conflict with common sense. To use Descartes's own example: if I fall asleep on the deck of a ship sailing from England to France across the Channel, then surely I move along with the ship, even if I am not the cause of my motion. It is not merely true that it is "possible to say" that I traveled to France; I genuinely did! Of course, in employing his distinction between the ordinary and the proper conceptions of motion, Descartes shows that he is perfectly well aware that his understanding of the earth's motion reflects the fact that his view conflicts with common sense. So he might be untroubled by this point.

The second objection is more serious. If properly speaking the earth is at rest, then why postulate the vortex theory of planetary motion in the first place? After all, the principal guiding reason to postulate a vortex surrounding the earth is that mechanical philosophers wish to explain the earth's solar orbit through some mechanism involving contact action—as Leibniz makes clear in his vortex theory in the *Tentamen*. The goal is ipso facto to explain why the earth exhibits a deviation from the tangent to that orbit, which is its expected trajectory given Descartes's own first two laws of nature. If the earth is truly at rest, it has no true solar orbit, and so there is no reason to postulate the vortex.

At it happened, Descartes's denial of the earth's motion puzzled his readers (Gaukroger 2002, 142), including Henry More, who just a few years later regarded Descartes as altering his theory of motion based on nonrational (political or theological) constraints.[10] But that is not the only interpretation.[11] The letters to Mersenne might suggest that Descartes reacted to a rational constraint on the theory of motion, or at least that he took himself to have a reason to alter his philosophy in a way that might eventually lead to a new conception of motion, whereby it would follow that according to the correct philosophical view, the earth does not move, although it does experience changing spatial relations with the vortical particles that swirl around it and indeed with the sun. In any event, there is no doubt that on Descartes's considered view, the proper philosophical understanding of motion, along with some empirical facts, indicates that the earth is at rest.

Stepping back, we find two different approaches in Galileo and Descartes to the problem of motion within nature and scripture.[12] Galileo's approach is to develop a theory of the earth's motion that is unconstrained by questions about scriptural interpretation—such as how to interpret the Joshua passage quoted earlier—and by the pronouncements of the Church. The next step is to provide a guide to scriptural interpretation that removes any tension between that theory of motion and the literal text of scripture. There are many means of doing so. One way of removing the tension is to say that scripture describes how things *appear* to be moving in various ways from the vantage point of the earth's surface, leaving the task of describing the actual motions of the planetary bodies to the mathematically inclined philosopher. Descartes's approach is distinct. He avoids one potential tension between what philosophers say about motion in nature and what scripture says about it (at least according to the Church) by developing a theory of motion according to which the earth is actually at rest within its vortex, which latter is itself postulated on philosophical grounds involving ideas about the laws of nature and the possible causal interactions that can produce certain physical situations. This maneuver may reflect Descartes's genuine belief that the Church's rejection of Copernican ideas actually tells against their potential truth, but it might also reflect aspects of his theory of motion that he endorses on distinct grounds. What is clear is this: what lies at the heart of Descartes's approach is his novel distinction between an ordinary and a philosophical way of thinking about motion, for the latter enables him to determine that according to the proper concept, the earth is truly at rest.

We are now in a position briefly to indicate what is so intriguing about Newton's position. He develops a unique blend of elements of Galileo's and Descartes's views. In particular, he strongly emphasizes the notion that whereas scriptural passages describe appearances involving the motions of objects, it is philosophers studying nature who describe the realities of motion connected with these appearances. In that way, he takes a leaf out of Galileo's book. But he also borrows Descartes's novel distinction between the ordinary and the proper way of thinking about motion (reconceived, of course). Finally, he decides to connect these two ideas in a unique way, contending that the ordinary person's ideas about space, time, and motion concern the appearances of objects; philosophers thinking about space, time, and motion deal instead with true quantities.

The fact that Newton's view reflects key elements of the Galilean and the Cartesian approach to thinking about motion within nature and scripture should not blind us to the deep differences in their respective historical contexts. Regardless of their various religious differences, Galileo and Descartes were both Catholic and obviously at least concerned with evading any conflict with theologians or the Vatican, if not convinced that Church doctrine was actually a guide to the truth. And Galileo's interlocutors in the Church hierarchy and their supporters were obviously concerned to ensure that he did not give succor to the Protestant notion that lay people can interpret scripture without the authority of the Church (Blackwell 1991, 36–39), especially given the fact that the Council of Trent had proclaimed the authority of the Church in such matters. Newton, on the other hand, was not only working within Anglican England, he was ferociously anti-Papist, and so such concerns could not have been further from his mind. Nonetheless, Galileo and Descartes were crucial to Newton for an obvious reason. He never took Aristotelian ideas about motion very seriously: he regarded these two predecessors as having vanquished Scholasticism and as having begun to articulate aspects of the correct theory of motion (with Galileo obtaining much of the official credit, but Descartes obviously playing a central role behind the scenes—see Cohen 1999,

113). Moreover, as we will see, the fact that Newton worked within Anglican England is less important than might at first appear: Newton did not need any institution such as the Catholic Church to impose any kind of constraints on his theorizing about motion, whether rational or nonrational, for he himself was deeply concerned with the question of how to reconcile scriptural descriptions of the motions of the heavenly bodies with the latest thinking about such matters in philosophy. With Descartes, as we have seen, there is the possibility that he regarded Church doctrine concerning Copernicanism as a guide to the truth, or at least as a rational constraint on a philosophical understanding of the solar system. But with Newton, there is no doubt that he regarded scripture itself as providing a direct rational constraint on theorizing. The reason, as we will see, is that Newton took the bible to be literally true.

Galileo and Descartes were not the only natural philosophers who could have provided Newton with examples of how natural philosophy might be conceived of as intersecting with theology in some way. Working in the generation after Galileo, and especially in the wake of Descartes's achievements in natural philosophy, the British natural philosopher Robert Boyle developed a novel conception of theology's relationship with natural philosophy, one that was influential in Newton's day. Since Boyle was not concerned with astronomy or celestial mechanics, as Galileo and Descartes were, but rather with what he called *chymistry*, or what we would regard as protochemistry, focusing on questions about the air and its features in particular, he was not confronted with the Copernican question. He was concerned instead with the relation between the two disciplines from a distinct point of view, one that tackled general questions about the relation between ideas issuing from faith and those issuing from the study of nature. In 1674, Boyle published his *Excellency of theology compared with natural philosophy*, a book that attempts to indicate the details of the distinction between these two fields (Boyle, *Works* 8: 12–28). Boyle seems to think that nature can disclose aspects of the divine being and that these can be learned by the natural philosopher, as Newton would argue later, but he also contends that scripture discloses much more about God's attributes than one can discover from studying the natural world as he does. To know the nature and will of God, we require revelation. And in tandem, he claims that it is revelation, and not nature or its philosophical interpreters, which provides us with insight into crucial topics like the immortality of the soul, the concept of sin, the ideas of heaven and hell, and so on.[13] Unlike the topics of natural philosophy—the nature of the *spring* of the air, the possibility of creating a vacuum, and so on—these topics are of universal interest and import. So in this text, Boyle's project is not so much to seek accommodation between theology and natural philosophy, but to indicate the superiority of the former over the latter in certain limited, yet central, respects. Elsewhere, he made the familiar point that Aristotelianism, which teaches that nature is eternal and which enables one to conceive of nature as autonomous from the divine, is a poor candidate for natural philosophers working within the context of early modern Christianity (Hunter 2009, 82–84). He took the new natural philosophy—*corpuscularianism* or the mechanical philosophy—to be much better suited for the project of accommodation. Boyle was certainly the most important natural philosopher in England in the middle of the century, so everyone else, including the young Isaac Newton, worked in his wake, and Newton took his views seriously.

Thus, in the 1670s, three influential but radically different approaches toward philosophy's relation to theology and its questions were available to Newton. First, Galileo's famous attempt to defend the autonomy of natural philosophy to answer questions about nature by arguing that scripture must be interpreted to cohere with truths found by philosophers ended in a distinct failure. Second, Galileo's failure dramatically altered Descartes's plans, ultimately leading him to develop a complex and novel conception of natural philosophy's dependence upon metaphysics, one that enabled him to evade the Copernican problems that had bedeviled Galileo. Third, philosophers such as Boyle were able to eschew the Copernican problem altogether, leaving them free to articulate a conception of theology's priority over natural philosophy in a way that would nonetheless leave philosophers autonomous when studying various aspects of nature lacking any theological import, such as the nature of the air. Despite having three influential models of theology's relation to philosophy available to him, beginning already in 1680, and continuing until the end of his life, Newton decided to develop his own unique conception of this relation by articulating an insightful theory of motion that enabled him to tackle the Copernican problem without encountering any theological difficulties, even while preserving a kind of autonomy for natural philosophy at the same time.

7.1   Newton's Unique Approach to Theology and Natural Philosophy

Newton was a good Protestant in so far as he firmly believed that an individual could develop his own detailed interpretation of scripture without the mediation of any institutional authority. Indeed, he greatly doubted the institutional authorities that existed in England at the time.[14] And on the basis of his reading of scripture, Newton concluded at an early age that there are questions about how one can render consistent what the Bible says about space, time, and motion with what the philosopher says about them on the basis of studying nature. Indeed, he shows interest in that theme even in his undergraduate days.[15] This poses a problem: if Newton develops a concept of true motion that accords with the newly discovered laws of nature, as we have seen in Chapters 4 and 5, then one wonders whether he can use that *same* notion to interpret the Bible's proclamations. His law-based conception of true motion, along with basic empirical facts, would seem to indicate that the earth truly moves, as Galileo had believed. One can be confident that Newton would not choose Descartes's escape route, but what other choice did he have?

As it turned out, Newton's first, detailed attempt to tackle these questions arose not in the context of *Principia Mathematica*, but earlier in that decade, when one of Newton's acquaintances from Cambridge,[16] Thomas Burnet, corresponded with him. In the beginning of 1681, Burnet published a book, *Telluris theoria sacra*, or the *Sacred Theory of the Earth*,[17] and he sought Newton's opinion on certain philosophical questions that intersected with questions concerning scriptural interpretation. The *Sacred Theory* became extremely popular: it went through several editions, was translated from Latin to English, and by 1700 had accrued no fewer than *thirty* published replies.[18] Among those replies were books by Erasmus Warren and William Whiston (Newton's successor as Lucasian Professor and a professed Newtonian), each of which led to book-length replies by Burnet and further replies by his critics (Force 1994, 196, Porter 1977, 83). Burnet tells us that his theory is *sacred* because it treats historical issues discussed in scripture, but he notes that using scripture rather than reason to understand the natural world is problematic because we might claim to find doctrines in scripture that we later discover through reason to be false. So reason will be Burnet's first guide, and scripture will be used only where it falls short (Reedy 1985, 43*ff*). To give one illustrative example: Burnet argues that Noah's flood—a topic of great interest also to Mersenne's circle (Popkin 1968, 13)—could not have involved a sufficient mass of water to cover the world's mountainous regions, so the early earth must have had a smooth surface. This conclusion is the result of rational argument, since scripture does not describe this natural fact. In his rational explanations of natural phenomena, Burnet appears to have followed many Cartesian ideas and built a reputation in England as an important Cartesian-influenced philosopher in the 1660s and 1670s, having discussed Cartesianism in his lectures on natural philosophy at Christ's College.[19]

On Christmas Eve in 1680, Newton wrote to Burnet with some criticisms of his attempt to accommodate the biblical description of the earth's creation with the current teachings of what Burnet calls *philosophy*.[20] Newton apparently informed Burnet of various reasons that *Divines* would resist his theory of the earth and its formation, especially on the grounds that the theory conflicts with the account of the creation found in Genesis. On January 13, 1681, Burnet wrote a lengthy reply, arguing that if scripture is interpreted correctly, it need not be understood as conflicting with his theory:

And if all Divines were as rational & judicious as your self I should not fear that this would retard the reception of the theory, as you suggest it may. For I would ask them in the first place whether Moses his Hexameron or 6 days description of the creation, doth respect the whole universe or only the sublunary world, all the heavens and the heaven of heavens, & all the host of them, stars or angels; or our Earth only & the orb or heaven that belongs to it: And I would not stir one step further till that was determined between us. Now it being demonstrable I think that the whole universe was not made out of the Mosaical Chaos, I would in the next place ask them whether the Sun,

Moon & stars mentioned [in] the fourth day, were made out of the Chaos, & then first brought into being when the Earth was formed? If they grant that this Chaos did not extend to the whole universe, then they must grant that the Sun, Moon & Stars were not made out of it; but are mentioned as things necessary to make this Earth an habitable world. From which concession I would infer two things, first that the distinction of 6 days in the Mosaical formation of the world is no physical reality, seeing one of the 6 you see is taken up with a non-reality, the creation of these things that existed before. Secondly I infer from this, that as the distinction of 6 days is no physical reality so neither is this draught of the creation physical but Ideal, or if you will, moral. Seeing it is not physically true that the Sun, Moon & Stars were made at that time, viz. 5 or 6000 years since when the Earth was formed. And if it be Ideal in one part, it may in some proportion be ideal in every part. (*Correspondence* 2: 323–324)

At the end of his letter, Burnet indicates what had spurred him on to write such a long and detailed account: Newton had insisted to Burnet (presumably in the lost letter) that we must regard the Mosaic characterization of the creation as a *physical description*. Burnet resists this view, contending instead that the Mosaic description—according to which, of course, the world was created in 6 days—cannot be squared with the teachings of philosophy and that we must therefore regard Moses as providing us not with a description of what Burnet calls *physical reality*, but rather with a *metaphorical* or *ideal* description. The business of *philosophy* is to describe physical reality.

After Burnet's extensive defense of this overarching conception of Biblical interpretation and its connection with philosophical truth, one might expect Newton to endorse the *Sacred theory*. Later that month, however, Newton strongly rejected Burnet's interpretive method in a lengthy and detailed letter:

As to Moses I do not think his description of the creation either philosophical or feigned, but that he described realities in a language artificially adapted to the sense of the vulgar. Thus where he speaks of two great lights I suppose he means their apparent, not real greatness. So when he tells us God placed those lights in the firmament, he speaks I suppose of their apparent not of their real place, his business being not to correct the vulgar notions in matters philosophical but to adapt a description of the creation as handsomely as he could to the sense and capacity of the vulgar. (January 1681, *Correspondence* 2: 331)

Later in the same letter, Newton elaborates:

Consider therefore whether any one who understood the process of the creation and designed to accommodate to the vulgar not an Ideal or poetical but a true description of it as succinctly and theologically as Moses has done, without omitting any thing material which the vulgar have a notion of or describing any being further than the vulgar have a notion of it, could mend that description which Moses has given us. If it be said that the expression of making and setting two great lights in the firmament is more poetical than natural: so also are some other expressions of Moses, as where he tells us the windows or floodgates of heaven were opened Gen 7 and afterwards stopped again Gen 8 and yet the things signified by such figurative expressions are not Ideal or moral but true. For Moses accommodating his words to the gross conceptions of the vulgar, describes things much after the manner as one of the vulgar would have been inclined to do had he lived and seen the whole series of what Moses describes. (January 1681, *Correspondence* 2: 333)

Newton forcefully rejects Burnet's tendency to rely on metaphorical or allegorical interpretations, arguing instead that Moses provides a description of the creation that is not metaphorical or poetical, but *literal*. Burnet insists that Moses accommodates the ordinary reader of Genesis by describing events in a way and in an order that they can understand, even if the real order was distinct and even if some of the events described were not physically real. Newton objects, contending that we cannot interpret Moses as describing something that happened *neither in reality nor in appearance*. He argues instead that Moses accommodates the common reader not by altering the order of events nor by providing an ideal description of events that were not physically real, but rather by accurately and literally describing the way that the real events would have *appeared* to the common person if she had been present when they occurred. Nothing is described that did not occur; what is described is the way that things appeared, and not how they really were.

But what distinction is Newton really making here? At one point in his letter, he focuses on the third day of creation. In Genesis 1: 9–13, we read that on the third day, God divided the land from the waters under the heavens, calling the gathering of the waters the *seas*. Now for Burnet, this description of what happened on the third day need not be understood as a description of *physical reality*, but rather as an ideal characterization, one that fits with what he later calls *an artificial scheme of narration*. In reply, Newton does not insist that Moses's description of the third day must be understood as a description of physical reality; rather, he objects to the idea that it is an *ideal* description in the precise sense that it is *neither* a description of reality nor a description of the appearances. That is, from Newton's point of view, where Burnet errs is in arguing that Moses provides a narrative about the creation that ordinary readers can understand by describing neither appearance nor reality. For Newton, if Moses does not describe reality it is precisely because he describes the appearances instead. His interpretive method is to say that Genesis tells the common person how things would have looked to them on the third day of creation, rather than how things really were on that day.

Whereas Burnet's hermeneutical approach is highly flexible, enabling him to argue that the Bible often describes neither appearance nor reality, but rather provides morally or metaphorically true narratives, Newton's approach is strictly limited, forcing him to say that the Bible describes the appearances. So in early

1681, Newton wished to endorse the literal truth of scripture, and he takes biblical language to be the commoner's language, which characterizes apparent places and sizes and, indeed, appearances more generally. As is also well known, Newton was working within the seventeenth-century Protestant tradition of providing literal interpretations of the Bible, rather than the metaphorical or allegorical interpretations favored by many interpreters working broadly in the Catholic tradition at that time. It is possible that Newton regarded Burnet as having been influenced by Cartesianism not just in his philosophical views, but also in his theological ones, especially in his penchant for finding accommodation between the two disciplines by favoring metaphorical or ideal interpretations of scripture.[21]

But this raises a serious problem for Newton: in a long and detailed correspondence with Burnet, he has argued that scriptural characterizations of space, time, and motion within nature (including its history, dating back to the creation) must not, in the first instance, be understood as metaphorically, allegorically, or morally true. They are to be read as literally true. The consequence would seem all too clear: if scripture is literally true and if, for example, Joshua describes a day when the sun stopped moving, then that would appear to conflict with the Copernican view of the world advocated by many of Newton's predecessors, including most prominently Galileo. And that would appear to box Newton in, requiring him to make something like Descartes's choice by developing a theory of motion according to which the earth is actually at rest (and, relatedly, according to which the sun moves). He could potentially avoid this fate if he borrowed another leaf from Galileo's book, arguing that the Copernican view of the solar system is in fact more closely compatible with the Joshua passage than any version of the Ptolemaic view could be. However, Newton chose instead to pursue a different path.

The issues discussed in depth with Burnet in 1680–1681 continued to preoccupy Newton over the next few years while he was working on the *Principia's* predecessor text, *De Motu corporum*, its original title before Halley and Newton agreed on altering it in 1686. As the title suggests, in this text Newton developed a general theory of motion, with concomitant ideas about space and time. In "De Motu corporum in mediis regulariter cedentibus," written in 1684–1685, we find the following intriguing passage:

> Definition 18: The representatives of times, spaces, motions, speeds and forces are any quantities whatsoever proportional to the things represented.

> The aim of explaining all these things at length is that the reader may be freed from certain vulgar prejudices and, imbued with the distinct principles of mechanics, may agree in what follows to distinguish carefully from each other quantities which are both absolute and relative, a thing very necessary since all phenomena depend on absolute quantities. But ordinary people who fail to abstract thought from sensible appearances always speak of relative quantities, so much so that it would be absurd for wise men or even Prophets to speak to them otherwise. Hence both the sacred writings and theological writings are always to be understood in terms of relative quantities, and he

who would on this account bandy words with philosophers concerning the absolute motions of natural things would be laboring under a gross misapprehension.[22] (Herivel 1965, 306, 312)

Here, we find a remarkable continuation of the argument Newton makes in his correspondence with Burnet, with Newton now adding a general distinction between absolute and relative quantities to his original distinction between real and apparent location and real and apparent size (*greatness*). In this manuscript, Newton also makes a key move: he connects the idea that ordinary people think about space, time, and motion in terms of *relative quantities* with the idea that scripture is written precisely in order to communicate with people who conceive of space, time, and motion in that way. Here, we see the connection between the Galilean claim—from the letter to Christina—that scripture describes only the way that things appear to us with the Cartesian claim—from the *Principles*—that ordinary people think about motion differently than philosophers.

This same issue made its way into the *Principia* already in its first edition of 1687 (the relevant passage is found in all three editions of the text). This passage—especially its sentence concerning scripture—is typically ignored by commentators (Cohen (1969) and Rynasiewicz (1995a, b) are exceptions), but it fits perfectly within the progression of texts outlined earlier:

> Relative quantities, therefore, are not the actual quantities whose names they bear, but are those sensible measures of them (true or false) that are commonly used in place of the quantities measured. But if the meanings of words are to be defined by usage, then by the names "time," "space," "place," and "motion" it is these sensible measures which should properly be understood; it will be out of the ordinary and purely mathematical if the quantities being measured are understood here. Accordingly those who there interpret these words as referring to the quantities being measured do violence to the Scriptures. And those who confuse true quantities with their relations and common measures corrupt no less mathematics and philosophy. (Newton 1972, vol. 1: 51–52)

There are aspects of Newton's discussion that can be confusing, so they demand explanation before larger issues can be tackled. First of all, Newton thinks of space, time, and motion as *quantities*. That may sound odd, but it is connected with his idea that we can measure (say) the space between two objects, the time between two events, and the motion of some object across space over time. There are many questions about the precise sense in which these three items should be thought of as quantities, but they are not relevant for our analysis. Second of all, Newton thinks of what he calls *relative* spaces, times, and motions as sensible *measures* of these quantities. For instance, when one looks at one's watch, one measures the quantity *time*, and one does so in virtue of the relations between the elements of the watch (the face, the hands, the numbers on the dial, etc.). It may be the case that in the *De Motu corporum* draft quoted earlier, Newton thought that there are both absolute and relative quantities; however, in *Principia Mathematica*, he contends that whereas absolute space and absolute time *are* the quantities themselves, relative spaces and relative times are *measures* of those quantities.

In an unpublished manuscript, "An Account of the Systeme of the World," which is a four-page English popularization of the principal themes of the *Principia*, Newton returns to the themes noted earlier.[23] What this text indicates, among other things, is that the brief discussion of scripture in the Scholium on space and time represents what Newton regarded as a key theme of his text. The correspondence with Burnet and the *De Motu* draft suggest that this represents a continuity of his thought. He writes:

> **I Scripture abused to prove the immoveableness of the globe of the Earth.**
> In determining the true systeme of the world the main Question is whether the earth do rest or be moved. For deciding this some bring texts of scripture, but in my opinion misinterpreted, the Scriptures speaking not in the language of Astronomers (as they think) but in that of the common people to whom they were written. So where tis said that [1] God hath made the round world so fast that it cannot be moved, the Prophet intended not to teach Mathematicians the spherical figure [2] & immoveableness of the whole earth & sea in the heavens but to tell the vulgar in their own dialect that God had made the great continent of Asia Europe & Africa so fast upon its foundations in the great Ocean that it cannot be moved therein after the manner of a floating Island.

Remarkably, in a mere four-page characterization of the principal themes of the *Principia*, Newton focuses on the debate between revealed theology and natural philosophy regarding the earth's motion. He indicates once again that he regards scripture as referring only to relative places and motions; in particular, it describes the relation between continents and oceans, rather than the absolute position of the earth within the solar system. It does not characterize the rest or motion of the earth as a whole, at least in the passages cited.

We can now more fully appreciate the way in which Newton unifies elements of the Galilean and the Cartesian approaches to motion. In 1681, Newton understood the old trope that scripture is written in the language of the *common person* to mean that scripture refers to apparent, rather than true, sizes and places. In the *De Motu corporum* draft of 1684–1685, he adds the idea that scripture characterizes relative motions, which are connected with sensible appearances, the very things that ordinary people emphasize when conceiving of motion (e.g., the earth's motion). In 1687, he develops this view further, contending that we ought to understand scripture as referring to *relative spaces* and *relative motions*. To understand these descriptions as holding of absolute space, according to Newton, does *violence* to the scriptures, presumably because it renders them suspect, if not false. Thus, when Joshua 10:12 proclaims that the sun miraculously stopped moving, we should not understand this as a change in what Newton calls its true motion, which would have to be accompanied by dynamical effects, but rather as a change in its apparent and relative motion, which need not be accompanied by such effects. Hence, for Newton, the Joshua passage is not describing the true or absolute motion of the sun or of the earth; rather, it is describing the fact that on a certain day in history, it appeared to ordinary people as if the sun had stopped moving through the sky, such that the day was extended (the period between sunrise and sunset was longer than expected). Now, of course, we would like Newton to explain in detail exactly what he takes this to mean: how could the true motions of the earth around the sun produce such an appearance? He disappoints us in that respect. But what we *do* know is what his approach must be: we should attempt to understand Joshua just as we would attempt to interpret any description of astronomical events that are restricted solely to the appearances available to ordinary people. (Philosophers might have such precious items as telescopes and microscopes to provide them with appearances, but ordinary people are left with basic sense perception.) For instance, scripture would describe astronomical events such as a solar eclipse or the passage of a comet through the solar system by appealing to the way these events would appear to an ordinary person looking up at the sky during the day or night. It might dramatically state that the sun disappeared one day, or that the sky went dark; to describe a comet, it might speak of a great streak of lightning across the sky. And so on. The point is that the true motions of the earth, sun, moon, and comet are irrelevant to the prophetic writer. They fall under the purview of the philosopher.

What about more regular astronomical phenomena? What about something as ubiquitous and seemingly straightforward as the sunset? Consider a simple statement, say, "The sun set last night in London at 7 pm." Newton wishes to say that scripture is literally true, so its descriptions of the timing of the sunset ought to be understood in that way. And indeed, given Newton's distinction between true and apparent motion, this statement can be literally true if it is interpreted *as a statement about apparent motion*. It is a true statement about the way that the sun appeared to people in London last night, nothing more. The corollary is that this statement is not to be read as a false or misleading statement about the true motion of the sun or the earth; indeed, it must not be understood as a statement about true motion at all. Moreover, statements concerning relative motion and the way that objects appear to be moving to people perceiving them at a given moment from a given vantage point can themselves be either true or false. It may be false, for example, to say that the sun set last night in London at 2 pm. Newton indicates the importance of this idea in his easily missed parenthetical remark in the Scholium: "Relative quantities, therefore, are not the actual quantities whose names they bear, but are those sensible measures of them (true or false) that are commonly used in place of the quantities measured." There can be true or false sensible measures of space, time, and motion. The statement about the sunset in London is a true sensible measure—this means that it is a true statement about relative motion, which is to say, a true statement about apparent motion.

Newton's view is clarified if we distinguish two distinctions from one another. These two distinctions can be conflated because each contains *truth* or *true* as one of its elements. The first distinction is important for understanding nature; the second for understanding scripture. The first is Newton's distinction between *true* and *apparent* time, place, space, and motion. We know that ordinary people use sense perception to conceive of *apparent* time, place, space, and motion and that the philosopher abstracts away from sense perception in various ways in order to conceive of *true* time, place, space, and motion. (This abstraction, incidentally, may require the *mathematical* idea of space available to philosophers from geometry.) The second is the distinction between *literal* truth and various *other* kinds of truth, especially metaphorical, allegorical, and moral truth. Now, if one argues, as Newton does, that certain scriptural passages in Genesis are literally true rather than metaphorically true, that does not entail that they are descriptions of true time, place, space, or motion. For the distinctions are orthogonal to one another. A literally true description can be a characterization of apparent, rather than of true, motion.

One might object here: how can Newton claim that it is *literally true* that the sun set last night in London at 7 pm? It cannot be literally true because it is surely false: the claim that the sun set at some time implies that the sun is moving around the earth, which we know, and which Newton knew, to be false. At best, this is a *facon de parler*, but certainly not a true statement.

Answering this objection requires a bit more precision than I have provided thus far. The claim here is not that Newton said that it is literally true that the sunset occurred at a certain moment in history; he may very well have believed that, but here, I contend only that it expresses the general character of his overarching approach toward interpreting scriptural descriptions of space, time, and motion. With that caveat aside, there is a reply to the objection available to Newton. By the time that he published the Scholium in 1687, he had developed the following idea: in fact, the claim that the sun set at some time, if interpreted correctly, need not imply that the sun is moving around the earth; rather, if interpreted as a statement about relative or apparent motion, it implies only that the sun *appears* to be moving around the earth. This statement does not broach the question of whether the sun is actually moving, for that concerns the true or absolute motion of the sun, which is a separate issue. This move is not undermined by the further fact that from Newton's point of view, the true motion of the sun and of the earth must ultimately explain—or at least be relevant for an explanation of—their apparent motions. For that is the philosopher's task.

This shows, in turn, that Newton's position reflects a more general concern in the late seventeenth century with distinguishing between appearance and reality. Consider this example: suppose one says that there was a rainbow yesterday afternoon in the sky over the Thames. One means this claim literally: one is not speaking metaphorically, and although rainbows might be understood as a sign of God's promise to Noah, and might mean much else besides, nonetheless, one is speaking literally of an appearance. But to say that this claim is literally true is not to commit oneself to any particular understanding of the nature of rainbows. Perhaps they are appearances that result from the interactions of photons with hydrogen and oxygen molecules. Regardless of what rainbows *really* are, it remains literally true that things appeared a certain way to certain people at a certain time in history. The same holds for the sunset. The rainbow example calls to mind so-called secondary qualities—first popularized in concept, though not in name, by Galileo himself in the *Assayer*. Ordinary perception of objects suggests that the leaves of an oak tree are green, but the early modern philosopher understands that in fact, our perception of greenness is the result of a causal interaction between rays of light, the physical surface of the leaf, and our visual system. The prophet who wishes to communicate with the commoner, however, is not engaged in a philosophical analysis of perceptually relative qualities, so she describes the lovely green tree before her, rather than patterns of light rays that bounce off congeries of material particles characterized by size, shape, and motion. We might then remind ourselves: the Prophet's description of the tree is not metaphorical; it is literally true that the tree appears green to us. Hence, the distinction between the literal and the metaphorical cannot be conflated with the distinction between reality and appearance.

Now, this is not to say that the characterization of the way that moving objects appear to certain people from a certain vantage point is a simple matter. Newton says, for instance, that the earth appears to be at rest, reminding us that commoners are not aware that an *equable* motion of an object carrying a perceiver is not perceptible. This idea is ripe for philosophical analysis: is it really obvious that commoners would not grasp this point, given, say, their experience of boats moving calmly along a river or a lake? And what of the tides? Is it obvious that the oceans do not appear to be sloshing? It is an aspect of the burden of Newton's interpretive approach that he must take such questions seriously, and by all accounts, he did, even if he failed to articulate what we would now regard as a satisfactory and systematic conception of such matters.

What was Newton's real achievement in this domain? Perhaps most importantly, his unique approach to the ancient problem of reconciling natural knowledge with scriptural exegesis lies in his systematic distinction within the theory of motion in natural philosophy between two separate ways of conceiving of space, time, and motion. As with many natural philosophers in the seventeenth century, not least Descartes, Newton grasped the fact that ordinary people think about space, time, and motion differently than astronomers and philosophers do, a fact that in the very least can hamper the latter's efforts to convince the former of the truth of the new cosmology. In some ways, the generally understood coherence of Aristotelian ideas with conceptions of nature arising from ordinary sense perception enabled the survival of the Scholastic consensus (McMullin 1998, 339, note 89). Thus, the new *science* had a burden that its predecessor lacked. But Newton's unique maneuver was to recognize the essential connection between the old slogan "Scriptura humane loquitur" and the new idea that the theory of motion must distinguish apparent from true motion within the *system of the world*. In analyzing and cementing this connection, Newton argued that the new cosmology could in fact be rendered consistent with scripture after all. In this way, the theory of motion within Newtonian natural philosophy could promote the new cosmology even while saving the truth of the very scriptures that Newton took so seriously and spent so much of his life studying.

Yet Newton's view of the divine is not exhausted by his interest in finding a means of rendering scriptural passages concerning space, time, and motion consistent with a philosophical view of those aspects of the natural world. Indeed, he developed an unusual, if not unique, approach to understanding God's relation to the world precisely by employing his threefold distinction between conceptions of space, time, and motion. As we have seen, scripture refers to apparent or relative motion, and natural philosophy to true motion, that is, motion with respect to absolute space. Intriguingly, although absolute space obviously plays no role in Newton's program of scriptural interpretation—indeed, one does harm to the Bible if one interprets it as referring to absolute motion or places at all—Newton employs that very notion in order to present what I will call a philosophical conception of God.

7.2 Newton's Philosophical God

In Chapter 4, we encountered Newton's rejection of Cartesian metaphysics, along with his insistence that space should become a fundamental concept of philosophy. One reason is that the philosopher studying nature, as we have seen, must think about space and time in the right way if she is to think about motion (and its causes) in the right way. Another reason is that the systematic philosopher, one not merely concerned with understanding nature, requires a proper conception of space in order to articulate a proper conception of the divine. This was not the case for Descartes, or for Leibniz, but it was the case for Newton. Indeed, as we will see, Newton was the most systematic in his philosophizing whenever he discussed the relation between God and the world, between the divine presence and the infinite space in which God is to be encountered. Newton provided an especially dramatic portrayal of this relationship in Query 31, added originally to the Latin translation of the *Opticks* (by Samuel Clarke) in 1706, and renumbered as thirty-one in subsequent English editions. His discussion generated an intense debate with Leibniz and his followers. After mentioning that the structure of the solar system, with its arrangement of planets that all travel in the same direction around the sun, even as comets traverse the system along various eccentric trajectories, must have been designed by an intelligent agent, and adding that the design of animals on earth also calls for a divine explanation, Newton writes that such things

> can be the effect of nothing else than the wisdom and skill of a powerful ever-living agent, who being in all places, is more able by his will to move

the bodies within his boundless uniform sensorium, and thereby to form and reform the parts of the universe, than we are by our will to move the parts of our own bodies. And yet we are not to consider the world as the body of God, or the several parts thereof, as the parts of God. He is an uniform being, void of organs, members or parts, and they are his creatures subordinate to him, and subservient to his will; and he is no more the soul of them, than the soul of man is the soul of the species of things carried through the organs of sense into the place of its sensation, where it perceives them by means of its immediate presence, without the intervention of any third thing. The organs of sense are not for enabling the soul to perceive the species of things in its sensorium, but only for conveying them thither; and God has no need of such organs, he being everywhere present to the things themselves. (*Opticks* 403)

This comment about God's relation to the world, especially Newton's particular way of characterizing God's presence to objects in nature, generated a famous and long-lasting controversy with the Leibnizians. They objected strenuously to Newton's idea that God has a sensorium, or anything like it, that is, anything like a perceiving capacity, since that would (according to a standard idea of perception at the time) render God a passive recipient of information from the world. Leibniz and his followers argued in contrast that God is never passive, for the divine is a purely active being that has no need of anything akin to sensory perception.[24]

Despite the fact that Leibniz and others objected to Newton's discussion in Query 31 to the *Opticks*, he forged ahead, presenting a similarly far-reaching and powerful characterization of God's relation to the world in the second edition of *Principia Mathematica*. In the General Scholium, which Voltaire called its *metaphysical appendix*, Newton clearly intended in part to respond to Leibniz's growing criticisms of his basic ideas (see Chapter 6).[25] In this text, Newton did not merely reply to Leibniz's criticisms by arguing against vortex theories of planetary motion and by defending his alternative theory involving universal gravity, but once again tackled aspects of the relation between space and the divine that require a discussion of issues within systematic philosophy. After indicating that God is not only the creator but also the ruler of the world, he then proceeds to describe the divine being in more detail, beginning with widely accepted divine attributes such as omniscience and ending with what turned out to be a controversial philosophical conception of God's presence within space (*Principia* 941; I have altered the translation slightly):

He is eternal and infinite, omnipotent and omniscient; that is, his duration reaches from eternity to eternity; his presence from infinity to infinity; he governs all things, and knows all things that are or can be done. He is not eternity and infinity, but eternal and infinite; he is not duration and space, but he endures and is present. He endures forever, and is everywhere present; and by existing always and everywhere, he constitutes duration and space. Since every particle of space is *always*, and every indivisible moment of duration is *everywhere*, certainly the maker and lord of all things cannot be *never* or *nowhere*. Every soul that has perception is still the same indivisible person, though in different organs of sense and motion. There are given successive parts in duration, co-existent parts in space, but neither the one nor the other in a person, or his thinking principle; and much less can they be found in the thinking substance of God. Every person, so far as he is a thing that has perception, is one and the same person during his whole life, in all and each of his organs of sense. God is the same God, always and everywhere. He is omnipresent, not only in power, but also in substance: for power cannot subsist without substance. In him are all things contained and moved; yet neither affects the other: God suffers nothing from the motion of bodies; bodies find no resistance from the omnipresence of God. It is allowed by all that the supreme God exists necessarily, and by the same necessity he exists *always* and *everywhere*.

Since Newton thinks of God as substantially omnipresent throughout space, it is essential to his systematic philosophical views—to the extent that he developed them—that space is understood in the right way. It was also essential to his views that God be understood in the right way. The two intersect in Newton in a way that they never do in Descartes and Leibniz: in Newton's eyes, to conceive of God properly, one must conceive of space properly. That is because God is everywhere, a claim he had already endorsed in *De Gravitatione* years before (see the following text).[26]

It is tempting to read the General Scholium as wading into theological waters, since it presents one of the most detailed published expressions of Newton's understanding of the divine and since it includes extensive citations to scriptural passages in its notes. Indeed, since Newton embraces a version of the design argument in the General Scholium—arguing that the elements of the solar system could not have arisen from mere *mechanical causes* but must have been arranged by the creator—he clearly delves into natural theology. The citations to scripture involve him in revealed theology, at least to a minimal degree, and his discussion of divine attributes might be thought to involve him in systematic theology. But Voltaire's description is prescient: all of these facts are compatible with the further fact that Newton's text also tackles important metaphysical topics—or topics in systematic philosophy—centered on the relation between space and the divine. More importantly, there is evidence to suggest that as far as theological topics in Anglicanism in the early eighteenth century were concerned, Newton's remarks in the General Scholium would have been widely accepted as standard ideas, and not as reflecting his anti-Trinitarian sentiments.[27] He shared those sentiments with a small circle of friends, including John Locke, but kept them reasonably private.[28] For instance, Newton's claim that God is everywhere, an idea for which he references St. Paul's line concerning God, "in him we live and move and have our being" (Acts 17: 27–28), was a widely cited and uncontroversial line in Newton's day.[29] And yet that very same idea, the notion of God's substantial omnipresence, was *highly* contested in metaphysics. Indeed, Newton's conception of the divine became a centerpiece of the philosophical debates that gathered steam in 1713 and continued unabated until the end of his life.

Newton's ideas about God's presence within nature were developed long before his debate with Leibniz began in earnest in the early 1690s, as is especially evident from his remarks in *De Gravitatione*. That text clearly shows that Newton developed his highly controversial ideas about God and space in the context of rejecting Cartesian metaphysics. He makes this point explicitly:

> For since the distinction of substances into thinking and extended, or rather into thoughts and extensions, is the principal foundation of Cartesian philosophy, which he contends to be known more exactly than mathematical demonstrations: I consider it most important to overthrow [that philosophy] as regards extension, in order to lay truer foundations of the mechanical sciences.

> Perhaps now it may be expected that I should define extension as substance, or accident, or else nothing at all. But by no means, for it has its own manner of existing which is proper to it and which fits neither substances nor accidents. It is not substance: on the one hand, because it is not absolute in itself, but is as it were an emanative effect of God and an affection of every kind of being; on the other hand, because it is not among the proper affections that denote substance, namely actions, such as thoughts in the mind and motions in body. (Newton 2014, 35–36)

In this passage, Newton has obviously waded into deep metaphysical waters. We find the negative view that space is neither substance nor property (accident), but we also find the much more confusing, positive view that space is something called *an affection* and an *emanative effect* of God. Later on in the text, Newton returns to this positive conception of space's ontology:

> 4. Space is an affection of a being just as a being. No being exists or can exist which is not related to space in some way. God is everywhere, created minds are somewhere, and body is in the space that it occupies; and whatever is neither everywhere nor anywhere does not exist. And hence it follows that space is an emanative effect of the first existing being, for if any being is posited, space is posited. (Newton 2014, 40)

Throughout his mature life, Newton argued that God must be conceived of as *everywhere*, as a substantially omnipresent being. As we have seen in Chapter 4, Newton was well aware that Descartes rejected this conception of God's omnipresence in his correspondence with More in 1648–1649. Indeed, a Cartesian reader, like a Leibnizian one, would reject not only this type of view, but also Newton's insistence that space itself is infinite and can be considered to exist independently of objects. (We have already seen Leibniz's profound objections to Newton's view of space in Chapter 6.) But for a Cartesian, Newton's view is doubly mistaken: first, Cartesians think that space is identical to matter; and second, they also think that matter or space cannot be infinite. Only God is actually infinite—space or matter is merely indefinite. Newton was well aware of these very points (Janiak 2014). So in both *De Gravitatione* and in the General Scholium, Newton developed a systematic philosophical conception of space and the divine to compete with its Cartesian and Leibnizian competitors.

Newton employs the notions of *affection* and *emanation* (or *emanative effect*) to clarify his understanding of space. What do these ideas mean? Just as Henry More's correspondence with Descartes helps to illuminate the later Newtonian idea that God is substantially omnipresent (not merely omnipresent in power), More's views help to indicate what Newton might mean when he speaks of *affections* and of *emanation*. According to "Axiome" xvi in More's *Immortality of the Soul*, an "Emanative Cause" is "such a cause as merely by Being, no other activity or causality interposed, produces an Effect."[30] Thus, for More, to say that something, or some attribute F, emanates from God is to say (perhaps among other things) that God is the cause of F in a nontemporal way, such that merely by being, God causes F to be. He adds that it is a *contradiction* that an emanative effect, F, should be *disjoined* from its cause (More 1712, 19). Hence, there is some sense in which it is not possible for an emanative cause *to be* and its emanative effect *to fail to be*. He clarifies this idea by distinguishing emanation from creation, noting that God the creator can exist without creating anything in particular, and perhaps, without creating anything at all. However, if it is the case that we can accurately apply the concept of emanation to God, then it must also be the case that if God exists, whatever emanates from God also exists, on pain of contradiction.[31]

This enables us to take our first step in understanding why Newton speaks of *emanation* or *emanative effects* in *De Gravitatione*. To say that space emanates from God, or indeed from any being, is to *deny* that God, or any being, *creates* space. And from Newton's point of view, whereas God creates bodies, space is not created. (For the Cartesian, of course, this is nonsensical, since body and space are identical.) In other words, body depends upon the divine will, but space does not. Similarly, in the General Scholium, although he speaks of God the creator and ruler of all things in considerable depth, he does not claim that God *creates* space; instead, he says that God *constitutes* duration and space. But what does that mean? Does Newton follow More in thinking that God *causes* space to exist in some way, even if God does not create space?

The best interpretive approach here is to highlight the connections among the otherwise confusing concepts that Newton employs in the second passage earlier (which Newton numbers paragraph four in *De Gravitatione*). Newton seems to be presenting the following connected points:

(1) Space is an *affection* of every kind of being.
(2) Point 1 is clarified by the claim that God is spatially ubiquitous, minds are spatial, and bodies are spatial.
(3) Point 1 is also clarified by the claim that an entity that is nowhere in space does not exist.

(4) The view that space is an affection of every kind of being entails the claim that space is an *emanative effect* of the first existing being.

(5) The claim about emanation is clarified by the claim that if any being is posited, space is posited.

Newton says that the affection thesis entails that "space is an emanative effect of the first existing being," and he explains this claim by saying that if any being is posited, space is posited—"quia posito quolibet ente ponitur spatium." What do these terms mean? This is one of those rare cases in which philosophical hay can be made out of the meanings of words. As we find in the Oxford English Dictionary, the term *emanation* in mid-seventeenth-century English was sometimes understood to have a causal meaning, but it was also used to mean a logical inference or a necessary consequence. The latter meaning also fits with the seventeenth-century meaning of *posit*: as a transitive verb, to *posit* is to "put forward or assume as fact or as a basis for argument, to presuppose; to postulate; to affirm the existence of." Thus to say that *if any being is posited, space is posited* may be to say that space is a logical consequence of the existence of any being. So Newton follows More in thinking that it is a contradiction for the *emanator* to exist and the *emanated* not to, but this may be a logical notion, rather than a causal one (or: rather than the consequence of a causal one).[32]

But if Newton does not follow More in employing a causal concept of emanation, what then causes space to exist? Surely space is not a *necessary* being, a being that is a cause of itself, so its existence must have *some* cause! It must be causally contingent in some way or other. If we consider the intersection of Newton's conception of God with his affection thesis, we find that he actually conceives of space as *uncaused*. But this does not follow from a general view of what Newton calls affections; it follows from God's specific relation to space. Since God exists necessarily, there is no time at which God fails to exist; since space exists just in case any entity exists, space has existed eternally because God has existed eternally. In that sense, space and time have always existed, and are therefore uncaused. Although space is *uncaused* and is not dependent on God's *will*—hence, space is not created, but rather *emanates*—this does not mean that Newton regards space as a necessary being, for he thinks that space is not a being at all and therefore not a necessary one. Unlike contingent beings such as objects and minds—which, from Newton's point of view, are substances that bear characteristic actions—space is causally inert and therefore fails the Newtonian criterion of substance-hood.[33]

We are now in a position to connect Newton's view of emanation with his understanding of the divine presence. Christia Mercer has helpfully shown one connection between the basic concept of emanation, in many of its guises, and the Platonic idea of divine ubiquity (Mercer 2002). It was often said that sunlight emanates from the sun: it exists just in case the sun exists. We might then use the idea of emanation, so conceived, to express the idea that creatures bear the mark of the divine in some way. Just as the light from the sun fills my room, God's wisdom fills the wise person—hence, God is in the wise person. Can we find such a connection in Newton's thinking about space and the divine? Very roughly put, the idea might be as follows: space emanates from the divine being in the sense that space exists just in case God exists; God is in all parts of space because all parts of space, to infinity, emanate from God, and in so emanating, God fills every region of space. The concept of emanation is therefore appropriate to Newton's conception of the divine being.

Even if Newton's idea of the divine was considered theologically unproblematic, it was rejected as *philosophically* heterodox. It was heterodox precisely because Newton's God has an intimate relation with space. And it was that same view, in turn, that led to another highly contested Newtonian idea, namely, that space itself is actually infinite. Newton was well aware of the contested nature of this idea. As he indicates already in *De Gravitatione*, Descartes worried that regarding space as actually infinite might threaten to lead to atheism or threaten the uniqueness of God, so Descartes claimed that space is only indefinite, that is, arbitrarily large but always still finite. For Descartes, only God, who is transcendent, is actually infinite.[34] Newton may reject this idea because if God inhabits space, then the potential infinitude of space would render God potentially infinite, rather than actually infinite. If God is to be ubiquitous, as Newton thinks, then to conceive of God as extended just is to conceive of God as occupying an uncountable set of places—that is, the set of places within the divinely inhabited space cannot be mapped onto the natural numbers, but it can be mapped onto the real numbers (to be somewhat anachronistic). Far from threatening the uniqueness of God, or undermining God's infinity, Newton thinks that the only way to express and understand the actual infinity of God is to imbed God in an infinite Euclidean space (Janiak 2014). God occupies space in a way that material objects do not—no matter what level we reach in thinking about the various parts of space, God is at that level. I regard this as an entailment of two premises: the view that God is actually infinite and Newton's heterodox view that God substantially occupies space.

7.3 The God of the Philosophers and the God of the Bible

The interpretation of Newton I have provided leaves us with a puzzle. We have seen that Newton developed a unique solution to the kinds of problem faced by his major predecessors Galileo and Descartes, articulating the novel idea that the philosopher's pronouncements about the true motions of celestial bodies are consistent with scripture's pronouncements about their apparent motions. We have also seen how he developed and defended a detailed and highly contested philosophical conception of the nature of God and of God's relation to the world, especially to the infinite space Newton postulates. What happens, then, when we consider the intersection of these two views? Perhaps, it is not difficult to grasp why this poses a puzzle. The solution to the problem of motion involves the idea that scripture describes only appearance and not reality; the philosopher focuses on the reality underneath the appearance (a view that obviously has roots in antiquity). But scripture does not merely, on occasion, describe the motions of celestial bodies, including the earth; it does not merely describe aspects of the creation; it describes the creator. The philosopher also describes the creator, and does so using classic metaphysical concepts such as *infinite*, *eternal*, *omnipresent*, and so on. So the question is, can scripture's descriptions of the creator be rendered consistent with the philosopher's? Do they fit together into a single picture of the world, as descriptions of space, time, and motion do?

As we have seen, in the Scholium on space and time—which was published and unchanged in all three editions of *Principia Mathematica*—Newton argues that the ordinary view of space and time conceives of them through appearances that are available to our perception. For instance, the ordinary perspective regards time as consisting of a series of minutes, hours, or days—it conflates the sensible measures of time with time itself (a one-dimensional quantity). Similarly, the ordinary point of view characterizes space in terms of the relations among various objects that we perceive—it conflates sensible measures of space with space itself (a three-dimensional quantity). Now, when we conceive of space and time through the lens of the measurements that we make of them and of the perceptible objects that inhabit them, it seems ipso facto that we conceive of them as merely potentially infinite. That is, both space and time on this perspective are finite but limitless.[35] Space is limitless in the sense that as we travel through it, we never reach a boundary—there is always some further place to be traversed; from any place, we can conceive of space as stretching another foot or another mile in any direction. Time is analogous: at any arbitrary point in history, we envision time as flowing for another hour or another day, never stopping. This is connected, of course, to Newton's view that commoners conflate sensible measures of space and time with those quantities themselves. The common view is that time itself *just is* a series of seconds, minutes, or hours, continuing on without end; space itself *just is* a collection of numerous places, stretching on without end. So the ordinary perspective is that space and time are potentially infinite.

Now from Newton's perspective, the common conception of space and time, which does not rigorously distinguish between those quantities and measurements of them, would appear to be sufficiently powerful to accommodate scriptural characterizations of space, time, and motion. If we are concerned with apparent—rather than true—motion, then we presumably do not require the idea of absolute motion and therefore do not need the idea of absolute space. But from Newton's point of view, this set of concepts is insufficient for natural philosophy. That is true both because of what Newton regards as the correct understanding of true motion—something missing from the Cartesian system, in his view—and because of what he regards as the correct understanding of the divine. For as we have seen, God is substantially omnipresent and actually infinite—therefore, the space that God occupies must also be actually infinite. So the common conception of space is *not* sufficiently powerful to accommodate the philosopher's characterization of the divine.

But now, we can appreciate the potential problem: if scripture describes the appearances; if it is limited to the relative or common conception of space, then it must describe space as potentially infinite (nothing more). And if that is the case, then scriptural descriptions of the divine cannot describe God's actual infinity in actually infinite space. But Newton has committed himself to that very idea. Is this a genuine problem for Newton? Does it mean that after all his efforts—beginning with his lengthy letter to Burnet in 1680—to render philosophy and revealed theology consistent, he has saddled himself with a deep tension?

Perhaps, he has not. Newton seems to be suggesting that the God of the Hebrew Bible—the God who speaks to Abraham and to Moses—is described in the common language, which means that the Biblical God is described as occupying the very large, but only potentially infinite, space of the commoner. The God of the philosophers is described as being omnipresent throughout an actually infinite space. And these two *might* be consistent. First of all, we should remember the well-known fact that infinity is not a scriptural concept; the attribute of infinity plays a key role in philosophical, and in theological, conceptions of the divine, but not in scriptural interpretation; it is therefore important to systematic rather than revealed theology. Second of all, Newton's own way of understanding this standard idea might be put as follows: it is not that scripture describes God as finite, when God is really infinite, just as it is mistaken to say that scripture describes the earth as motionless, when it is really moving. Instead, scripture does not employ the concept of infinity at all because scripture does not describe the divine reality; instead, it describes the *appearances* of God through history (just as it describes other appearances). And it might very well be that an actually infinite God would appear to an ordinary person in just the way that scripture describes. The relevant point here is not that it is metaphorical to say, for example, that God places his hand in front of Moses to block his gaze; the point, rather, is that Biblical characterizations of the divine employ relative concepts of space and descriptions of the appearances. Third and finally, we might speculate a bit further: if Newton is right in thinking that scripture describes appearances in a language that ordinary people can understand, then perhaps, it follows that scripture must describe the actually infinite God as appearing to human beings in the guise of a being that is merely finite in some way or other. For after all, if ordinary people think about space, time, and motion through the lens of sense perception, then even if an actually infinite being were to appear to them, they would not perceive it as an actually infinite being. They could not do so.

Intriguingly, Newton tackles this very topic in the very next sentences of the General Scholium, after articulating a few details of his philosophical conception of the divine. Right after indicating the philosopher's idea that God exists necessarily, and exists "always and everywhere," Newton adds this description of God (*Principia* 942–943; I have altered the translation slightly):

Whence also he is all similar, all eye, all ear, all brain, all arm, all power to perceive, to understand and to act; but in a manner not at all human, in a manner not at all corporeal, in a manner utterly unknown to us. As a blind man has no idea of colors, so have we no idea of the manner by which the all-wise God perceives and understands all things. He is utterly void of all body and bodily figure, and can therefore neither be seen, nor heard, nor touched; nor ought he to be worshipped under the representation of any corporeal thing. We have ideas of his attributes, but what the real substance of anything is, we know not. In bodies we see only their figures and colors, we hear only the sounds, we touch only their outward surfaces, we smell only the smells, and taste the savours; but their inward substances are not to be known, either by our senses, or by any reflex act of our minds; much less, then, have we any idea of the substance of God. We know him only by his most wise and excellent contrivances of things and final causes; we admire him for his perfections, but we revere and adore him on account of his dominion. For we adore him as his servants, and a God without dominion, providence and final causes is nothing else but fate and nature. Blind metaphysical necessary, which is certainly the same always and everywhere, could produce no variety of things. All that diversity of natural things which we find, suited to different times and places, could arise from nothing but the ideas and will of a being that necessarily exists. But by way of allegory, God is said to see, to speak, to laugh, to love, to hate, to desire, to give, to receive, to rejoice, to be angry, to fight, to frame, to work, to build. For all our notions of God are taken from the ways of humanity, by a certain similitude that, though not perfect, has some likeness. Enough concerning God, to discourse of whom from the phenomena certainly belongs to natural philosophy.

Newton's remarks cover a vast landscape. One aspect of his interpretive method here adds to the views he presents to Burnet: when scripture describes space, time, and motion, it provides literally correct characterizations of the appearances. But God of course is not an appearance, not a phenomenon, not a corporeal entity at all. So perhaps scripture cannot describe God by characterizing the appearances of anything, but instead must employ "allegory" to describe God in a language that employs "the ways of humanity" so that ordinary people can understand something about the divine.[36] This means that Newton must have a more nuanced Biblical hermeneutics than one might think: he is clearly not claiming that the Bible is always *literal*, for at least when describing God, it must sometimes be read allegorically. Rather, the point is that when the Bible is literal, it always describes the appearances. Since scripture must sometimes use allegories to describe God and since it must employ human emotions and states to do so, it can never describe the actually infinite God. And so it leaves that task to the philosophers, just as it leaves the true motions of the heavenly bodies to them.

Famously, Newton ends the section on God in the General Scholium with the comment that it is proper to discuss God within natural philosophy if one bases one's discussion on the phenomena.[37] Earlier in the General Scholium, Newton had provided a version of the design argument for God's existence. Leaving aside the merits of that argument, which came in for serious criticism at the hands of David Hume later in the century, one might see why Newton thinks that studying the phenomena of planetary motion might give one a reason to think that a divine agent had created the solar system so that it has a certain stable structure. The planets are neither too far from the sun to fly off along the tangents to their orbits nor too close (at least in earth's case) to make life impossible. Perhaps, one can also see, in a general way, why Newton would often insist that if we study the causes of some natural phenomenon, such as the earth's solar orbit, then we will eventually reach the *first cause*. For the design argument itself seems to presuppose that if we have sought out every natural cause for some phenomenon, then we are licensed ultimately to refer phenomena to God's causal activity, for the creator is the first cause.[38] In any event, this case could be made, and to be charitable, we can grant Newton these two points for the sake of argument. But even so, there remains a deeper question about the General Scholium lurking here.

We might put the deeper question like this: how could our investigations into natural phenomena ever, under any circumstances, give us knowledge of an actually infinite God in actually infinite space? If you like, how does the philosopher come to know about God's actual infinity? We have already seen that scripture cannot describe God directly, but must do so using allegories involving human likeness, or else must describe the finite appearance of an infinite God. And we have already seen, in tandem, that scripture cannot describe God's actual infinity throughout space, because it limits itself to relative characterizations according to which space is only potentially finite. So the philosopher cannot rely on scripture here. But how can she rely on *nature*? Surely, even if nature is actually infinite, or even if space is actually infinite, it is difficult to see how a philosopher studying it could possibly come to know about an actually infinite God occupying all of space. Our knowledge of any phenomenon is surely finite; even if we inhabit an infinite space, we cannot learn about its infinity by studying phenomena. So how does Newton come to his knowledge of God? If I could travel back in time and meet him on the streets of London, then that is what I would ask him.

notes

1 See Newton's unpublished manuscript, "Principles of Philosophy," CUL MS. Add. 3970.3, ff. 479r-v, written between 1700 and 1704—this text was published and helpfully analyzed by McGuire (1970).
2 The General Scholium in the second edition says that studying God through phenomena is certainly part of experimental philosophy and in the third edition that it belongs to natural philosophy—see *Principia* 943.
3 This famous line is from Newton's unpublished manuscript, "Seven statements about religion," which was probably written in 1715 (Keynes MS 6), that is, not long after the second edition of *Principia Mathematica*, with its General Scholium's discussion of God, was published.
4 The fact that natural philosophy included discussions of humans is significant, because those discussions tackled not only the body, but also the mind as well.

As we have seen in Chapter 6, Newton certainly believed that analyses of the mind constituted a proper part of natural philosophy.

5   Descartes explores the distinction between theology and first philosophy—that is, metaphysics—rather than natural philosophy in his dedicatory letter to the Faculty of Theology in Paris in his *Meditations* (AT VII: 1–2).

6   As Galileo knew from such sources as Ludovico della Colombe's *Contro il moto della terra* of 1611, numerous other scriptural passages were interpreted as declaring or implying the earth's immobility. See Blackwell (1991, 60). For his part, Newton, too, was aware of all such passages and cited many of them in one of his own manuscripts—see Newton (1687), which is analyzed in the following.

7   See Blackwell (1991, 29); Westfall (1989, 17–20) argues that Galileo actually wrote the letter to Christina with Bellarmine explicitly in mind, and there is reason to believe that he read it.

8   That aspect of Descartes's view is emphasized in Garber (1992). In Janiak (2012), I provide a distinct and less sympathetic interpretation of Descartes's understanding of the earth's immobility. Thanks to Oliver Pooley for raising insightful objections against that interpretation, which prompted me to present the view outlined here.

9   Newton criticizes the idea that a body carried along by a body or bodies that surround it—like a peanut in its shell—does not participate in the motion of that body or bodies; Newton argues, following common sense, that if I throw a shell across the room, the peanut inside moves as well. In the Scholium, he directly challenges the Cartesian theory of the earth's immobility within its moving vortex and explicitly references Descartes's idea in his proper concept of motion that the moving body must change its relation to a vicinity that is regarded as being at rest. He writes (*Principia* 411): "It is a property of motion that parts which keep given positions in relation to wholes participate in the motions of such wholes. For all the parts of bodies revolving in orbit endeavor to recede from the axis of motion, and the impetus of bodies moving forward arises from the joint impetus of the individual parts. Therefore, when bodies containing others move, whatever is relatively at rest within them also moves. And thus true and absolute motion cannot be determined by means of change of position from the vicinity of bodies that are regarded as being at rest. For the exterior bodies ought to be regarded not only as being at rest but also as being truly at rest. Otherwise all contained bodies, besides being subject to change of position form the vicinity of the containing bodies, will participate in the true motions of the containing bodies and, if there is no such change of position, will not be truly at rest but only be regarded as being at rest. For containing bodies are to those inside them as the other part of the whole to the inner part or as the shell to the kernel. And when the shell moves, the kernel also, without being changed in position from the vicinity of the shell, moves as a part of the whole." See the illuminating discussion in Belkind (2007).

10 See Gabbey (1982, 193, 216) and More (1662, xi in the "preface general"); also see More's letter to Clerselier, Descartes's editor, from 1655 (AT 5: 644). More's letters to Descartes himself are available in Lewis (1953).

11 Several interpreters have rejected this basic approach. For instance, Gaukroger (2002, 142–145) argues that other aspects of Descartes's theory in the *Principles* are heliocentric, which means that he asserts the earth's immobility because

of his more general understanding of motion and not because of Galileo's condemnation. Garber argues (1992, 184–188) that Descartes's theory of motion drives the view of the earth's rest and that the theory, in turn, reflects Descartes's belief that motion is a mode of a body, which implies that there must be a genuine distinction between motion and rest and that each body has only a single true motion.

12 For Catholics like Galileo and Descartes, of course, it is standard to think of scriptural interpretation as heavily influenced and mediated by the Church.

13 Boyle argues in particular that even if Descartes is right to think that the mind and the body are distinct in some sense, we cannot know that the soul is immortal unless we appeal to revelation, because immortality requires specific actions by God that cannot be known through the study of nature (*Works* 8: 23–25). For an illuminating discussion of Boyle's views on such matters, see Hunter (2009, especially 82–84).

14 Newton deviated radically from any Anglican interpretive consensus that may have existed in his lifetime (see Iliffe 2006, Mandelbrote 1993, Snobelen 2006).

15 For instance, in his *Quaestiones* of 1664, written as an undergraduate at Trinity College, Cambridge, he writes: "Whither Moses his saying Gen the 1st that the evening & the morning were the first day &c do prove that God created time." See CUL Add. Ms. 3996, p. 73.

16 Burnet and Newton knew one another personally: Burnet was the senior proctor at the University of Cambridge in 1668, when Newton sat for his MA degree (Mandelbrote 1994, 157). Many see Burnet, unlike Newton, as a rather traditional Anglican thinker, although Gascoigne calls him "theologically avant-garde" (1985, 47).

17 The text had a printed date of 1681 but was available already toward the end of 1680, when Newton read it.

18 For discussions of Burnet, his influence on early geology in England, and reactions to his work, see Redwood (1976, 119–129, 248, note 42) and Porter (1977, 71–83).

19 See, inter alia, Mandelbrote (2006), Redwood (1976, 129), Roger (1982, 100–103), and Porter (1977, 71). On Burnet's lectures, see Gascoigne (1985, 65–66).

20 Unfortunately, Newton's letter is lost, save for a short quotation from it within Burnet's reply in early January 1681 (by the new calendar).

21 I owe this important point to Scott Mandelbrote; for his analysis of Burnet's relation to Newton and of Newton's work in biblical criticism more generally, see Mandelbrote (1993, 1994). Burnet's status as a Cartesian theologian and philosopher, or at least as a Cartesian-influenced theologian and philosopher, is discussed by Gascoigne (1985, 65–67) and Redwood (1976, 129).

22 The original reads: "Def. 18. Exponentes temporum spatiorum motuum celeritatum et virium sunt quantitates quævis proportionales exponendis. Hæc omnia fusius explicare visum est ut Lector præjudicijs quibusdam vulgaribus liberatus et distinctis principiorum Mechanicorum conceptibus imbutus accederet ad sequentia. Quantitates autem absolutas et relativas ab invicem sedulò distinguere recesse fuit eò, quod phænomena omnia prendeant ab absolutis, vulgus autem qui cogitationes a sensibus abstrahere nesciunt semper loquuntur de relativis, usque adeo ut absurdum foret vel sapientibus vel etiam Prophctis apud hos aliter loqui. Vnde et sacræ literæ et Scripta Theologorum de relativis semper intelligenda sunt, et crasso laboraret præjudicio qui inde de

rerum naturalium motibus absolutis philosophicis disputationes moveret." Many thanks to Karin Verelst for discussion of this passage.

23   This is CUL Add. Ms. 4005, ff. 39–42, written in 1687 or later.

24   See Cohen and Koyré (1961). Leibniz objected in part by citing the relevant entry from Goclenius (1613).

25   Roger Cotes, the young natural philosopher appointed by Bentley and Newton to edit the second edition of *Principia Mathematica*, wrote Newton a letter on March 18, 1713, in which he said: "I think it will be proper to add some things by which your book may be cleared from some prejudices which have been industriously laid against it. As that it deserts mechanical causes, is built upon miracles and recurs to occult qualities. That you may not think it unnecessary to answer such objections you may be pleased to consult a weekly paper called *Memoirs of Literature* sold by Ann Baldwin. In the 18th number of the second volume of those papers, which was published May 5th, 1712 you will find a very extraordinary letter of Mr. Leibniz to Mr. Hartsoeker which will confirm what I have said" (*Correspondence* 5: 392). Responding to Leibniz's charges against Newton was an important aspect both of Cotes's editor's preface to the second edition, and of the General Scholium. As it turned out, however, Newton's remarks about space and the divine in the latter merely led Leibniz to articulate further criticisms.

26   Newton presents the same conception of God in a manuscript from the 1690s that has been transcribed, translated, and discussed in McGuire (1978).

27   Few readers of the General Scholium took it to indicate any commitment to anti-Trinitarian ideas or to related doctrines of scriptural interpretation. Some interpreted Newton as expressing views that were consistent with, or perhaps reflected, some of the ideas in Samuel Clarke's 1712 work, *The Scripture-Doctrine of the Trinity*, which contributed to Clarke's reputation for endorsing views that were not completely standard or orthodox, but certainly far from embracing Unitarianism. There were exceptions to this trend: Newton's successor as Lucasian Professor of Mathematics at Cambridge University, William Whiston, implicated him in anti-Trinitarian views in 1711–1712, which angered Newton, and he then argued that the General Scholium should be read in that light. In 1714, John Edwards claimed that Newton had derived some of the ideas in that appendix to the second edition from well-known Unitarian writers. But these were not common sentiments. For a different perspective, see especially Snobelen (2001), who views the General Scholium as advocating anti-Trinitarian ideas, and who also links this text to Clarke's view of Jesus in the *Scripture-Doctrine*, and cf. Stewart (1996), who discusses various interpretations of the General Scholium in the eighteenth century.

28   There is no doubt that Newton himself held strongly anti-Trinitarian views (Snobelen 2006). He shared those views with Locke in his very long essay, "Two Notable Corruptions of Scripture," which argues in part that the original Greek text of the Bible did not include passages supporting the Anglican or the Catholic view of the Trinity; these passages were added in later editions, perhaps by St. Jerome, and therefore represent a *corruption* of the original text. This idea connects, in turn, with Newton's penchant for finding straightforward, literal interpretations of Biblical passages, for he apparently believed that the original Biblical text had a simple meaning that was corrupted by complex, allegorical insertions made by Catholic authorities (Iliffe 2006, 148–150). Newton was not

alone, for many late seventeenth-century English authors thought that allegories were important for pagan religion but unnecessary in Christianity. For his part, Locke denied that he was a Socinian or any other kind of anti-Trinitarian; he apparently thought that although the Trinity was not in scripture, it was deduced from scripture (Iliffe 2006, Reedy 1985, 133–140). On Socinianism more generally, see Scholder (1990, 32–44). Intriguingly, the Cambridge Platonists, who were often *Latitudinarians*, were also sometimes accused of being Socinians (see Cassirer 1953, 38, Tulloch 1874, 34), which may connect with philosophical views that they held in common with Newton.

29 This is not to deny that Paul's work itself was philosophical: it certainly can be read in that way, since he may have been speaking in part of Epicureans and Stoics and therefore taken himself to be contributing to a philosophical conversation (French and Cunningham 1996, 16). Koyré notes that Newton read the passage from Acts more literally than some others (1957, 227).

30 All references to More's *Immortality* and *Antidote* are to the pagination of these texts within More (1712). Newton owned a copy of an earlier edition of this text (the 1662 version). The quotation in the text earlier is from More (1712, 18).

31 These points are raised in *Antidote* and in *Immortality* at More (1712, ix, 22).

32 This issue is the subject of substantial controversy in the secondary literature, so the interpretation that I present here is certainly not universally endorsed. According to one interpretive camp, which includes John Carriero, emanation in Newton is just what we find in More, namely, it names a kind of efficient causation in which a cause and its effect exist simultaneously, which distinguishes emanation from creation, since creators exist prior to their creations. According to another camp, founded by J.E. McGuire, who engaged in a famous dispute with Carriero, emanation is not a causal relation at all, but rather a relation of ontic dependence, such that space somehow depends for its existence on God. According to the third camp, represented by Howard Stein, emanation in Newton is neither a causal nor an ontological relation, but rather a logical one: space is taken here to be a consequence of the existence of some entity, such as God, but a logical consequence rather than a causal one. See Carriero (1990), McGuire (1990, 2007), and Stein (2002). More's profound influence on Newton supports Carriero's view. But Carriero's interpretation carries a burden: it must be rendered consistent with the fact that Newton seems to apply the concept of emanation not only to God's relationship with space, as we find in More, but more surprisingly, to every entity's relationship with space. That is, Newton clarifies his claim about emanation by noting that if *any being* is posited, space is posited—this is not a claim specifically about God, but rather about all beings. On Carriero's reading, that would have to mean that space is caused to exist by whatever entity is the first to exist, and then Newton would have to be arguing that a finite entity's causal influence could range over an infinite area (many thanks to Nick Huggett for discussion of this point). The principal reason to think that infinite space (and therefore an infinite area) emanates from the first existing being is this: Newton's discussion of extension involves a series of numbered discussions. In the first discussion, we read that space bears geometric properties; in the second, we find that space is extended infinitely in all directions. After adding, in the third discussion, that the parts of space are motionless, Newton outlines his views of emanation in the fourth discussion. Hence, there is no doubt that for Newton, *infinite geometric space* is an affection of every kind of being and emanates from the first existing being.

33 See the discussion in Stein (2002, 266–267). This leaves us with one last pressing question. Why then does Newton say that space is *as it were* an emanative effect of God: "sed tanquam Dei effectus emanativus"? Like many interpretive questions, this may lack a definitive answer. I think that Newton employs *tanquam* here to signal his distance from More, who contends that space is an emanative effect of God in the sense that God efficiently causes space to exist, as Carriero indicates. Newton wishes to employ the very idea of emanation but to insist that space is not the sort of item that *acts* or that is *acted upon*; hence, it is not caused at all. Thus, *in Newton's sense*, space emanates from God, *full stop*; but from Newton's point of view, it is only *as it were* an emanative effect of God *in More's sense* of the term. However, this is a speculative answer, because earlier in *De Gravitatione*, we do not find any use of *tanquam*.

34 See Newton (2014, 39). For an insightful discussion of Descartes's views of infinity in the light of Newton's reactions to them, see McGuire (2007).

35 It is presumably no accident that this is also the Cartesian view, at least of space, since Newton explicitly regards the Cartesian *proper* view of motion, according to which motion through space involves a change in the moving object's relations with other objects, as falling under the category of *relative* views of space.

36 This is clearly not the complete picture, for one might think that Newton would have to believe that God did in fact appear to someone like Moses at a specific moment in history.

37 Newton emphasizes the overarching importance in his philosophizing of focusing solely on phenomena in a number of texts from this period. For instance, in an unpublished draft preface to *Principia Mathematica*, written around 1713–1715, Newton writes: "What is taught in metaphysics, if it derived from divine revelation, is religion; if it is derived from phenomena through the five senses, it pertains to physics [*ad Physicam pertinent*]; if it is derived from knowledge of the internal actions of our mind through the sense of reflection, it is only philosophy about the human mind and its ideas as internal phenomena likewise pertain to physics. To dispute about the objects of ideas except insofar as they are phenomena is dreaming. In all philosophy we must begin from phenomena and admit no principles of things, no causes, no explanations, except those which are established through phenomena." (ULC MS Add. 3968, fol. 109, transcribed and translated in Cohen (1999, 54)).

38 In Query 31 to the *Opticks*, which was first published in the 1706 Latin edition of the text, and then renumbered in the later 1717 English edition, Newton describes the process of thinking about the first cause: "And for rejecting such a Medium, we have the Authority of those the oldest and most celebrated philosophers of *Greece* and *Phoenicia*, who made a *Vacuum*, and Atoms, and the Gravity of Atoms, the first Principles of their Philosophy; tacitly attributing Gravity to some other Cause than dense Matter. Later Philosophers banish the Considerations of such a Cause out of natural Philosophy, feigning Hypotheses for explaining all things mechanically, and referring other Causes to Metaphysicks: Whereas the main Business of natural Philosophy is to argue from Phaenomena without feigning Hypotheses, and to deduce Causes from Effects, till we come to the very first Cause, which certainly is not mechanical" (Newton 1952, 369).

bibliography

1. Works by Isaac Newton

Unknown date, *De Gravitatione et Aequipondio Fluidorum*, University Library, Cambridge, MSS Add. 4003.

1664, *Questiones Quædam Philosophicæ*, University Library, Cambridge, MSS Add. 3996.

1672, "A Letter of Mr. Isaac Newton, Professor of the Mathematiks in the University of Cambridge; containing his New Theory about Light and Colors," *Philosophical Transactions of the Royal Society* 6: 3075–3087.

1687, "An Account of the Systeme of the World described in Mr. Newton's Mathematicall Principles of Philosophy," University Library Cambridge, MSS Add. 4005, ff. 39–42.

1715, [anonymous], "An Account of the Book Entitled *Commercium Epistolicum Collinii & aliorum, De Analysi promota*," *Philosophical Transactions of the Royal Society* (January–February): 173–224.

1717, *Opticks, or A Treatise of the Reflections, Refractions, Inflections & Colours of Light*, 2nd English ed., London: Printers to the Royal Society.

1729, *The Mathematical Principles of Natural Philosophy*, translated by Andrew Motte, London: Benjamin Motte.

1731, *De Mundi Systemate*, London: J. Tonson.

1731, *A Treatise of the System of the World*, 2nd ed., London: F. Fayram.

1756, *Four Letters from Sir Isaac Newton to Doctor Bentley Concerning Some Arguments in Proof of a Deity*, London: R. and J. Dodsley.

1759, *Principes mathématiques de la philosophie naturelle*, translated by Madame la Marquise du Châtelet, with *Exposition Abregége du Systeme du Monde, et explication des principaux phénomenes astronomiques tirée des principes de M. Newton*, by Châtelet and Clairault, Paris: Desaint & Saillant.

1779/1785, *Isaaci Newtoni Opera quae exstant omnia*, edited by Samuel Horsley, London: J. Nichols.

1952, *Opticks, or A Treatise of the Reflections, Refractions, Inflections & Colours of Light*, based on the fourth edition of 1730, New York: Dover.

1958, *Isaac Newton's Papers and Letters on Natural Philosophy*, edited by I. Bernard Cohen and Robert Schofield, Cambridge: Harvard University Press.

Newton, First Edition. Andrew Janiak.
© 2015 Andrew Janiak. Published 2015 by John Wiley & Sons, Ltd.

1959/1977, *The Correspondence of Isaac Newton*, edited by H.W. Turnbull et al., Cambridge: Cambridge University Press.

1960, *Sir Isaac Newton's Mathematical Principles of Natural Philosophy and His System of the World*, The Andrew Motte translation [1729] revised and edited by Florian Cajori, Berkeley: University of California Press.

1967/1981, *The Mathematical Papers of Isaac Newton*, edited by D.T. Whiteside, with the assistance of M.A. Hoskin, Cambridge: Cambridge University Press.

1972, *Philosophiae Naturalis Principia Mathematica*, edited by Alexandre Koyré and I. Bernard Cohen, with Anne Whitman, the third edition with variant readings, Cambridge: Harvard University Press.

1983, *Certain Philosophical Questions: Newton's Trinity Notebook*, edited by J.E. McGuire and Martin Tamny, Cambridge: Cambridge University Press.

1984, *The Optical Papers of Isaac Newton*, vol. 1, edited by Alan Shapiro, Cambridge: Cambridge University Press.

1999, *The Principia: Mathematical Principles of Natural Philosophy*, translated by I. Bernard Cohen and Anne Whitman, Berkeley: University of California Press. Cited throughout as *Principia*.

2014, *Newton: Philosophical Writings*, 2nd ed., edited by Andrew Janiak, Cambridge: Cambridge University Press.

2. Works by others

Ablondi, Fred and J. Aaron Simmons, 2010, "Heretics Everywhere: On the Continuing Relevance of Galileo to the Philosophy of Religion," *Philosophy and Theology* 22: 49–76.

Aiton, Eric, 1972, *The Vortex Theory of Planetary Motions*, New York: American Elsevier.

Anstey, Peter, 2011, *John Locke and Natural Philosophy*, Oxford: Oxford University Press.

Anstey, Peter, editor, 2013, *The Oxford Handbook of British Philosophy in the Seventeenth Century*, Oxford: Oxford University Press.

Anstey, Peter and John Schuster, editors, 2005, *The Science of Nature in the Seventeenth Century*, Dordrecht: Springer.

Barrow, Isaac, 1734, *The Usefulness of Mathematical Learning Explained and Demonstrated*, London: Austen.

Barrow, Isaac, 1961, *The Geometrical Lectures of Isaac Barrow*, translated by J.M. Child, Chicago: Open Court Press.

Beiser, Frederick, 1996, *The Sovereignty of Reason*, Princeton: Princeton University Press.

Belgioioso, Giulia et al., editors, 1990, *Descartes: il metodo e I saggi*, Rome: Istituto della Enciclopedia Italiana.

Bennett, Jonathan and Peter Remnant, 1978, "How Matter Might at First be Made," in Jarrett, King-Farlow, and Pelletier, editors.

Bensaude-Vincent, Bernadette, 2003, "Chemistry," in Cahan, editor.

Bentley, Richard, 1842, *The Correspondence of Richard Bentley*, edited by Christopher Wordsworth, London: John Murray.

Bentley, Richard, 1976, *Eight Boyle Lectures on Atheism, 1692*, New York: Garland.

Berkeley, George, 1975, *Philosophical Works*, edited by M.R. Ayers, London: Dent.

Berkeley, George, 1992, *De Motu and the Analyst*, edited and translated by Douglas Jesseph, Dordrecht: Kluwer.

Bertoloni Meli, Domenico, 1993, *Equivalence and Priority: Newton vs. Leibniz*, Oxford: Oxford University Press.

Bertoloni Meli, Domenico, 1999, "Caroline, Leibniz, and Clarke," *Journal of the History of Ideas* 60: 469–486.

Bertoloni Meli, Domenico, 2002, "Newton and the Leibniz-Clarke Correspondence," in Cohen and Smith, editors.

Bertoloni Meli, Domenico, 2006, "Inherent and Centrifugal Forces in Newton," *Archive for History of Exact Sciences* 60: 319–335.

Biarnais, Marie-Françoise and François DeGandt, editors and translators, 1995, *Isaac Newton: De la gravitation, suivi du mouvement des corps*, Paris: Gallimard.

Biener, Zvi and Chris Smeenk, 2012, "Cotes's Queries: Newton's Empiricism and Conceptions of Matter," in Janiak and Schliesser, editors.

Blackwell, Richard, 1991, *Galileo, Bellarmine and the Bible*, South Bend: University of Notre Dame Press.

Blair, Ann, 2006, "Natural Philosophy," in Park and Daston, editors.

Blay, Michel, 1995, *Les "Principia" de Newton*, Paris: Presses universitaires de France.

Boas, Marie, 1952, "The Establishment of the Mechanical Philosophy," *Osiris* 10: 412–541.

Böhme, Gernot, 1989, "Philosophische Grundlagen der Newtonschen Mechanik," in Hutter, editor.

Boyle, Robert, 1744, *The Works of the Honourable Robert Boyle*, edited by T. Birch, London.

Boyle, Robert, 1772, *A Free Enquiry into the Vulgarly Received Notion of Nature*, in *The Works of the Honourable Robert Boyle*, vol. 4, London: W. Johnston.

Boyle, Robert, 1999, *The Works of Robert Boyle*, edited by Michael Hunter and Edward Davis, London: Pickering & Chatto.

Brading, Katherine, 2012, "Newton's Law-Constitutive Approach to Bodies: A Response to Descartes," in Janiak and Schliesser, editors.

Bricker, Phillip and R.I.G. Hughes, editors, 1990, *Philosophical Perspectives on Newtonian Science*, Cambridge: MIT Press.

Brooke, John and Ian Maclean, editors, 2005, *Heterodoxy in Early Modern Science and Religion*, Oxford: Oxford University Press.

Broughton, Janet and John Carriero, editors, 2008, *A Companion to Descartes*, Oxford: Blackwell.

Buchwald, Jed and I. Bernard Cohen, editors, 2001, *Isaac Newton's Natural Philosophy*, Cambridge: MIT Press.

Buchwald, Jed and Sungook Hong, 2003, "Physics," in Cahan, editor.

Cahan, David, editor, 2003, *From Natural Philosophy to the Sciences*, Chicago: University of Chicago Press.

Cannon, Susan Faye, 1978, *Science in Culture: the Early Victorian Period*, New York: Science History.

Cantor, G.N., 1983, *Optics after Newton: Theories of Light in Britain and Ireland, 1704–1840*, Manchester: Manchester University Press.

Carnap, Rudolf, 1950, "Empiricism, Semantics and Ontology," *Revue international de Philosophie* 4: 20–40.

Carriero, John, 1990, "Newton on Space and Time: Comments on J.E. McGuire," in Bricker and Hughes, editors.

Casini, Paolo, 1984, "Newton: The Classical Scholia," *History of Science* 22: 1–58.

Cassirer, Ernst, 1911, *Das Erkenntnisproblem in der Philosophie und Wissenschaft der neuren Zeit*, Berlin: Bruno Cassirer.

Cassirer, Ernst, 1953, *The Platonic Renaissance in England*, translated by James Pettegrove, Austin: University of Texas Press.

Charleton, Walter, 1654, *Physiologia Epicuro-Gassendo-Charltoniana*, London.

Chomsky, Noam, 2013, "The Dewey Lectures 2013: What Kind of Creatures Are We?" *Journal of Philosophy* 110: 645–700.

Clarke, Desmond, 1989, *Occult Powers and Hypotheses: Cartesian Natural Philosophy under Louis XIV*, Oxford: Oxford University Press.

Clarke, Samuel, 1998, *A Demonstration of the Being and Attributes of God*, edited by Ezio Vailati, Cambridge: Cambridge University Press.

Clarke, Samuel and Gottfried Wilhelm Leibniz, 1717, *A Collection of Papers, which Passed between the late Learned Mr. Leibnitz and Dr. Clarke, in the Years of 1715 and 1716*, London: Printed for James Knapton.

Cohen, I. Bernard, 1956, *Franklin and Newton: An Inquiry Into Speculative Newtonian Experimental Science and Franklin's Work in Electricity as an Example Thereof*, Philadelphia: American Philosophical Society.

Cohen, I. Bernard, 1966, "Hypotheses in Newton's Philosophy," *Physis: Rivista Internazionale di Storia della Scienza* 8: 163–184.

Cohen, I. Bernard, 1969, "Isaac Newton's *Principia*, the Scriptures, and the Divine Providence," in Morgenbesser, Suppes, and White, editors.

Cohen, I. Bernard, 1971, *Introduction to Newton's "Principia,"* Cambridge: Harvard University Press.

Cohen, I. Bernard, 1980, *The Newtonian Revolution*, Cambridge: Cambridge University Press.

Cohen, I. Bernard, 1982, "Newton's copy of Leibniz's *Théodicée*," *Isis* 73: 410–414.

Cohen, I. Bernard, 1990, "Newton and Descartes," in Belgioioso et al., editors.

Cohen, I. Bernard, 1992, "The Review of the First Edition of Newton's *Principia* in the *Acta Eruditorum*, With Notes on the Other Reviews," in Harman and Shapiro, editors.

Cohen, I. Bernard, 1999, "Guide to Newton's *Principia*," in Newton 1999.

Cohen, I. Bernard and Alexandre Koyré, 1962, "Newton and the Leibniz-Clarke Correspondence," *Archives internationales d'histoire des sciences* 15: 63–126.

Cohen, I. Bernard and George Smith, editors, 2002, *The Cambridge Companion to Newton*, Cambridge: Cambridge University Press.

Costello, William, 1958, *The Scholastic Curriculum at Early Seventeenth-Century Cambridge*, Cambridge: Harvard University Press.

Cunningham, Andrew, 1988, "Getting the Game Right: Some Plain Words on the Identity and Invention of Science," *Studies in History and Philosophy of Science* 19: 365–389.

Cunningham, Andrew, 1991, "How the *Principia* Got its Name; or, Taking Natural Philosophy Seriously," *History of Science* 29: 377–392.

Cunningham, Andrew, 2000, "The Identity of Natural Philosophy: A Response to Edward Grant," *Early Science and Medicine* 5: 259–278.

Danielson, Dennis, 2001, "Scientist's Birthright," *Nature* 410: 1031.

De Gandt, François, 1995, *Force and Geometry in Newton's "Principia,"* translated by Curtis Wilson, Princeton: Princeton University Press.

Densmore, Dana, 1999, "Cause and Hypothesis: Newton's Speculation about the Cause of Universal Gravitation," *St. John's Review* 45: 94–111.

De Pierris, Graciela, 2012, "Newton, Locke and Hume," in Janiak and Schliesser, editors.

DeRisi, Vincenzo, editor, 2015, *Mathematizing Space: The Objects of Geometry from Antiquity to the Early Modern Age,* Basel: Birkhaüser.

Descartes, René, 1644/1982, *Principia Philosophiae,* edited by Charles Adam and Paul Tannery, Paris: Vrin.

Descartes, René, 1647/1989, *Principes,* edited by Charles Adam and Paul Tannery, Paris: Vrin.

Descartes, René, 1954, *The Geometry of Rene Descartes,* translated by David Eugene Smith and Marcia L. Latham, New York: Dover.

Descartes, René, 1991, *Principles of Philosophy,* translated and edited by V.R. and R.P. Miller, Dordrecht: Kluwer.

Descartes, René, 1996, *Oeuvres de Descartes,* edited by Charles Adam and Paul Tannery, 11 volumes, Paris: Vrin.

Desmaizeaux, Pierre, 1720, *Recueil de diverses pieces, sur la philosophie, la religion naturelle, l'histoire, les mathematiques, &c.,* Amsterdam: Chez H. Du Sauzet.

DeSmet, Rudolf and Karin Verelst, 2001, "Newton's Scholium Generale: The Platonic and Stoic Legacy," *History of Science* 39: 1–30.

Detlefsen, Karen, 2013, "Émilie du Châtelet," *Stanford Encyclopedia of Philosophy.*

DiSalle, Robert, 2002, "Newton's Philosophical Analysis of Space and Time," in Cohen and Smith, editors.

DiSalle, Robert, 2006, *Understanding Space-time,* Cambridge: Cambridge University Press.

Dobbs, Betty Jo Teeter, 1975, *The Foundations of Newton's Alchemy,* Cambridge: Cambridge University Press.

Dobbs, Betty Jo Teeter, 1988, "Newton's Rejection of the Mechanical Aether," in Donavan, Laudan, and Laudan, editors.

Dobbs, Betty Jo Teeter, 1991, *The Janus Faces of Genius: The Role of Alchemy in Newton's Thought,* Cambridge: Cambridge University Press.

Dobbs, Betty Jo Teeter, 1994, "Newton as Final Cause and First Mover," *Isis* 85: 633–643.

Dobre, Mihnea and Tammy Nyden, editors, 2014, *Cartesian Empiricisms,* Dordrecht: Spinger.

Dobzhansky, Theodosius, 1973, "Nothing in Biology Makes Sense Except in Light of Evolution," *The American Biology Teacher* 35: 125–129.

Domski, Mary, 2003, "The Constructible and the Intelligible in Newton's Philosophy of Geometry," *Philosophy of Science* 70, 1114–1124.

Domski, Mary, 2010, "Newton's Empiricism and Metaphysics," *Philosophy Compass* 5: 525–534.

Domski, Mary, 2012, "Newton and Newtonianism," *The Southern Journal of Philosophy* 50: 363–369.

Donavan, Arthur, Larry Laudan, and Rachel Laudan, editors, 1988, *Scrutinizing Science,* Dordrecht: Kluwer.

Downing, Lisa, 1997, "Locke's Newtonianism and Lockean Newtonianism," *Perspectives on Science* 5: 285–310.

Drake, Stillman, 2001, *Galileo: A Very Short Introduction*, Oxford: Oxford University Press.

Du Châtelet, Émilie, 1740, *Institutions de physique*, Paris.

Du Châtelet, Émilie, 1742/1988, *Institutions physiques, nouvelle edition*, reprinted in Christiaan Wolff, *Gesammelte Werke*, Jean Ecole, editor, Abt. 3, Band 28, Hildesheim: Olms.

Ducheyne, Steffen, 2011, "Newton on Action at a Distance and the Cause of Gravity," *Studies in History and Philosophy of Science* 42: 154–159.

Ducheyne, Steffen, 2012, *The Main Business of Natural Philosophy*, Dordrecht: Springer.

Dunlop, Katherine, 2012, "The Mathematical Form of Measurement and the Proof of Proposition I in Newton's *Principia*," *Synthese* 186: 191–229.

Earman, John, 1989, *World Enough and Space-time: Absolute versus Relational Theories of Space and Time*, Cambridge: MIT Press.

Edelston, J., editor, 1850, *Correspondence of Sir Isaac Newton and Professor Cotes*, London.

Euler, Leonard, 1748, "Réflections sur l'Espace et le Temps," *Mémoires de l'Académie des Sciences de Berlin* 4: 324–333; reprinted in *Leonhardi Euleri Opera Omnia*, vol. 2, edited by Ferdinand Rudio et al., Leipzig.

Feingold, Mordechai, 2004, *The Newtonian Moment: Isaac Newton and the Making of Modern Culture*, New York and Oxford: New York Public Library and Oxford University Press.

Figala, Karin, 2002, "Newton's Alchemy," in Cohen and Smith, editors.

Force, James, 1985, *William Whiston: Honest Newtonian*, Cambridge: Cambridge University Press.

Force, James, 1994, "The God of Abraham and Isaac (Newton)," in Force and Popkin, editors.

Force, James and Richard Popkin, editors, 1994, *The Books of Nature and Scripture*, Dordrecht: Kluwer.

Fox, Robert, 1974, "The Rise and Fall of Laplacian Physics," *Historical Studies in the Physical Sciences* 4: 89–136.

French, Peter, Howard Wettstein, and Bruce Silver, editors, 2002, *Midwest Studies in Philosophy*, vol. 26, Boston: Blackwell.

French, Roger and Andrew Cunningham, 1996, *Before Science: The Invention of the Friars' Natural Philosophy*, Brookfield: Scholar's Press.

Friedman, Michael, 1992, *Kant and the Exact Sciences*, Cambridge: Harvard University Press.

Friedman, Michael, 2000, *A Parting of the Ways: Carnap, Cassirer, Heidegger*, Chicago and LaSalle: Open Court.

Friedman, Michael, 2008, "Descartes and Galileo: Copernicanism and the Metaphysical Foundations of Physics," in Broughton and Carriero, editors.

Friedman, Michael, 2012, *Kant's Construction of Nature: A Reading of the Metaphysical Foundations of Natural Science*, Cambridge: Cambridge University Press.

Funkenstein, Amos, 1986, *Theology and the Scientific Imagination from the middle ages to the Seventeenth Century*, Princeton: Princeton University Press.

Gabbey, Alan, 1980, "Force and Inertia in the Seventeenth Century: Descartes and Newton," in Gaukroger, editor.

Gabbey, Alan, 1982, "Philosophia Cartesiana Triumphata: Henry More (1646–1671)," in Lennon, Nicholas, and Davis, editors.

Gabbey, Alan, 2002, "Newton, Active Powers, and the Mechanical Philosophy," in Cohen and Smith, editors.

Gabbey, Alan, 2004, "What was Mechanical about the Mechanical Philosophy?" in Palmerino and Thijssen, editors.

Galilei, Galileo, 1890/1909, *Opere di Galileo*, edited by Antonio Favaro, Florence: Giunti-Barbera.

Galilei, Galileo, 1953, *Dialogue Concerning the Two Chief World Systems*, translated by Stillman Drake, Berkeley: University of California Press.

Galilei, Galileo, 1959, *Discoveries and Opinions of Galileo*, translated by Stillman Drake, New York: Doubleday.

Galilei, Galileo, 2010, *The Essential Galileo*, edited and translated by Maurice Finocchiaro, Indianapolis: Hackett.

Garber, Daniel, 1992, *Descartes's Metaphysical Physics*, Chicago: University of Chicago Press.

Garber, Daniel, 2000, "A Different Descartes: Descartes and the Program for a Mathematical Physics in his Correspondence," in Schuster, Gaukroger, and Sutton, editors.

Garber, Daniel, 2002, "Descartes, Mechanics, and the Mechanical Philosophy," in French, Wettstein, and Silver, editors.

Garber, Daniel, 2006, "Physics and Foundations," in Park and Daston, editors.

Garber, Daniel, 2012, "Leibniz, Newton and Force," in Janiak and Schliesser, editors.

Garber, Daniel and Michael Ayers, editors, 1998, *The Cambridge History of Seventeenth Century Philosophy*, Cambridge: Cambridge University Press.

Garber, Daniel and Sophie Roux, editors, 2013, *The Mechanization of Natural Philosophy*, Dordrecht: Springer.

Gascoigne, John, 1985, *Cambridge in the age of the Enlightenment*, Cambridge: Cambridge University Press.

Gaukroger, Stephen, 1980, *Descartes: Philosophy, Mathematics and Physics*, Sussex: Harvester Press.

Gaukroger, Stephen, 2002, *Descartes' System of Natural Philosophy*, Cambridge: Cambridge University Press.

Gaukroger, Stephen, 2005, "The Autonomy of Natural Philosophy," in Anstey and Schuster, editors.

Gaukroger, Stephen, 2008, "Life and Works," in Broughton and Carriero, editors.

Gill, Mary Louise and James Lennox, editors, 1994, *Self-Motion: From Aristotle to Newton*, Princeton: Princeton University Press.

Goclenius, Rodolphus, 1613, *Lexicon Philosophicum*, Frankfurt.

Gorham, Geoffrey, 2011, "How Newton Solved the Mind-Body Problem," *History of Philosophy Quarterly* 28: 21–44.

Grant, Edward, 1981, *Much Ado about Nothing: Theories of Space and Vacuum from the Middle Ages to the Scientific Revolution*, Cambridge: Cambridge University Press.

Grant, Edward, 2000, "God and Natural Philosophy: The Late Middle Ages and Sir Isaac Newton," *Early Science and Medicine* 5: 279–298.

Grant, Edward, 2007, *A History of Natural Philosophy*, Cambridge: Cambridge University Press.

Gravesande, W. Jacob's, 1747, *Mathematical Elements of Natural Philosophy*, translated by J.T. Desaguliers, London.

Guicciardini, Niccolò, 1999, *Reading the Principia: The Debate on Newton's Mathematical Methods for Natural Philosophy from 1687 to 1736*, Cambridge: Cambridge University Press.

Guicciardini, Niccolò, 2009, *Isaac Newton on Mathematical Certainty and Method*, Cambridge: MIT Press.

Hakfoort, Casper, 1995, *Optics in the Age of Euler: Conceptions of the Nature of Light, 1700–1795*, Cambridge: Cambridge University Press.

Hall, A. Rupert, 1980, *Philosophers at War: The Quarrel between Newton and Leibniz*, Cambridge: Cambridge University Press.

Hall, A. Rupert, 1993, *All was Light: An Introduction to Newton's Opticks*, Oxford: Clarendon Press.

Hanson, Norwood Russell, 1958, *Patterns of Discovery*, Cambridge: Cambridge University Press.

Harman, P.M. and Alan Shapiro, editors, 1992, *The Investigation of Difficult Things: Essays on Newton and the History of the Exact Sciences in Honour of D.T. Whiteside*, Cambridge: Cambridge University Press.

Harper, William, 2011, *Isaac Newton's Scientific Method: Turning Data into Evidence about Gravity and Cosmology*, Oxford: Oxford University Press.

Harper, William and George Smith, 1995, "Newton's New Way of Inquiry," in Leplin, editor.

Harrison, John, 1978, *The Library of Isaac Newton*, Cambridge: Cambridge University Press.

Harrison, Peter, 2005, "Physico-theology and the Mixed Sciences: The Role of Theology in Early Modern Natural Philosophy," in Anstey and Schuster, editors.

Hatfield, Gary, 1990, "Metaphysics and the New Science," in Lindberg and Westman, editors.

Hatfield, Gary, 1996, "Was the Scientific Revolution a Revolution in Science?" in Ragep and Ragep, editors.

Heidegger, Martin, 1962, *Die Frage nach dem Ding*, Tübingen: M. Niemeyer.

Heilbron, J.L., 1982, *Elements of Early Modern Physics*, Berkeley: University of California Press.

Heilbron, J.L., 2010, *Galileo*, Oxford: Oxford University Press.

Henry, John, 1994, " 'Pray Do Not Ascribe that Notion to Me': God and Newton's Gravity," in Force and Popkin, editors.

Henry, John, 2011, "Gravity and *De Gravitatione*: the development of Newton's Ideas on Action at a Distance," *Studies in History and Philosophy of Science* 42: 11–27.

Henry, John, 2013, "The Reception of Cartesianism," in Anstey, editor.

Henry, John, 2014, "Newton and Action at a Distance between Bodies: A Response to Andrew Janiak's 'Three Concepts of Cause in Newton'," *Studies in History and Philosophy of Science*.

Herivel, John, 1965, *The Background to Newton's Principia: A Study of Newton's Dynamical Researches in the Years 1664–1684*, Oxford: Clarendon Press.

Hessayon, Ariel and Nicholas Keene, editors, 2006, *Scripture and Scholarship in Early Modern England*, Hampshire: Ashgate.

Hesse, Mary, 1961, *Forces and Fields: The Concept of Action at a Distance in the History of Physics*, London: Nelson.

Hobbes, Thomas, 1656, *Six Lessons to the Professors of the Mathematiques One of Geometry the Other of Astronomy, in the Chaires Set Up by the Noble and Learned Sir Henry Savile in the University of Oxford*, London.

Hobbes, Thomas, 1839 (1655), *Elements of Philosophy, the First Section, Concerning Body*, edited by William Molesworth, London.

Hooke, Robert, 1665, *Micrographia: Or Some Physiological Descriptions of Minute Bodies Made by Magnifying Glasses, with Observations and Inquiries Thereupon*, London: Royal Society.

Hooykass, R., 1972, *Religion and the Rise of Modern Science*, Grand Rapids: Eerdmans Pulishing Company.

Huggett, Nick, 2012, "What did Newton Mean by 'Absolute Motion'?" in Janiak and Schliesser, editors.

Hume, David, 1739/2007, *A Treatise of Human Nature, a Critical Edition*, edited by David Fate Norton and Mary Norton, Oxford: Clarendon Press.

Hume, David, 1777/1993, *An Enquiry Concerning Human Understanding*, edited by Eric Steinberg, Indianapolis: Hackett.

Hume, David, 1854, *The History of England from the Invasion of Julius Caesar to the Abdication of James the Second, 1688*, New York.

Hunter, Michael, 2009, *Boyle: Between God and Science*, New Haven: Yale University Press.

Hutter, K., editor, 1989, *Die Anfänge der Mechanik: Newtons Principia gedeutet aus ihrer Zeit und ihrer Wirkung auf die Physik*, Berlin: Springer Verlag.

Hutton, Sarah, 1994, "More, Newton and the Language of Biblical Prophecy," in Force and Popkin, editors.

Hutton, Sarah, 2004, "Emilie Du Châtelet's Institutions de physique as a Document in the History of French Newtonianism," *Studies in the History and Philosophy of Science* 35: 515–531.

Hutton, Sarah, 2006, "Iconisms, Enthusiasm and Origen: Henry More Reads the Bible," in Hessayon and Keene, editors.

Huygens, Christiaan [Anonymous], 1673, "An Extract of a Letter Lately Written by an Ingenious Person from Paris," *Philosophical Transactions of the Royal Society* 96, 21 July: 6086–6087.

Huygens, Christiaan, 1690, *Discours de la cause de la Pesanteur*, in *Oeuvres complètes*, vol. 21.

Huygens, Christiaan, 1888/1950, *Oeuvres complètes*, edited by Johan Adriaan Vollgraff, The Hague: Nijhoff.

Iliffe, Rob, 1994, " 'Making a Shew': Apocalyptic Hermeneutics and the Sociology of Christian Idolatry in the Work of Isaac Newton and Henry More," in Force and Popkin, editors.

Iliffe, Rob, 2006, "Friendly criticism: Richard Simon, John Locke, Isaac Newton and the *Johannine Comma*," in Hessayon and Keene, editors.

Iliffe, Rob, 2007, *Newton: A Very Short Introduction*, Oxford: Oxford University Press.

Jacob, Margaret, 1986, "Christianity and the Newtonian Worldview," in Lindberg and Numbers, editors.

Janiak, Andrew, 2008, *Newton as Philosopher*, Cambridge: Cambridge University Press.

Janiak, Andrew, 2010, "Substance and Action in Newton and Descartes," *The Monist* 93: 657–677.

Janiak, Andrew, 2012, "Newton and Descartes: Theology and Natural Philosophy," *Southern Journal of Philosophy* 50: 414–435.

Janiak, Andrew, 2013, "Three Concepts of Cause in Newton," *Studies in History and Philosophy of Science* 44: 397–407.

Janiak, Andrew, 2014, "Mathematics and Infinity in Descartes and Newton," in DeRisi, editor.

Janiak, Andrew and Eric Schliesser, editors, 2012, *Interpreting Newton: Critical Essays*, Cambridge: Cambridge University Press.

Jarrett, Charles, John King-Farlow, and F.J. Pelletier, editors, 1978, *New Essays on Rationalism and Empiricism*, Guelph: Canadian Association for Publishing in Philosophy.

Jesseph, Douglas, 1999, *Squaring the Circle: The War between Hobbes and Wallis*, Chicago: University of Chicago Press.

Joy, Lynn, 2006, "Scientific Explanation from Formal Causes to Laws of Nature," in Park and Daston, editors.

Kant, Immanuel, 1786/1997, *Metaphysische Anfangsgründe der Naturwissenschaft*, edited by Konstantin Pollok, Hamburg: Felix Meiner Verlag.

Kant, Immanuel, 1787/1956, *Kritik der reinen Vernunft*, edited by Raymund Schmidt, Hamburg: Felix Meiner Verlag.

Kochiras, Hylarie, 2009, "Gravity and Newton's Substance Counting Problem," *Studies in History and Philosophy of Science* 40: 267–280.

Kochiras, Hylarie, 2011, "Gravity's Cause and Substance Counting: Contextualizing the Problems," *Studies in History and Philosophy of Science* 42: 167–184.

Koyré, Alexandre, 1957, *From the Closed World to the Infinite Universe*, Baltimore: Johns Hopkins University Press.

Koyré, Alexandre, 1968, *Newtonian Studies*, Chicago: University of Chicago Press.

Koyré, Alexandre and I. Bernard Cohen, 1961, "The Case of the Missing *Tanquam*: Leibniz, Newton & Clarke," *Isis* 52: 555–566.

Kuhn, Thomas, 1957, *The Copernican Revolution*, Cambridge: Harvard University Press.

Kuhn, Thomas, editor, 1977, *The Essential Tension*, Chicago: University of Chicago Press.

Kuhn, Thomas, 1977, "Mathematical versus Experimental Traditions in the Development of Physical Science," in Kuhn editor.

Kuhn, Thomas, 1996/1962, *The Structure of Scientific Revolutions*, 3rd ed., Chicago: University of Chicago Press.

Langton, Rae and David Lewis, 1998, "Defining 'Intrinsic'," *Philosophy and Phenomenological Research* 58: 333–345.

Leibniz, Gottfried Wilhelm, 1722a (1712), "A Letter of M. Leibnitz to M. Hartsoeker," *Memoirs of Literature* 3: 453–460.

Leibniz, Gottfried Wilhelm, 1722b (1712), "A Second Letter of M. Leibnitz to M. Hartsoeker, Dated July 12, 1711," *Memoirs of Literature* 5: 62–65.

Leibniz, Gottfried Wilhelm, 1765/1921, *Nouveaux Essais sur l'Entendement Humain*, Paris: Flammarion.

Leibniz, Gottfried Wilhelm, 1849, *Mathematische Schriften*, edited by C. Gerhardt, Berlin: A. Asher.

Leibniz, Gottfried Wilhelm, 1890, *Die Philosophischen Schriften*, edited by C. Gerhardt, Berlin: Weidmann.

Lennon, Thomas, John Nicholas and John Davis, editors, 1982, *Problems of Cartesianism*, Kingston and Montreal: McGill-Queen's University Press.

Leplin, Jarrett, editor, 1995, *The Creation of Ideas in Physics*, Dordrecht: Kluwer.

Lewis, Genevieve, editor, 1953, *Descartes: Correspondance avec Arnauld et Morus, texte Latin et traduction*, Paris: Librairie philosophique Vrin.

Lindberg, David and Ronald Numbers, editors, 1986, *God and Nature: Historical Essays on the Encounter between Christianity and Science*, Berkeley: University of California Press.

Lindberg, David and Robert Westman, editors, 1990, *Reappraisals of the Scientific Revolution*, Cambridge: Cambridge University Press.

Locke, John, 1690/1975, *An Essay Concerning Human Understanding*, edited by P. Nidditch, Oxford: Oxford University Press.

Locke, John, 1699, *Mr. Locke's Reply to the Right Reverend the Lord Bishop of Worcester's Answer to his Second Letter: Wherein, Besides Other Incident Matters, what his Lordship has Said Concerning Certainty by Reason, Certainty by Ideas, and Certainty of Faith*. London.

Locke, John, 1823, *The Works of John Locke*, 10 volumes, London.

LoLordo, Antonia, 2007, *Pierre Gassendi and the Birth of Early Modern Philosophy*, Cambridge: Cambridge University Press.

Lüthy, Christoph, 2000, "What to do With Seventeenth-Century Natural Philosophy? A Taxonomic Problem," *Perspectives on Science* 8: 164–195.

Machamer, Peter, editor, 1998, *The Cambridge Companion to Galileo*, Cambridge: Cambridge University Press.

Machamer, Peter, J.E. McGuire, and Hylarie Kochiras, 2012, "Newton and the Mechanical Philosophy: Gravitation as the Balance of the Heavens," *Southern Journal of Philosophy* 50: 370–388.

Maclaurin, Colin, 1748, *An Account of Sir Isaac Newton's Philosophical Discoveries in Four Books*, London.

Mahoney, Michael, 1998, "The Mathematical Realm of Nature," in Garber and Ayers, editors.

Mandelbrote, Scott, 1993, "A Duty of the Greatest Moment: Isaac Newton and the Writing of Biblical Criticism," *The British Journal for the History of Science* 26: 281–302.

Mandelbrote, Scott, 1994, "Isaac Newton and Thomas Burnet: Biblical Criticism and the Crisis of Late Seventeenth-Century England," in Force and Popkin, editors.

Mandelbrote, Scott, 2006, "Isaac Newton and the Flood," in Mulsow and Assmann, editors.

Manuel, Frank, 1968, *A Portrait of Isaac Newton*, Cambridge: Harvard University Press.

Marks, Herbert, editor, 2012, *The English Bible, King James Version*, 2 volumes, New York: W.W. Norton and Company.

Martinich, A.P., 1999, *Hobbes: A Biography*, Cambridge: Cambridge University Press.

McGuire, J.E., 1970, "Newton's 'Principles of Philosophy': An Intended Preface for the 1704 *Opticks* and a Related Draft Fragment," *British Journal for the History of Science* 5: 178–186.

McGuire, J.E., 1972, "Boyle's Conception of Nature," *Journal of the History of Ideas* 33: 523–542.

McGuire, J.E., 1978, "Newton on Place, Time and God: An Unpublished Source," *British Journal for the History of Science* 11: 114–129.

McGuire, J.E., 1990, "Predicates of Pure Existence: Newton on God's Space and Time," in Bricker and Hughes, editors.

McGuire, J.E., 1994, "Natural Motion and its Causes: Newton on the 'vis insita' of Bodies," in Gill and Lennox, editors.

McGuire, J.E., 2007, "A Dialogue with Descartes: Newton's Ontology of True and Immutable Natures," *Journal of the History of Philosophy* 45: 103–125.

McMullin, Ernan, 1978, *Newton on Matter and Activity*, Notre Dame: University of Notre Dame Press.

McMullin, Ernan, 1985, "The Significance of Newton's *Principia* for Empiricism," in Osler and Farber, editors.

McMullin, Ernan, 1998, "Galileo on Science and Scripture," in Machamer, editor.

McMullin, Ernan, 2001, "The Impact of Newton's *Principia* on the Philosophy of Science," *Philosophy of Science* 68: 279–310.

Mercer, Christia, 2002, "Platonism and Philosophical Humanism on the Continent," in Nadler, editor.

Metzger, Hélène, 1938, *Attraction universelle et religion naturelle chez quelques commentateurs anglais de Newton*, Paris: Hermann et cie.

Miller, David Marshall, 2014, *Representing Space in the Scientific Revolution*, Cambridge: Cambridge University Press.

More, Henry, 1655, *An Antidote Against Atheism*, London: J. Flesher.

More, Henry, 1659, *Immortality of the Soul, So Farre Forth as It Is Demonstrable from the Knowledge of Nature and the Light of Reason*, London: J. Flesher.

More, Henry, 1662, *A Collection of Several Philosophical Writings*, London: J. Flesher.

More, Henry, 1712, *A Collection of Several Philosophical Writings*, 4th ed., London.

Morgenbesser, Sidney, Patrick Suppes, and Morton White, editors, 1969, *Philosophy, Science and Method: Essays in honor of Ernest Nagel*, New York: St. Martin's Press.

Mulsow, Martin and Jan Assmann, editors, 2006, *Sintflut und Gedächtnis*, Munich: Wilhelm Fink Verlag.

Murdoch, John, 1982, "The Analytic Character of Late Medieval Learning: Natural Philosophy without Nature," in Roberts, editor.

Musgrave, Alan and Imre Lakatos, editors, 1968, *Problems in Philosophy of Science*, Cambridge: Cambridge University Press.

Nadler, Steven, editor, 2002, *A Companion to Early Modern Philosophy*, Oxford: Blackwell.

Neiman, Susan, 1997, "Metaphysics, Philosophy: Rousseau on the Problem of Evil," in Reath, Herman, and Korsgaard, editors.

Nelson, Alan, 1995, "Micro-Chaos and Idealization in Cartesian Physics," *Philosophical Studies* 77: 377–391.

Osler, Margaret, 2010, *Reconfiguring the World: Nature, God and Human Understanding from the Middle Ages to Early Modern Europe*, Baltimore: Johns Hopkins University Press.

Osler, Margaret and Paul Lawrence Farber, editors, 1985, *Religion, Science and Worldview: Essays in Honor of Richard Westfall*, Cambridge: Cambridge University Press.

Palmerino, Carla-Rita, 2006, "Galileo and the Mathematical Characters of the Book of Nature," in van Berkel and A.J. Vanderjagt, editors.

Palmerino, Carla-Rita and J.M.M.H. Thijssen, editors, 2004, *The Reception of the Galilean Science of Motion in Seventeenth-Century Europe*, Dordrecht: Kluwer.

Palter, Robert, editor, 1970, *The Annus Mirabilis of Sir Isaac Newton 1666–1966*, Cambridge: MIT Press.

Panza, Marco, 2003, *Newton*, Paris: Societé d'édition les Belles Lettres.

Pardies, Ignatio [Anonymous], 1670, *A Discourse of Local Motion*, London.

Park, Katherine and Lorraine Daston, editors, 2006, *The Cambridge History of Science: Volume 3: Early Modern Science*, Cambridge: Cambridge University Press.

Popkin, Richard, 1968, "Scepticism, Theology and the Scientific Revolution in the Seventeenth Century," in Musgrave and Lakatos, editors.

Porter, Roy, 1977, *Making of Geology: Earth Science in Britain, 1660–1815*, Cambridge: Cambridge University Press.

Quine, W.V.O., 1951, "Two Dogmas of Empiricism," *The Philosophical Review* 60: 20–43.

Ragep, F. Jamil and Sally Ragep, 1996, *Tradition, Transmission, Transformation*, Leiden: E.J. Brill.

Reath, A., B. Herman, and C. Korsgaard, editors, 1997, *Reclaiming the History of Ethics: Essays for John Rawls*, Cambridge: Cambridge University Press.

Redwood, John, 1976, *Reason, Ridicule and Religion*, Cambridge: Harvard University Press.

Reedy, Gerard, 1985, *The Bible and Reason*, Philadelphia: University of Pennsylvania Press.

Reid, Jasper, 2008, "The Spatial Presence of Spirits among the Cartesians," *Journal of the History of Philosophy* 46: 91–118.

Richards, Robert, 2003, "Biology," in Cahan, editor.

Roberts, L.D., editor, 1982, *Approaches to Nature in the Middle Ages*, Binghamton: Center for Medieval and Early Renaissance Studies.

Roger, Jacques, 1982, "The Cartesian Model and its role in Eighteenth Century 'Theory of the Earth'," in Lennon, Nicholas, and Davis, editors.

Rogers, G.A.J., 1978, "Locke's Essay and Newton's Principia," *Journal of the History of Ideas* 39: 217–232.

Rohault, Jacques, 1671/1697, *Physica*, London: Jacobi Knapton [includes Samuel Clarke's *Annotata*].

Rohault, Jacques, 1723, *System of Natural Philosophy: Illustrated with Dr. Samuel Clarke's Notes, Taken Mostly Out of Sir Isaac Newton's Philosophy*, translated by John Clarke, London: James Knapton.

Roux, Sophie, 2014, "Was there a Cartesian Experimentalism in 1660's France?" in Dobre and Nyden, editors.

Ruffner, James, 2000, "Newton's Propositions on Comets: Steps in Transition, 1681–1684," *Archive for the History of the Exact Sciences* 54: 259–277.

Ruffner, James, 2012, "Newton's *De gravitatione*: A Review and Reassessment," *Archive for the History of the Exact Sciences* 66: 241–264.

Rynasiewicz, Robert, 1995a, "By Their Properties, Causes and Effects: Newton's Scholium on Space, Time, Place and Motion—I. The Text," *Studies in History and Philosophy of Science* 26: 133–153.

Rynasiewicz, Robert, 1995b, "By Their Properties, Causes and Effects: Newton's Scholium on Space, Time, Place and Motion—II. The Context," *Studies in History and Philosophy of Science* 26: 295–321.

Sabra, A.I., 1981, *Theories of Light from Descartes to Newton*, 2nd ed., Cambridge: Cambridge University Press.

Salusbury, Thomas, editor and translator, 1661, *Mathematical Collections and Translations*, vol. 1, London: William Leybourn.

Schaffer, Simon, 1986, "Scientific Discoveries and the End of Natural Philosophy," *Social Studies of Science* 16: 387–420.

Schliesser, Eric, 2007, "Hume's Newtonianism and Anti-Newtonianism," *Stanford Encyclopedia of Philosophy*, Edward Zalta, editor.

Schliesser, Eric, 2011, "Newton's Substance Monism, Distant Action, and the Nature of Newton's Empiricism," *Studies in History and Philosophy of Science* 42: 160–166.

Schliesser, Eric and George Smith, forthcoming, "Huygens's 1688 Report to the Directors of the Dutch East Indian Company on the Measurement of Longitude at Sea and the Evidence it Offered Against Universal Gravity," *Archive for History of Exact Sciences*.

Schmaltz, Tad, 2008, *Descartes on Causation*, Oxford: Oxford University Press.

Scholder, Klaus, 1990, *Birth of Modern Critical Theology*, translated by John Bowden, London: SCM Press.

Schuster, John, Stephen Gaukroger, and John Sutton, editors, 2000, *Descartes's Natural Philosophy*, London: Routledge.

Shabel, Lisa, 2005, "Apriority and Application: Philosophy of Mathematics in the Modern Period," in Shapiro, editor.

Shapin, Steven and Simon Schaffer, 1985, *Leviathan and the Air-pump: Hobbes, Boyle and the Experimental Life*, Princeton: Princeton University Press.

Shapiro, Alan, 1993, *Fits, Passions and Paroxysms: Physics, Method, and Chemistry and Newton's Theories of Colored Bodies and Fits of Easy Reflection*, Cambridge: Cambridge University Press.

Shapiro, Alan, 2004, "Newton's Experimental Philosophy," *Early Science and Medicine* 9: 185–217.

Shapiro, Lisa, editor, 2007, *The Correspondence between Princess Elisabeth of Bohemia and René Descartes*, Chicago: University of Chicago Press.

Shapiro, Stewart, editor, 2005, *Oxford Handbook of Philosophy of Mathematics and Logic*, Oxford: Oxford University Press.

Sklar, Larry, 1974, *Space, Time and Space-Time*, Berkeley: University of California Press.

Smith, George, 2001, "The Newtonian Style in Book II of the Principia," in Buchwald and Cohen, editors.

Smith, George, 2002, "The Methodology of the *Principia*," in Cohen and Smith, editors.

Smith, George, 2012, "How Newton's *Principia* Changed Physics," in Janiak and Schliesser, editors.

Snobelen, Stephen, 2001, "'God of Gods, and Lord of Lords': The Theology of Isaac Newton's General Scholium to the *Principia*," *Osiris* 16: 169–208.

Snobelen, Stephen, 2005, " 'The True Frame of Nature': Isaac Newton, Heresy, and the Reformation of Natural Philosophy," in Brooke and Maclean, editors.

Snobelen, Stephen, 2006, " 'To us there is but one God, the Father': Antitrinitarian Textual Criticism in Seventeenth and Early-Eighteenth Century England," in Hessayon and Keene, editors.

Snobelen, Stephen, editor, 2009, "Isaac Newton in the Eighteenth Century," special issue of *Enlightenment and Dissent*, No. 25.

Snyder, Laura, 2011, *The Philosophical Breakfast Club*, New York: Broadway.

Stedall, Jacqueline, editor, 2010, *The Arithmetic of Infinitesimals*, by John Wallis, Dordrecht: Springer.

Stein, Howard, 1970, "Newtonian Space-Time," in Palter, editor.

Stein, Howard, 1993, "On Philosophy and Natural Philosophy in the Seventeenth Century," *Midwest Studies in Philosophy*, vol. 18, Minneapolis: University of Minnesota Press.

Stein, Howard, 2002, "Newton's Metaphysics," in Cohen and Smith, editors.

Steinle, Friedrich, 1991, *Newtons Entwurf "Über die Gravitation": Ein stück entwicklungsgeschichte seiner mechanik*, Stuttgart: Franz Stiner Verlag.

Stewart, Larry, 1996, "Seeing through the Scholium: Religion and Reading Newton in the Eighteenth Century," *History of Science* 34: 123–165.

Tamny, Martin, 1979, "Newton, Creation, and Perception," *Isis* 70: 48–58.

Tulloch, John, 1874, *Rational Theology and Christian Philosophy in England in the Seventeenth Century, vol. 2: The Cambridge Platonists*, Edinburgh/London: Blackwood and Sons.

Vailati, Ezio, 1997, *Leibniz and Clarke: A Study of their Correspondence*, Oxford: Oxford University Press.

van Berkel, K. and A.J. Vanderjagt, editors, 2006, *The Book of Nature in Modern Times*, Leuven: Peeters.

Voltaire, 1738/1992, *Eléments de la philosophie de Newton*, vol. 15, edited by Robert Walters and W.H. Barber, Oxford: The Voltaire Foundation.

Westfall, Richard S., 1962, "Newton and his Critics on the Nature of Colors," *Archives internationales d'histoire des sciences* 15: 47–58.

Westfall, Richard S., 1971, *Force in Newton's Physics*, New York: Wiley.

Westfall, Richard S., 1980, *Never at Rest*, Cambridge: Cambridge University Press.

Westfall, Richard S., 1989, *Essays on the Trial of Galileo*, Vatican City State: Vatican Observatory Press.

Whewell, William [Anonymous], 1834, "Review of Mary Somerville, *On the Connexion of the Physical Sciences*," *The Quarterly Review* 51: 54–67.

Wilson, Catherine, 1995, *The Invisible World: Early Modern Philosophy and the Invention of the Microscope*, Princeton: Princeton University Press.

Wilson, Margaret, 1999, *Ideas and Mechanism*, Princeton: Princeton University Press.

Yoder, Joella, 1988, *Unrolling Time: Christiaan Huygens and the mathematization of nature*, Cambridge: Cambridge University Press.

index

Newton, First Edition. Andrew Janiak.
© 2015 Andrew Janiak. Published 2015 by John Wiley & Sons, Ltd.

calculus, 1, 6, 7, 24, 25, 30, 60, 90, 94, 101, 118, 137
correspondence with Bentley, 95, 96
correspondence with Burnet, 152–6
correspondence with Cotes, 174
calculus priority dispute with Leibniz, 11, 12, 14, 92, 117, 118, 121, 124
correspondence with Leibniz, 129–37
De Gravitatione, 14, 26, 63, 69, 72, 75, 78, 80, 82–4, 87, 131, 163–5, 167, 176
De Motu corporum, 7, 8, 14, 30, 70, 137, 155, 157
debate with Hooke, 49–60
debate with Pardies, 50, 51, 57, 62
doctrine of light, 53–9
experimentalist, 49–60
founder of modern mathematical physics, ix, 3
Grantham School, 5, 6
hypothesis of nature of light, 41, 47, 50, 53, 55, 59
hypotheses non fingo, 50
interpretation of scripture, 151–61, 167–71
laws of motion, 17, 65, 67–88, 103–106, 127, 128, 136
Lucasian professor of mathematics, 3, 6, 7, 100, 114, 130, 152, 174
mathematical physics, 3, 7, 9, 20, 25, 31, 33, 85
Mathematical Principles of Natural Philosophy, 2, 171, 172
mathematical treatment of force, 100, 102, 104–12, 118, 119, 136
mathematics, ix, 1, 3–7, 17, 22, 25, 100–113, 118, 156
metaphysics, 60, 78–85, 117–38, 149–76
natural philosopher, 4, 9, 18, 19, 24, 27, 29, 32, 33, 39, 42, 44, 85, 90, 100, 101, 110, 114, 140
"New theory about light and colors", 50
Optical Papers, 114
optics work in 1670s, 49–60
president of Royal Society, 2, 10, 11, 13

relation to Descartes, 63–88, 96–100
relation to Halley, 8, 9
relation to Leibniz, 11–13, 117–38
relation to Locke, 3, 4, 9, 13–15, 21–3, 26, 37, 8, 39, 51, 60, 84, 86, 89, 109, 110, 115, 125–30, 163, 174, 175
scientist, ix, 1, 2, 17–20, 22–37, 39, 89, 112
space, 78–85, 96–100, 129–37, 159
theology, 149, 151–61
Theory about light and colors, 40, 50–62
theory of motion, 69–78, 117–29
time, 12, 25, 26, 63–5, 69–73, 133, 135, 137, 149, 151, 155–7, 159, 160, 166, 168, 170, 173
Two Notable Corruptions of Scripture, 174
undergraduate at Trinity College, 2, 3, 5, 6, 61, 63, 88
Warden of the Mint, ix, 3, 10, 11
Woolsthorpe, 5–7
normal science see science, normal

observation, 19, 22–4, 27, 28, 38–40, 42, 50, 62, 115, 123
occasionalism, 21, 80, 86
occult qualities see quality, occult
Oldenburg, Henry, 24, 50, 54, 57, 62
opticks, 10, 11, 17, 26, 29, 31, 108, 115, 161, 162, 176
first edition, 10
Latin edition, 115, 161
queries, 10, 108, 162, 176
Query thirty-one, 115, 161, 162, 176
optics, 2, 3, 7, 8, 10, 17, 19, 22, 23, 31, 33, 40, 41, 50, 51, 55, 56, 60–62, 90, 100, 104, 107, 113
orbit, 8, 14, 24, 26, 32, 34, 98–100, 102, 103, 107, 114, 118–20, 122, 124, 126, 135–7, 139, 147, 148, 171, 172
Keplerian, 122, 137
planetary, 8, 14, 26, 32, 34, 114, 118–20, 124, 126, 136, 139, 147
paradigm, 22, 52, 87, 112,
Pardies, Ignatius, 50, 51, 57, 62